Nigel,

It was fun reliving my Southeast Tours days.

Hope you enjoy it.

The Road to
Sedona

by
Robert Louis DeMayo

2/1/18

This book can be ordered on: Amazon, Kobo, ACX,
Ingram, Kindle and other retailers.

Available in print, audio book
and as an eBook.

Cover Design: Andrew Holman
On our Way lyrics by: Steven Pile
Interior Images: Robert Louis DeMayo

Edited by: Nina Rehfeld

Also by Robert Louis DeMayo:

The Wayward Traveler
The Making of Theodore Roosevelt
Pledge to the Wind, the Legend of Everett Ruess
The Light Behind Blue Circles
The Cave Where the Water Always Drips
Random Thoughts from the Road

Robert Louis DeMayo

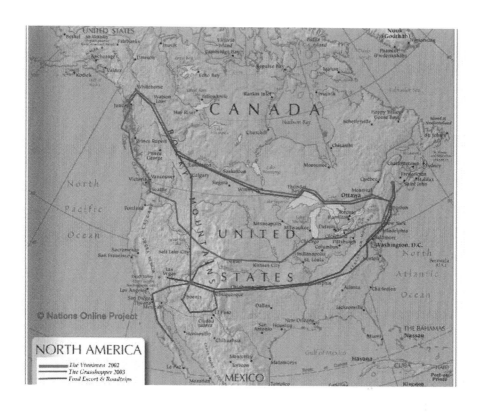

NORTH AMERICA
The Vinnimau 2002
The Grasshopper 2003
Ford Escort & Roadtrips

Table of Contents

3

The DeMayo family - 2003

This is a work of fiction

This is our story. I've changed some names and tried to round things out the best I could, but the following pages are filled with as much truth as I could muster. Over a two year stretch we crossed North America six times, logging over twenty thousand miles, before sinking solid roots.

We completed these travels with little money and two very young children, and for much of this time I felt we were victims — one step above refugees while we sought out a new home. But in the years since I've grown to believe that these were some of the best days of my life, and I'm thankful for the chance to share them with you.

I've used the word 'story' to describe these events because however closely the narrative may fit my recollections, or those of my wife or daughters, the fictional process has been at work.

by Tom Fish

Robert Louis DeMayo

for

Martika Louise DeMayo
my little traveller.

I am lucky to be surrounded by talented people. Many, like my steadfast editor, Nina Rehfeld, have been with me for five novels now. Drew Holman completed the cover, using one of his own pictures for the reflection in the train window; and the image of Tavy in front of the bull moose was completed by former Disney artist, Tom Fish.

My readers, whose feedback helped inspire me, will always have my gratitude: Dave Egan, Anne Luchtenveld, Lucinda Sylvester, Mary Johnson, Gayle Pace, Tim Glover, Rebecca Uphold, Steve & Sally Douglas, Robert & Jan Soper, Charlie Haithcock, Marilee Stemmler, Heidi Benson, Bettina Peyton, Cheryl Wasley, Liz Stevens, Cindy Wilmer, Jill Mandell, Katherine Connors, Bette Byrnes, Keith Okie, Steve Donovan, Debra Peth, James Triplett, Sherri O'Neil and Chris Fitzpatrick. And also those who helped me remember the past: Yvonne Fischer, Brian Lewandoski, Joanne Sheehan, Amanda Dehling, Nigel Glover, Paul Beebe, Kevin Dockter, Margaret Perry, Joni MacKinnon, Martin Gray, Dave Lee, Mark Patton, Steven Pile and Robert Moore.

A writer has a tough battle ahead if he doesn't have a good support, and my wife, Diana, and three daughters: Tavish, Saydrin and Martika, have always encouraged me, and helped me keep the act of storytelling fun. My parents, Pat and Ron, and my siblings, David and Kathleen, have also been incredibly supportive and I'd like to thank them here.

The Chase House, East Alstead, New Hampshire

Prologue

East Alstead, New Hampshire
(September 2001)

The canoe glided across the water, silently, and caused barely a ripple. The lake was quiet in the predawn hour, except for the occasional dip of the paddle, and a thick layer of mist floated over the water. The air was cold and not a fish jumped. Oak trees lined the shore; they still held their leaves, but the red and yellow splashes of color looked restrained in the gloomy light.

The canoe was moving west, away from the rising sun.

In the back sat Louis. He was thirty-six, clean-shaven with light blue eyes, and wearing an L.L. Bean flannel-lined jacket over a short-sleeve button-up shirt. He peered through the soft indigo dawn. This quiet morning canoe ride was the highlight of his day, and he wanted it to continue forever.

The first glint of sunlight shot through the trees and illuminated the oaks on the shore and the foliage burst forth brilliantly.

In the front Pinky leaned way over the edge of the canoe and trailed her finger in the water. For a two–year-old she had remarkable balance. She was blue-eyed also, but hers were large saucers of deep azure. She looked up at Louis, smiled, and tilted her head sideways as she hummed the theme from *Bear in the Big Blue House*.

Pinky wasn't her name of course, but when you're surrounded by people who treat nicknames like rites of passage you get used to them.

Some you treasure, some you just live with, and others you evade wherever you can. Louis had nicknames from his past that I've heard: Barn Rat, Kiboko and H-bear, to name a few, but at this point in his life Louis fit the best. So for now it's gonna be Pinky sprawled over the bow of the canoe, and Louis paddling.

"Time to head in," he said with a sigh and turned the craft back in the direction they'd come from.

Pinky frowned and backed up, and then twisted around and settled into the middle of the bench. She sat there quietly, watching Louis paddle.

"My turn?" she asked hopefully.

He shook his head and smiled. "Not today."

She had begun to speak very young, and now issued commands in short staccato bursts.

If you got in her way when she wanted to do something she'd hold up a finger and shout, "My do it!"

The sun crept over the trees on the east side of the lake and lit up a small house on a grassy hill directly in front of them. Through the morning haze its gables poking up out of the fog gave it the appearance of a chalet; but the rough-cut, unpainted siding and numerous quirky windows were distinctively New Hampshire. Smoke twirled from a chimney and the windows on the lower levels glowed warmly. Louis dipped the paddle in the water and propelled the boat towards it.

He looked around and inhaled deeply.

Louis had spent most of his twenties crisscrossing Africa and Asia. For years he'd chased that nomadic, peripatetic lifestyle, and was always telling travel stories, but he was settled now, and it was obvious he was proud of the stability of his quiet home.

He once told me he believed Pinky's confidence originated in the structured life he'd created in the little house by the lake.

"You can't figure out much while you're on the road," he said. "You need a quiet place to process it all."

I'm not in the boat with them, and I don't even come into this tale for quite a long time so don't start looking for me, but I've heard all the stories so many times that I feel like I was. I can imagine Louis staring off into the mist, contemplating, and Pinky drying her cold fingers on a yellow fleece vest.

"Look!" whispered Pinky. She extended her arm and pointed beyond the bow.

Between the house and the shoreline grew several clusters of blueberry bushes, and by one a doe was nibbling at the ripe fruit. With the sun now above the horizon, the mist and shadows had only just burnt away and they saw her clearly.

Pinky began to stand but Louis coaxed her back down with a whisper. They coasted closer, the deer unaware.

When the canoe ground up onto the gravely sand the doe stiffened.

She turned and stared at them for a moment, and slowly became unafraid. She dropped her head and extended her delicate muzzle to grab a few more berries.

Pinky said, "Hi!" and her ears pricked up as she stared at them.

And then time stopped.

Well, it probably didn't for the doe. But it did for Louis and Pinky. And it did for me. Because over the years I heard about it so many times: the lake, the canoe ride, the deer, the blueberries, all of it. I listened to that one story so often that I've now come to believe that that was when everything changed. That was when one thing ended and another thing began.

The screened back door of the little house opened and a woman called, "Coffee's ready!"

Suddenly the deer sprang away, out of sight in three bounds.

Louis pulled the canoe ashore, picked up Pinky, and sat her on one shoulder as he walked through the wet grass. "Coming!"

I imagine Louis was quietly counting the window panes as he came up the hill, life jackets and paddle in one hand, the other resting on Pinky's leg as she clung to his neck. Every window in the house had multiple panes, and many were made from the old glass that rippled when you looked through it. He always claimed he would count them all someday, but there were quite a few: the windows, the storm windows covering them, the sun porch and basement. He always seemed to get to the door before he had even counted half.

Only the trim of the house had ever been painted, the coarse sideboards had aged, making it look ancient—like something out of a fairy tale. An old road ran along one side of the house. It was the kind of road that you could never imagine paved.

The house had been built in the 1930s by Heman Chase. He was a surveyor, writer, and inventor of sorts. He seemed like one of those people who always stared back into the past when he visited a place. He'd had an office in the basement where his books were on display next to several collections of poetry written by his wife, Edith. Even though he'd lived in the house up until the late 70's, the spacious office felt distinctly pre-World War II.

His writings revealed a man who was proud of the morals of his community, and the good, strong-willed men who had come before him. He believed that the finest things were handmade, and that the best inventions helped reduce the day's toil.

A quarter mile from the house a stream flowed out of the lake. There were once a lot of old mills along it where the old-timers had created dams and mill wheels to harness the latent power of the falling water. Whenever Heman surveyed a lot and saw a timeworn mill stone, he'd try to obtain it through purchase or barter. Over the years he had decorated the house and yard with so many hand-made objects and chiseled stones that many considered the property to be a museum in its own right.

The exterior of the front door landing of the Chase house featured a large flat, circular millstone embedded in the ground; three inches of the stone rose above the surrounding lawn and guests stepped up onto it before knocking on the door.

Propped up next to the shed and other outbuildings were numerous stone or metal items whose onetime functions Louis could only guess at. And the stone walls that surrounded the lot had lots of interesting pieces in them that probably hadn't sprung up in the fields naturally, pushed out of the earth by the frost.

By the garage entrance a cord of wood had been split and stacked. The house had an oil furnace, but oil was expensive and the winter was long, so Louis burnt wood to keep them warm. Around the bend stood a shed with a large pile of unsplit logs that he planned to use if they ran short.

Louis leaned the paddle against the wood pile and reached for the garage door, but Pinky wiggled down from his shoulder, shouting, "My do it!"

She grabbed the bottom of the heavy door and effortlessly lifted the entire thing up. Simultaneously a thick plank on the side of the building descended, led by a large smooth stone that had been mounted to the end. The counterweight was a typical Heman Chase invention; with it a child could easily open the door.

They entered the house through the garage, followed a rickety flight of stairs up, and then shut the door behind them. When they came into the living room Pinky shouted, "We saw a deer!"

By a crackling fireplace sat Dee with the baby, lazily swaying in an antique rocker. An old black lab lay between them and the fire, worrisomely close to it.

"Come tell me!" said Dee, pointing to a cushion by the dog.

Pinky stared at the baby, and then eyed the fire.

"My do this," she said as she reached up, just below the mantle, and grabbed a heavy metal screen to lower it. Dee slid the dog's paws out of the way.

"Sorry Missy," she said and the dog glanced up and appeared to smile.

The fireplace grid was also counterweighted by a heavy stone that dangled by a chain in the basement. Dee absolutely loved it, although Louis claimed the stone almost conked him once when he happened to be walking through the basement as someone hitched the grid up above.

Dee smiled warmly at her oldest as she settled down. She was twenty-seven, with long blond hair and soft brown eyes. She looked content and rested, despite the fact that the bundled infant by her side had kept her up most of the night.

"Me and Stinky have been loving this fire," she said.

"Stinky? Really?" asked Louis.

Dee shrugged and then buried her nose in the soft folds of the three-month-old's neck.

"But she smells so good!"

Pinky stared at the little neck, but lost interest.

"I'll warm up the Vinniman," said Louis.

The *Vinniman* was actually a Dodge *Caravan* and owed its nickname to Pinky. Two months after the baby had been born Dee had driven to Nashua and purchased it.

It was dark green with a clean interior, and at only three years old, it was as good as new to them. Louis had had a small heart attack when she showed up with the car, dreading a big monthly payment, but they were both employed, and Dee reminded him of this.

In fact, their jobs at a local touring company were why they'd moved to this remote part of New Hampshire, not far from Walpole, near the Connecticut River that formed the border between New Hampshire and Vermont. The company created tours for scientific organizations: Antarctic voyages, archaeological tours, deep sea dives, and African safaris.

Louis was in heaven. Like I said, he'd been just about everywhere, and he was nuts about exploration. Now he was answering emails from Robert Ballard's office concerning a submersible dive to the wreck of the *Bismarck*, or receiving photos from the Leakey Foundation in Africa for an *Origins of Man* tour. He was in charge of marketing.

Dee worked in sales, and although she excelled in her job, it wasn't her dream. She liked seeing Louis happy, but found the long hours away from her baby and office pecking order annoying.

They loaded up the Vinniman and began the forty-minute drive to work. On the way they'd drop off both girls with their nanny, Sue Sue, and eight hours later they'd commute back to the little house on the lake.

On this day, however, things changed. The tragedies that shook America on September 11th would alter the travel industry dramatically, and when Louis dragged himself home that night they had both been given their notice.

Louis never liked to talk about it. He'd say, "Heck, people lost their lives—we only lost our jobs."

But the fact remained that they were now living in a remote place with no jobs and two extra mouths to feed. And a big car payment.

He looked over the lake sadly. A cold wind blew at him, and he felt it penetrate deep as he thought, What the hell am I gonna do now?

Healy, Alaska

Chapter One

East Alstead, New Hampshire
(February 2002)

The metal *Tink!* echoed across the frozen lake, and then returned, just before another let loose. Dee sat in a window, looking down at the shed, and thought of Louis out there, pounding away, trying to split a stubborn log.

After the Twin Towers came down high-end travel came to a standstill, but Louis's boss found a few week's work for him converting current tours to the Middle East to safer destinations like Europe. But they weren't creating new tours, so there was only limited work. The owner would do all the marketing himself for the near future, and they only kept one woman on sales who'd been there longer than Dee.

Louis had taken it pretty hard, both because he lost his dream job, and he knew they could no longer stay in the quiet home by the lake. He wanted to move immediately, somewhere he could find work, but winter had set in early, and heavily, and soon the only sensible thing to do seemed to be to wait for spring.

"We should go back to Denali," he had said hopefully. "If we get there early in the spring we can work the full season."

Three years ago they had spent the summer in the town of Healy, just outside Denali National Park. They had made good money working at the local bar for their friends, Ryan and Simone, who had told them to come back anytime. It was a lucrative gig: Louis bartended and Dee waitressed. The tips were good and they worked long hours during the high season. But the park closed in the winter, and there was no work for almost five months, until April came around.

Tink!

They had no money for flights to Alaska, so eventually they decided to drive there.

"That's a long drive, isn't it?" asked Dee.

Louis scratched his head. "I'd guess roughly five thousand miles."

"When should we leave?"

"In February some of the roads will still be snowed in," he had replied. "But we should go as early in March as we can."

They cut as much cost as they could and used their meager savings to pay the remaining rent until March. Dee helped winterize the house, doubling the curtains and scrounging up thick duvets for the beds, while Louis searched the woods for dry logs or kindling. A few times he landed jobs as a day laborer for his friend Bone, and Dee took a waitressing shift in Keene, but even combined the money was barely enough to keep the fridge stocked with the basics.

She glanced at the shed, waiting for the sound of the heavy mall hitting the splitting wedge. She worried about him. A light had gone out of his eyes when he'd lost this precious job. Suddenly he would agree to anything, but he appeared to care about nothing.

Alaska would be good, she thought. She remembered camping in a boreal forest on the outskirts of Healy. A sparse grove of spruce had surrounded them—some of the trees leaning drunkenly—and the ground was covered with a thick layer of sphagnum moss that felt like a mattress under their little two-man tent. The airy, green scent of the spruce trees had been intoxicating and Dee could still smell it if she closed her eyes and concentrated.

The soft moss has no roots which is why some of the spruce, whose roots were anchored in it, leaned. The trees weren't too tall, maybe twelve feet, and finches, warblers and sparrows were perching in their crowns, watching them. There were jays in the treetops, too, and they'd steal any unguarded snacks that you left out.

This is another place where time stood still. Louis talked about it a lot, and over the years Dee repeatedly promised Pinky she'd bring her back there one day — you'll soon understand why.

Louis had strung a hammock up between two of the trees, and when you lay in it you could hear the wind whistle through the spruce crowns, making the hammock sway. Just beyond these sounds there was always the gurgle of the Teklanika River which flowed a hundred feet away.

Their campsite was alongside the Stampede Trail where a few years before a young traveler named Christopher McCandless had perished when he'd tried to rough it in the wilderness and ate the wrong berries.

He had tried to return to civilization, but the river, swelled with meltwater, had cut him off. The locals had thought him foolish because the river — which was wide and braided by the camp — is fed by the Cantwell glacier, and if he'd waited until the next morning he could have most likely crossed when the flow was less.

Louis understood McCandless, but didn't necessarily agree with him. The young man didn't like maps or want advice on the local terrain. He wanted the world to be a blank slate. He also sought to escape society and before he went into the wild he always burned what little money he had.

Louis laughed and thought, I can't afford to burn my cash. He also believed that when you went into the wilderness you should be prepared — to the best of your abilities. If McCandless had had a local map with him he would have seen that there was a bridge over the river only a few miles away.

Dee hadn't cared much for discussing the morbid story. She preferred listening to the birds and the river, and the wind that never seemed to descend on them. One large raven took to perching on a tree that overlooked their quiet camp; she decided it was a female, named her Donna, and talked to the bird like it was an old friend.

"Quiet down, Donna," she'd say to the cawing creature as she wiggled deeper into the hammock.

At the end of that summer she was pregnant with Pinky. As she was now staring out of the window of their little house in New

Hampshire, she looked forward to bringing her back to the spot where her oldest had been conceived: a beautiful camp in the Alaskan taiga.

Taiga — they almost named her after it.

But her name had instead come from a different place; a lonely slope where mountain goats hid behind ghostlike, wispy clouds and the wind told secrets. I'll tell you about it, I will, but I don't think we're ready for that story right now.

She saw him exit the shed, walk to a wooden box and grab another wedge, and then disappear into the shed again. He moved slowly, weighed down, and his breath jumped before him in thick white puffs.

Tink!

At first he'd been upbeat about making it through the winter with their existing supplies, pointing at the stacked wood confidently, but November was unusually cold and they soon used it up. They burned through the oil, too, and before January had to resort to keeping the thermostat just high enough so the pipes wouldn't freeze.

There was still the backup pile of cut logs in the shed, ten feet tall and fifteen wide.

One afternoon, she had found him in the shed, staring at one of the logs in disbelief.

"What the hell?" he said, pointing at the log which was gnarly and twisted and had three large metal wedges buried in it.

"Looks like you started with the wrong log," she'd said.

He shook his head. "They're all like that!"

Over the years, they realized, all the crappy logs — those that were curved, or forked, or knotted — had been thrown onto this pile. "Do you know how long it's gonna take me to get a wheelbarrow full of wood from logs like that?"

Tink!

That had been a month ago and now there were only a few logs left. He'd already raked up the entire area where he had stacked the other cord, and burnt all of it, and they were burning every scrap of trash that wasn't toxic.

Pinky appeared in the kitchen, wearing a fluffy pink bathrobe and matching slippers. She looked out the window at the thickening gloom. There were no lights in the shed. Dee frowned.

"Can you tell your father that dinner's ready?" asked Dee.

Pinky nodded, but then glanced at her slippers. "I need my boots."

Pinky found him trying to whack either of two wedges loose that were buried in the log that he was working. He cursed as he scraped his knuckle, attempting to pull the log apart with brute force.

Ten feet away Missy lay on a thick blanket, watching his efforts as curiously as Pinky.

"Are we gonna have a fire?" she asked.

Louis's face was wracked with frustration.

"Stand by the door," he said to Pinky. "And get Missy."

Pinky called the dog, and Missy stood up stiffly. Over the last few months she'd been moving ever slower. Louis had had her since she was a puppy and he hated to see the onetime vivacious hunter drag herself through her final years.

All that was left of the pile was the log he was working on and a big one underneath it which he used as a chopping block. He lost his temper and grabbed the log, lifted it high, and then smashed the whole thing onto the base.

The log burst open, into three pieces, sending one of the metal wedges flying.

"Yeah!" shouted Pinky.

The other wedge was still stuck. Louis looked it over, and then placed the log precariously on the base.

"Why don't you take Missy back inside. Tell mom I'll be there in a minute."

She stomped her left foot. "Missy! Come!" she ordered and the dog obediently limped behind her.

While he lined up his shot Louis thought: I can't believe how big Pinky has gotten. It seemed like yesterday that he had been camping along the Stampede Trail with Dee when she became pregnant.

*

They had planned the pregnancy. One month after the Cantwell Music Festival they began trying, and as it turned out she conceived almost immediately.

They had waited a month because at the festival Ryan had given Louis some mushrooms, and after a psychedelic experience in his tent — which I only ever heard him refer to as the "belly of the whale incident" — they decided to clean up for a month.

Dee's first trimester had been difficult, and Louis had done everything he could to make things more accommodating. Ryan had lent him a wall tent with a solid base, and he borrowed a wood stove and stove pipe that fit inside it, poking through a fitted hole in the ceiling. He outfitted their simple home with a cast iron pan, a crate book shelf, and a few rickety chairs that had been left behind by other campers.

On one of his hikes he had discovered a vein of coal and over several trips he assembled a good supply outside the tent.

Dee smiled at each improvement, but she was pale and threw up a lot. Her sense of smell haunted her. The salmon special at the restaurant made her heave, and the odor of the burning coal soon became unbearable to her.

Louis pointed at the glowing stove in frustration.

"But Dee, this is so much easier than collecting wood and cutting it without a chainsaw. We just have to throw a couple lumps in the stove in the morning and it's warm all day!"

But she just scowled and said, "But it stinks," and so he hauled the coal away, and then scrubbed the wall tent clean from the lingering scent.

Instead he talked the foreman at a nearby construction site into letting him collect the wood scraps at the end of each day.

Late one night they awoke with start when something large rubbed against the side of the wall tent. At first Louis thought it was one of the prep cooks, drunk, stumbling to his tent.

"Hey! Back off!" he shouted, but got no response.

He threw a book at the tent wall and a low growl sounded. In the morning they discovered Grizzly tracks outside the tent. Apparently the discarded throw up had attracted the bear; and over the next few nights he came back, sniffing around, looking for more.

Back in Maine, August was still a warm month, so Dee decided to fly home to visit her mother while Louis finished the season bartending double shifts.

Louis loved the Alaskan fall with its crisp weather and vibrant colors; the tundra was ablaze with oranges and reds and deep gold, and the birch and willow turned a fierce yellow. The peaks around him were covered with snow, but it hadn't descended yet to the lower valleys.

It made him feel alive as he sensed the animals preparing for the long winter; many would have young in the spring, like him. They came down from the high country to escape the deep snow, and on his way to work he regularly passed moose and deer, now carrying a heavy winter coat. The moose lost the soft felt on their antlers and the deer began to move through the woods in regular patterns while the bucks fought for dominance.

Most of all he enjoyed the northern lights which danced in the night sky. All summer they'd been immersed in almost constant daylight, but as the season wore on the sun had started to dip behind the horizon again at night, and now sunset arrived a full eight minutes sooner each day, bringing the lights earlier and earlier.

Plenty of bar patrons slept the day away and didn't show up at the bar until eleven at night. At that hour the sky was dusky and it wasn't until the wee hours of morning that it was dark enough to see the lights; by then they'd be good and drunk and in no mood to clear out. Ryan typically let people stay at the bar as long as they kept buying drinks.

Louis knew Ryan and his wife, Simone, from when she had worked with Dee at a bar in southern New Hampshire a few years earlier — you'll hear more about them later.

There were also two bar backs who worked closely with Louis: Daniel and Killer. Daniel was from Tennessee; he had a scraggy beard and mustache and looked a little bit like a demon, which was fitting since he claimed to be a devil worshipper.

Whenever he had a chance, Daniel changed the restaurant's usual vintage Johnny Cash to hard, angry metal, and ran around screaming crazy stuff like: "Burn in hell, slaves of the masochistic liar, Jehovah! Repent or be damned in heaven!"

Killer was a giant of a man with fire-engine red hair. He looked like an Irish Conan the Barbarian, and when he chopped wood for the smoker he'd often heft the axe high and shout, "Give me a slave girl and a big axe and I will be a happy man!"

But he had a surprisingly, gentle nature. He was studying to be a guide and constantly spouted interesting facts about Alaska.

A few weeks after Dee left, the Bartender's Bash marked the end of the season. The bartenders, waitresses and other restaurant workers sent it off with a midnight party in the woods by a roaring fire.

Louis had stumbled to the party with the bar backs and a half-empty bottle of Jack Daniels which he'd been nursing all afternoon. He'd felt not just the season coming to an end, but maybe the wild and carefree part of his life as well. He would soon return to the lower forty-eight to meet his pregnant wife and set up life as a family man.

Everyone was drunk by the time they showed up. Ryan went around with a bag of mushrooms and gave everyone a few caps. He had a challenging look in his eyes.

He opened the bag for Louis to take some, and when he hesitated Ryan said, "Don't be a fuckin' pussy! Take a 'shroom!" But then he softened and broke into a grin and added, "Come on, man, I had to drive to Talkeetna to get these."

"Well, I won't be fathering another child anytime soon, so I might as well," said Louis.

The fire was over five feet tall and a crowd of roughly fifty people stood around watching some of the younger guys dive over it, through the flames.

Suddenly Daniel tore off his shirt, screamed at the heavens and charged toward the fire, shouting, "Lucifer!!!!"

He tripped a few feet away and fell right into it with an explosion of sparks, but scrambled back out with surprisingly little damage.

24

For the rest of the night you could smell that his eyebrows and the hair on his forearms had been singed.

Soon after a group of twenty people made their way to a nearby hill to watch the northern lights that wavered overhead in long ribbons of green and yellow. They twisted and glowed as if they were alive and for a while they all watched silently.

Daniel yelled at the lights and they appeared to move in response. "You see that?" he said, pointing. "I control them!"

Killer laughed. "You don't have that kind of power. They're forty miles above us, in the ionosphere — there's no chance you caused that."

Daniel shouted again, and again the ripples of light danced in response.

"Just look!"

"Daniel, you're ridiculous," said Killer, waving his hand in front of his face, "and you stink, too."

Louis had been swaying in place, the effects of liquor and mushrooms combining to make him feel like he was on a ship in rolling seas.

He took a Roman candle from his back pocket.

The sky was alive with color as the lights danced about. To Louis they were magical, powerful visions that had been placed there just for him.

There was a trace of light on the horizon, but the sky above them was deep blue. One twisting ribbon of green stood out clearly, bending like kelp in a retreating tide, and Louis yearned to be floating next to it, swaying in the Heavens while the universe rippled.

He could see how the lights could inspire legends, and understood how the native cultures of North America lived in awe of the powerful forces.

"Anybody got a light?" he asked and Daniel produced a Zippo with a grinning devil on the side.

He flicked it open, rolled the striker, and put flame to the fuse.

Louis pointed the candle toward the heavens.

A ball of fire shot up and the lights appeared to dance out of its way.

The others jumped back, surprised. "Wow!"

Louis shouted at the top of his lungs, coaxing the lights to dance more. I'm sure it was his "Barbaric Yawp" which he claimed came straight from Walt Whitman.

Killer shook his head. "You guys aren't doing that."

"Didn't you see them jump?" asked Daniel.

A half-dozen more fireballs shot out of the candle, and then it sputtered out. Louis continued to stare at the lights in the sky, mesmerized.

*

Louis remembered that night well as he was cutting wood in his shed in New Hampshire. It seemed to be one of the last wild, free things he'd ever done. For the rest of his life those ribbons of color would dance in his mind. He had returned to New Hampshire and gotten an amazing job at the travel office—and soon after he'd become a father. Life had been good for a few years, until the towers collapsed.

The prospect of returning to Alaska reinvigorated his sad soul. He lined up his last shot and the maul connected with the buried wedge and two chunks of wood flew off in different directions.

Guess we'll have a good fire tonight after all, he thought as he collected the wood.

Over the next few weeks they got the Vinniman ready. In the far back Louis took out the bench and stuck in twelve milk crates filled with camping gear, pots, plates and cutlery, guide books and maps, paper, envelopes, and baby clothes. There was even a crate for toys. He cut and primed a piece of plywood to fit over the crates as a platform for more luggage.

They had a good supply of dry food like rice, mac and cheese, and granola bars, and six cans of propane for their Coleman stove.

He mounted a Thule roof box on top of the van and stuck the tent, roll mats and sleeping bags up in there.

"That way we don't have to unload the entire van whenever we stop to camp," he explained to Pinky who watched everything skeptically.

At night he lay awake in bed, worrying about the journey. Would they have enough money to get there? Would the Vinniman hold up for the long journey? Would Ryan and Simone be able to give them good shifts so they could earn enough money to make it worth it?

One night he heard a thumping on the wall in the room next to his and walked over to investigate.

An inch-thick pipe ran vertically from floor to ceiling along the wall in Pinky's room, four inches away from the wall itself. When Louis entered the room he spotted Pinky close to the ceiling, holding the pipe with both hands as she walked up the wall.

She beamed proudly, "Hi!"

Louis moved to help her down and her eyebrows furrowed.

He stepped back and watched her down-climb, thinking: she's literally climbing the walls — I guess we're not that different.

Missy also seemed restless and watched as the family packed more boxes to go into the storage bin. A week before they were to depart Dee found her lifeless, sprawled out in front of the warm fire.

"She knew we weren't going to take her with us," said Dee.

Louis patted her head. "She was a good dog."

He wrapped Missy in her warm blanket and took her outside. The ground was frozen solid and even a heavy pick axe wouldn't open it up. A hole in the woods by an uprooted tree had to do.

After tenderly placing the dog inside the depression, he collected stones to cover her.

"Wish I could have done better, Missy," he said as he tried not to tear up.

When the house was empty and the Vinniman just about ready, Louis took one final walk through the place. His favorite room had always been Heman's office in the basement, which was usually off limits to any renters. But Heman's daughters, who owned the house, didn't mind him using the space because they appreciated his respectfulness.

Three rows of windows in the basement provided a view outside at lawn-level, when you looked out the window your eye-level was a foot above the grass. The house had been designed so that if you stood in the office you had a perfect panorama of the lake—as long as the lawn had been mowed recently.

There were no electrical devices in the office, and Louis didn't see a single piece of plastic in the room. The tools, and even the furniture, all looked hand-made, out of wood or metal.

Drafting and surveying tools were neatly aligned on a shelf, each drawer had a hand-written label on it, and an assortment of mysterious tools hung from pegs on the wall. Each item seemed to have a story to tell, but although Louis stared at the apparatuses for hours, he couldn't fathom the functions of most of them—as if the bygone era they came from had secrets that were lost to time.

A very large rectangular desk occupied the center of the room and Louis often came down here to write poetry. Over the eighteen months they had lived there he had compiled a collection of works about his days abroad, called *Random Thoughts from the Road*, and often Dee would find him sitting at the desk pondering a verse.

Louis looked around the room one last time, as if expecting to see someone standing there.

He had broken away from the Catholic Church at a young age, and as a result had his own definition for certain things. He didn't believe in ghosts, but sometimes felt a strong connection to the past.

One time he said to me, "We each contain an assortment of memories of departed ones that we have loved, or others that we've learned about. When you find yourself talking to them you've moved out of the realm of memories and into the world of spirits."

To Louis, these spirits were different from what others called ghosts because they existed solely in your mind. He once told me he thought God was a spirit too, not a conscious entity that controlled our lives.

Often when he was in the basement office he sensed that Heman's spirit was the strongest in him, just under his subconscious, almost willing itself to the surface.

He addressed Heman, "I'm sorry we couldn't stay longer—I liked it here."

The old building creaked as a strong wind blew off the lake.

He straightened up the chairs before turning off the light.

In the hallway he reached for another light switch when a large round rock, suspended by a chain, descended from above and missed him by a hair. He screamed.

Dee called from upstairs: "Sorry! Just burning the last of the trash!"

He chuckled and looked back at the office. "Okay, I guess I had that coming for running out on you. But I don't have a choice."

He sighed. "I'll come back some day."

On the Annapurna Circuit, Nepal

Chapter Two

Chicago, Illinois
(March 2002)

The highway was blanketed with snow and the only vehicles moving on it were dinosaur-like plows that roared by every ten minutes. The Vinniman, parked in the breakdown lane, was slowly sinking into the accumulating whiteness.

It was late at night, past midnight, and between the dense flurries in the headlights of the plows and the murky darkness around them, they could see little. All was silent, until Louis turned the key and the engine whirred on.

The wipers struggled to clear the snow from the windshield, skipping over a few frozen clumps, while the heater slowly warmed the interior. In the passenger seat Dee slept with the back tilted all the way down. Her seatbelt spanned the empty space above her.

Louis glanced at Pinky and Stinky in the rearview mirror, both in their car seats, asleep. Pinky was clutching a doll, smiling, unaware that they were on the verge of being snowed in.

The doll was a boy, and dark brown. For some reason she'd named it after Louis's father, and called it Baby Pip.

"Baby Pip drinks too much alcohol," she'd say as she pretended to clean it up.

In a month she would turn three. Over the last few months she had started using full sentences; a fact that often surprised strangers who addressed her.

Sleep tried to get a hold on Louis but he shook it off. His nerves lay bare. The plan had been to somehow make it to Alaska, but he didn't think the little money they had would stretch far enough.

And he tried to hide that worry from Dee.

He thought back to their little home on the lake in New Hampshire for solace, but the image that greeted him was the frozen woods and a shrill *Tink!*

Ryan and Simone had been glad to hear from them, and promised them work at their restaurant when they got there. He now leaned toward Alaska like he was a laser beam. If they could only get there, things would work out. He would make enough money to provide for his family, and the shadows would lift.

But since their initial contact they'd been unable to reach their friends. Over the last few months they'd tried to call Simone repeatedly, but her mailbox was full, and then the number was cancelled. Just before departing, Louis had mailed off a letter, informing them of their arrival.

They had intended to camp along the way to Alaska, but this whiteout prevented them from even reaching an exit.

A plow screeched by and Louis grabbed the steering wheel at ten and two o'clock, as if his white knuckles might make them all safer. I can see him there, clearly, trying to protect his family by sheer will.

Dee opened her eyes and stared at him. She thought, we'll be okay as long as he stays calm.

"You should get some sleep," she said.

"Here?" he asked. "Are you crazy?"

He looked at the highway. "We have to get out of here."

The gas gauge read a quarter tank. Even with the windshield clear of snow he couldn't see anything. He didn't dare get back on the freeway.

Louis sighed and turned off the engine.

"I was just warming up," said Dee.

"I'll turn it on again in twenty minutes. We might be stuck in this storm all night — or longer — and if we run out of gas we'll really be screwed."

Another plow came by, this time close enough to deposit a load of slush on the hood and side windows.

Louis cursed and fought to control his breathing. He was glad the girls weren't awake to see him panic. He looked at Dee and thought, we'll be fine, as long as she doesn't freak out.

He closed his eyes and tried to think of something else, anything to keep his mind off their current situation. The last five months had felt like a living nightmare, so his mind drifted further back, seven years before, to his first time abroad with Dee.

*

They'd flown to Nepal together, stopping in Southeast Asia for a month before continuing on to Kathmandu. Louis claimed they were still strangers when they set out to travel together, even though he'd known Dee for six months.

"How can you really know someone by just dating them," he'd said. "It all seems so superficial."

His best friend, Bone, had remarked that he was romanticizing travel.

"Not at all!" he replied, defiantly. "I just don't want to see someone once a week, for a dinner and a movie, and claim to know them."

"What's wrong with that? It's called a relationship."

Louis had shaken his head. "I want more than that. I want to see her hit her highest high — and her lowest low. This could be the woman I marry and I want to know what she's made of before I jump into that."

So after two months of dating, they had set off for southern Thailand, where they'd lived in a little bungalow for a month, soaking up the sun and exploring the islands. It wasn't until they landed in Nepal that things got challenging.

On the way from the airport Dee stumbled and twisted her ankle. They had wanted to hike in western Nepal, on the Annapurna circuit, but this injury threatened to derail those plans.

For the next week Louis massaged her ankle every night, kneading his worry into the inflamed tissue in the hope it would mend quickly. By the time they had bussed across the country to the town of Pokhara, and obtained their hiking permits, the swelling had subsided and they decided to try.

A few men had approached them, offering their service as porters, but Louis had waved them away.

"After a few days you won't even notice the weight of your pack," he told her. After all, he stated, they were mostly carrying warm clothing — thermal underwear, fleece and outer shell, hats and mittens — and the higher they got the more they'd be wearing.

The route they intended to hike was over one hundred and fifty miles, which was ambitions, and maybe foolish, considering that Dee had never hiked more than five miles in one stretch. But she went along with the plan, confident that it would be an adventure.

Louis had hiked the circuit a few years before but had to turn back before the high pass because it had been closed for the winter by heavy snow drifts. This time he was determined to complete it. They would do the hike in the reverse direction — counterclockwise — to see the side of the range he'd missed.

"The back side of the Annapurna circuit is in Nepal, but it goes right along the edge of the Tibetan plateau," he said. "Many of the villages we'll pass through are culturally more Tibetan than Nepalese."

The trail circled the Annapurna Range with twenty-three peaks over twenty thousand feet high. Above them all towered Annapurna I, more than twenty-six thousand feet above sea level. Thorung La pass, the midpoint in the circuit, crossed a saddle at just under eighteen thousand feet.

Springtime wasn't the best time of the year to hike the circuit, with much wet weather still lingering, so they purchased umbrellas and lots of plastic bags to store their gear in. They also had waterproof covers that fit snugly over their backpacks.

Louis had massaged Dee's ankle every night leading up to their departure, and now she claimed the sprain was completely healed.

It was hot in Pokhara, except when a rare breeze blew in off the beautiful lake that the town was built next to. In the morning the water seemed alive with dancing swirls of mist. When they blew away the massive, snow-covered peaks in the distance reflected clearly in the water.

Behind the town were lots of fields which were cropped by cows and water buffalos that seemed more numerous than people, and beyond that the mountain peaks glittered. Dee was mesmerized by the scenic location.

"Do we really have to go anywhere?" she asked. "Why not just rent a rowboat and float around on the lake?"

Louis laughed at her suggestion, and the way he kept looking toward the Annapurnas left no doubt he couldn't wait to get deeper into them.

"We'll do that when we get back."

They stowed most of their belongings at the guest house, and the proprietor locked away their passports and extra traveler's checks until their return.

The sun was still behind the big peaks the morning they started out.

At the edge of town they found a well-marked path that led to the trailhead, five miles away. There was a local bus that made the journey, but they were restless and didn't feel like waiting.

The brush along the trail was filled with twittering birds.

They passed through some low foothills where a series of ancient stone aqueducts gurgled pleasantly alongside them.

I can do this, thought Dee. It's so beautiful, and there's a buzz of spring in the air. She adjusted her pack and tightened the strap a little, but silently wished they had hired a porter.

*

In the Vinniman stuck in an Illinois snow storm, Louis smiled at these memories. He looked out the window at the horizon, which was beginning to lighten with a cold rosy glow. The snowfall had stopped. The plows had done a good job clearing the highway, and there was now only an inch of hard-packed snow covering the pavement.

He put the vehicle in gear and coaxed it onto the highway, exhaling with relief when it broke free of the snow and ice encrusting the tires.

Poor Louis worried about everything back then, and I can feel his relief as they began driving again. A few minutes later he pulled off the freeway and followed another highway south.

"Where are we going?" asked Dee.

"Southwest. I'm going to head down to Kansas to see if we can get under this weather." Louis bit his lip, wondering how much additional gallons of gas the detour would cost them.

The highway was still empty. He thought, we've probably got an hour before the morning commuters begin to show. The girls were still sleeping and he hoped he could knock out some miles before they woke.

*

They had started out slowly into the Annapurnas. Louis didn't want to wear Dee out early, plus he was still nervous about her ankle. Every mile or so, they passed through a small village where people smiled and greeted them. At the entrance to each town and at its exit there was always a row of Tibetan prayer wheels and Dee took to spinning them all, each and every one, while Louis patiently waited.

Often a villager would offer a blessing to her when they saw her spinning the wheels, and inevitably they would then be asked to sit and have some mint tea. Dee happily accepted every invitation and seemed to genuinely enjoy the conversations. Meanwhile, Louis would smile and grow restless with the long journey ahead in mind.

On his first visit here, people had been nice to Louis and the hikers he had fallen in with, but also somewhat guarded. His fellow travelers had been his age, mid-twenties, dirty young people in worn clothing; and they'd also smoked a lot of hash.

Now, however, everywhere they went people were opening their homes and asking them to stay. He watched Dee trying to communicate with the few words of Hindi she'd learned, and took pride in the smiles they showered on her for her efforts. He had really liked her since the first month they began to date, but now, watching her laugh and joke with the Nepalese they encountered, he felt a deep love sweep over him.

But he still had to refuse countless invitations to stop and visit.

"I'm sorry," he would say, "we would love to stop, but we have a long way to go and we should knock out some miles before the rain starts."

When they got on the trail again, Dee glanced at the blue sky and teased him. "Before the rain starts?"

He looked up as well. "Sure, this time of year they have afternoon showers here."

The playful look she gave him left no doubt she thought he was making this up.

Later that day they stopped again for mint tea and hardboiled eggs. Louis consulted a map and realized they still had four miles to go to get to the next village. "We shouldn't stay long."

Dee humored him and paid for their lunch, but a mile down the road she wanted to stop again. Louis got frustrated and kept pushing to move. When they summited a hill later he saw the village in the distance. It was only a mile away, but a mass of dark clouds was hovering over it, moving their way.

They were hit by a heavy downpour ten minutes from the village. Soaking wet, they stumbled into a small stone building with a metal roof.

The keeper was a quiet little man with kind eyes. He set them up with a tiny room in the back. It had one bed that squeaked loudly when you moved on it. The ceiling was very low, only six feet above the rough wooden plank floor. Soon it began to rain again, and the sound of the heavy drops hitting the metal roof was deafening.

Dee looked out the one small window and saw more dark clouds. "We got here just in time," she said.

"An hour ago would have been better," said Louis as he peeled off his dripping clothes. A fireplace was crackling in the lobby and they hung their clothes on a wooden rack there to dry.

Later, the keeper knocked on their door and handed Dee two steaming bowls of soup. He said something about the rain, but it was impossible to understand him in the noise.

He glanced at the roof, smiled, and backed away.

They ate in silence, the din of the rain making even simple conversation difficult.

After, they zipped their sleeping bags together and crawled in, cuddling to get warm. It began to hail and the level of noise seemed so obscene that they both laughed. The hail drowned the sound of their love making on the squeaking bed, and when they stepped outside the next morning the steaming, glittering world that greeted them seemed perfect.

*

Just outside of Springfield, Illinois the Vinniman stopped at a McDonalds so the girls could burn off some energy on the playground. Louis watched them while Dee prepared a bottle; she plugged a small heater into the cigarette lighter socket to warm the milk.

"Go easy with her!" shouted Louis as he saw Pinky trying to drag her sister up a slide. The little one was bundled in thick one-piece pajamas and seemed content to be hauled around.

Dee came with the bottle, and Louis picked the infant off the slide and told Pinky to run off.

"I'll take care of Stinky," he said.

Pinky shook her head. "She's called The Shrimp now."

"The Shrimp?"

Pinky nodded seriously, then climbed up the slide and disappeared into a plastic tunnel. A moment later she reappeared, sliding down backwards and upside down, and again Louis flashed back to Nepal.

*

They had pressed deeper into the mountains, gaining altitude and slowly leaving the traces of civilization behind. Industrial items like coca cola and bags of chips soon began to disappear from the roadside stalls, and instead, fruit, chapattis, hard boiled eggs and more tea stalls appeared. Dee lamented when she no longer found chocolate bars on the shelves.

"I should have stocked up at that big village we passed through two days ago."

After a week they were starting to slim down. Louis tightened his belt a notch. Dee was already skinny, but she glowed with the experience of traveling, and they fantasized about future meals.

"I'm gonna eat so much *pad Thai* when we get back to Southeast Asia," said Dee as she peeled her fourth hardboiled egg of the day.

They were high in the mountains now, surrounded by soaring, snow-covered peaks. Reports were trickling back from other travelers that the pass was closed and might be for several weeks. But they continued on, happily, in love and lost in the beautiful scenery.

Then on the morning they left Pisang—only a few miles from the pass—Louis fell down a flight of stone steps. He'd slipped on the top step of a double flight of stairs that led to a courtyard where Dee waited. Unable to stop his momentum, he had roughly tumbled downward.

Dee saw him from the courtyard and screamed, and Louis heard the worry in her voice. Later in his life he would remember plummeting through the air with her concerned cries warming his heart, and he would claim that was when he "fell" in love.

He came to a stop on the bottom, backwards and upside down—just like Pinky on the slide. With Dee's help he slowly struggled to his feet, and although he was bruised, they were both surprised that he hadn't broken any bones.

They left with high intentions to force their way over the pass. The sun was shining and they hoped that other travelers would try to tramp through the five-foot snow drifts that currently blocked the way.

They planned to stay in one last village before attempting the pass. A lot of other travelers were also waiting there. Just outside the small settlement Louis asked Dee for a quick stop to grab something out of his pack.

Dee sat down on a log, shivering. The waterproof hood of her jacket was pulled up over her head, and her face was hidden behind a pair of sunglasses and a white scarf.

Louis was crouched before his pack.

She watched him zip it up, then turn and kneel before her. In his hand was a small ring he'd bought in Kathmandu. It was silver, with two pieces of mother of pearl embedded in it.

"Will you marry me?" he asked.

"Yes!" she said.

He gave her a blank stare, and grinned. "Really?"

Her eyes lit up as she knelt beside him and hugged him.

"Of course!" she said. "Do you think I'd follow you into these mountains if I wasn't willing to marry you?"

They stood and looked over the snow-covered peaks. It seemed the entire world consisted of only the Annapurna Range, and as they leaned against each other, it contracted even more until it was only them.

*

A sendoff gift from Louis's friend, Bone, saved the girls from going stir crazy when they passed through Kansas. He'd given them a VHS player that ran off the DC plug in the back of the Vinniman. It buckled into the seat between the girls and together they watched Disney movies on a little five-by-three screen.

They played them over and over: *Robin Hood*, *The Jungle Book*, *The Little Mermaid* and *Peter Pan*. Soon Louis and Dee knew just about every line of dialogue. The girls were happy and occupied so they just kept watching as the miles ticked away.

The deep, jolly-base of Baloo the bear from the *Jungle Book* boomed through the car and lightened everyone's mood.

> *Look for the bare necessities*
> *The simple bare necessities*
> *Forget about your worries and your strife*
> *I mean the bare necessities*
> *That's why a bear can rest at ease*
> *With just the bare necessities of life*

*

The high pass didn't open during their first week in the little village. More and more travelers arrived and soon food became scarce and accommodations were sold out.

Louis and Dee were grateful to have a small room to themselves when the lobby started to fill up with travelers who had to sleep on the floor. Dee witnessed the supplies disappearing from the one store in the village and quickly bought the last roll of toilet paper.

They lived off boiled rice, tea, and hardboiled eggs that never seemed fully cooked. It was difficult to boil water in the thin air at thirteen thousand feet.

A few times, earlier on the trail, Dee had been tempted to drink from one of the crystal clear streams that flowed by them, but Louis had stopped her.

"You don't know where that water comes from," was his warning.

Dee had thought him paranoid, but she saw his point when she used the outhouse for the inhabitants of the guest house. The stone structure with a wooden door sat over a rushing stream. It afforded little privacy for lack of caulking between the stones, and the wind whistled loudly when you sat down on the worn plastic seat covering the hole.

Despite their caution, they both caught dysentery.

"Could be they washed our salad in the water," he said when doubled-over in pain, "or they didn't boil the tea water long enough."

Late one night, Louis was shivering in the outhouse, miserable and weak. Through the course of the night he'd made close to a dozen trips there.

By the first morning light he was seated in the courtyard, leaning against a wall, watching two Italian travelers return from an attempt at crossing the pass.

"No good!" said one of them.

Dee sat next to him, her skin ashen. She shivered from weakness and the chill deep in her bones caused by the altitude.

"How long do you want to wait?" she asked.

Louis stared at the outhouse. "Not much longer." He'd wanted to reach the other side of the pass — a temple called Muktinath where he'd stopped before — but now that Dee had agreed to marry him he just wanted to enjoy life with her.

"What do you want to do when we get out of here?" he asked.

Right away she said, "Go back to a beach — maybe Thailand?"

She looked at him, trying to gage how badly he'd wanted to complete the circuit. "How 'bout you?"

He laughed. "Right now I wish we'd just rented a row boat for the day and cruised on that lake next to Pokhara."

He looked at the two Italians limping to a room on the second floor.

"Let's go now," he said. "Let's just hike back the way we came and get out of here."

A flicker of life lit up Dee's tired eyes. "You'd do that?"

Louis drew his knees up and wrapped his arms around them.

He said, "It feels like we're forcing things with this pass."

She painfully straightened up, and then extended a hand to help him to his feet, saying, "Then what are we waiting for?"

"Okay then," he said and smiled, "let's get to a beach."

Dee paused. "Hey, if I had said no to your proposal, what would you have done?"

Louis smirked. "You weren't gonna leave these mountains without saying yes — if you hadn't agreed to marry me I'd still have seventy or eighty miles to talk you into it before we got back to civilization."

*

Kansas was cold and rainy and Louis grudgingly checked them into a cheap motel for the night. A cross wind had thrown the Vinniman all over the place, making him grip the wheel tightly so they didn't get blown right into the oncoming traffic, and he was exhausted.

After paying for the room he had one hundred and fifty dollars left.

This was their first night of not sleeping in the van. Pinky was so excited she wouldn't stop jumping on the bed.

"Calm down, Pinky!" pleaded Louis, but it did no good.

She laughed, looked at Dee, and said, "I'm not Pinky anymore. My name is Pookey Bear now."

"Pookey Bear? Really?"

Dee chuckled and snuggled up to her, sniffing her neck.

"Yes," she said, "she's my Pookey Bear."

The room had one bed and they stuck Pookey Bear in the middle of it and slept one on each side. The Shrimp was wrapped in a blanket and nested into one of the dresser draws they'd pulled out and stuck by the bed.

Dee cranked up the heat and they slept like they were drugged.

*

They were elated to be leaving the mountains, but still had a long way to go to get out. Soon after they began to descend a stomach virus got a hold of them and about once an hour one of them had to throw up.

They talked less, and their motions turned robotic. One moment it would be the bowels, the next the stomach.

At first they looked for a secluded place to let the spasms pass, but the fits came on so suddenly that they often found themselves squatting on the side of the trail, miserably retching at the same time.

The sickness pulled them closer and even though they talked seldom, they seemed strangely in sync with each other.

By the third day of their descent they were sitting by the side of the trail, too weak to move, when a caravan of yaks came by. The local men looked away as they passed and pretended not to notice the two travelers squatting in the dust and retching.

The pounds continued to fall off them.

At a guest house approximately fifty miles away from the end of the trail Dee started to fever up.

Louis consulted several other travelers and late one night a group of five stood looking down at Dee as she twisted in her fever dreams. Her skin was burning hot and Louis now had a panicked look in his eyes.

An older German man said, "If her fever climbs any higher you must do something."

"What should I do?" Louis asked.

The man's girlfriend said, "If you cannot get the fever down then you must put her in the water."

By the entrance to the guest house was a small stream that flowed down from the mountains. It was incredibly cold and the thought of dunking Dee in it filled him with dread.

The woman had some medicine—a German equivalent of Tylenol—and they managed to get Dee to swallow a few tablets.

She had a thermometer, too, and after sticking it in Dee's mouth she eyed it and said, "Forty-one degrees."

Louis gave her a confused, panicked look, and she paused, then said, "That would be almost 105 degrees on your Fahrenheit scale."

Louis blanched. The German woman looked down at Dee. "She seems very dehydrated. You should make her drink much water, then you must wait and see."

The next morning the fever broke, but Dee was miserably weak. Louis didn't think she could walk out. There were no roads and the closest place she could have flown out of was on the far side of the pass, at Muktinath, which they had now left far behind.

They rested for a day, but both felt they would only get better once they were out of the mountains. They needed more nutritious food, and to get some medicine to help with the dysentery.

The next morning they packed their few belongings. Dee was lethargic, and Louis loaded her pack for her and carried it down the stairs to the lobby. He watched her, feeling helpless.

He was taking items out of her pack, stowing them in his own, when an older Australian couple approached them.

"We heard about your girlfriend and want to help," said the woman.

Louis stared at her, barely hearing her words.

The man continued, "Last year our daughter got sick on this trail and someone paid for a donkey to take her out—we want to do the same for you."

They motioned to the courtyard where an old man stood next to a small donkey. He gave Louis a toothless grin and pointed his chin at the animal.

"We've paid for the donkey to take you to the trail entrance," said the Australian.

Louis stumbled through thanking them, later wishing he'd gotten their address, and walked into the courtyard. The old man strapped Dee's pack to the side of the donkey, then helped her to climb into the rickety, home-made saddle.

The last fifty miles seemed to take an eternity. The little old man left them alone, sometimes appearing on a rock ahead of them as he waited for them to catch up, other times coming up from behind and overtaking them.

They moved slowly, as if in a daze. Dee gripped the saddle and held on, not really aware where she was. When the trail became steep, Louis tried to talk her into getting off, but she wouldn't.

The path led across several high suspension bridges. Far below icy rivers rushed by and the spectacle was dizzying. One bridge was in terrifyingly poor shape; some of the foot boards had broken away.

Shouting over the wind, Louis tried in vain to get Dee off the donkey.

A strong gust whipped through the canyon below them and made the donkey skittish; halfway across the bridge it stopped before a gap in the boards. Through it they could see the river rushing a hundred feet below.

Louis leaned against the donkey to force it forward, but it wouldn't budge. He looked around helplessly.

The wind howled down the canyon, swaying the bridge. A sudden blast tore the plastic cover off Dee's pack and sent it tumbling away with the wind, and for one horrible moment Louis thought it was Dee falling off the bridge.

All of a sudden the donkey jumped over the gap, almost unseating Dee in the process. She screamed and swung her arms wildly, searching for the railing.

Louis jumped over the opening and was at her side, his heart pounding, a sick feeling in his stomach from the quick glimpse of the rapids far below.

They continued, moving slower each day. Their clothes hung loosely on them and neither of them spoke a word.

*

The Vinniman passed by Denver, and then Boulder, without stopping. By the time they made it to Rocky Mountain National Park the Shrimp had had enough and was screaming inconsolably, while Pookey Bear continuously unclipped her safety harness and attempted to get out of her child seat.

The sunset was fading and it was cold out when they pulled up to the park entrance gate at an elevation of over eight thousand feet; the craggy mountain peaks around them stretched to fourteen thousand.

An orange glow hovered over the snow.

Dee rolled down her window and the scent of pine whooshed through the vehicle with an icy blast. The Shrimp got quiet. Pookey Bear sat back and eyed the surrounding forest.

They stopped by a booth, and both girls looked apprehensively at the ranger as he collected their information and assigned a campsite.

Louis and Dee set up the tent with frozen fingers and they all piled inside.

In the tent's small vestibule Louis got the propane stove going and cooked some macaroni and cheese.

Dee watched him put the stove away after it had cooled off. He shook the canister he'd been using and was about to throw it away when he stopped and set it by the stove.

"There might be one meal left in it," he said.

"Just relax," said Dee. "If you act like you're having fun the girls will have fun."

He took a deep breath and faced Pookey Bear.

"Do you want to make a fort?" he asked.

The young girl nodded seriously. "Of course."

They zipped two sleeping bags together and hid inside from Dee and the Shrimp, pretending they were in an igloo hiding from polar bears.

Dee and the girls soon fell asleep, but Louis stayed up late, staring at the ceiling of the tent while he contemplated the road ahead. After the long day in the vehicle it felt strange to not be moving. He'd tried to take Dee's advice and act relaxed, like a tourist on vacation, but the reality was he felt more like a refugee.

*

Eventually they staggered out of the Annapurnas. Louis had lost a quarter of his body weight, and Dee looked pale and fragile. The trailhead didn't seem real to either of them. Louis looked at the paved road, a quarter mile away, and thought it was a trick.

At the trailhead they met three English girls who were on their way to Kathmandu.

"You don't look good — you should come with us," said one of them to Dee as she gave Louis a disapproving glance. "We're gonna catch the night bus when it passes by and we'll be in Kathmandu in the morning."

Louis was determined to get to the city quickly, too, and find a doctor. Unfortunately, their luggage and passports were stored in Pokhara. It was only five miles to the west, but in the opposite direction of Kathmandu, and he doubted there was time to return there and still make the night bus.

"I wish we could," he said, "but our things are in Pokhara."

"Well, it won't take both of you to get your stuff," said the woman. "She could still come with us." The other two stared at him while Dee gazed off, barely aware of the conversation.

Louis took their dark glances as an admonishment and wasn't surprised at the suggestion. It seems they thought he was to blame for Dee's condition.

He volunteered to bus back to Pokhara and grab their packs, while Dee went directly to Kathmandu, even though it felt wrong to leave her.

His mind had slowed down in the mountains and now nothing made sense. It seemed to him that the women had unfairly judged him.

The local bus to Pokhara stopped and one of the woman waved with both arms so he would stay. The driver hit the horn and gestured for Louis to hurry up.

He kissed Dee goodbye and staggered to the road, barely able to walk or hold up his backpack.

In the beginning of the ride he thought he might actually get their belongings and make it back in time for the night bus, but the local bus stopped every half mile, and sometimes remained waiting at the stops for an eternity.

It got dark, and when a merchant came in with six large sacks of grain he lost his seat. Somewhere during the murky, bumpy ride he sank to the ground and just lay there.

The only thing that lightened his mood was the chickens on the floor, loose. Whenever the bus hit a violent bump they burst into the air like popcorn.

Late in the night he found the guest house in Pokhara. The inn was full so he slept on the open roof on a roll mat. In the morning he woke under a layer of frost.

He claimed their luggage, ate a big breakfast, and then boarded a ten-hour bus ride to Kathmandu.

Throughout the journey he thought of Dee, slowly moving with him, side by side, the enormous peaks all around them, icy white and glittering in the heavens like angels.

He laughed at the thought, thinking, it didn't seem like anyone was protecting us. Ever since he'd proposed to her, everything had gone downhill: the pass had remained closed, they'd each gotten sick, and Dee had worsened to the point that he'd had to lead her out on a donkey.

But then he remembered her walking beside him, silently, and he again felt that connection, that oneness, like they were each other's shadow. He hoped she would be at the guest house they had agreed on, but he was weak, and his thoughts scattered, and their reunion seemed more and more like a fever dream.

*

Early the next morning Louis and Pookey Bear crawled out of the tent. There was a chill in the air and the grass was covered in frost. A sign read "Moraine Campground" and a short distance away was a wide open grassy area carved by an ancient glacier.

They had a picnic planned for breakfast, with yoghurt, an orange, and peanut butter and jelly sandwiches. The little girl's attention was fading until Louis said, "And I've got chocolate, too."

She stared up into his eyes. "Let me see it."

Louis pulled out the Hershey bar that had melted and been refrozen several times now, and let her handle it.

She half opened the wrapper and inspected it, then folded it back up and handed it to Louis. "Okay, let's go."

Their choice of picnic spots on the moraine was limited; a strong wind was blowing and he wanted something sheltered. In the middle of the moraine, a quarter mile off, sat a cluster of pines on a rocky island.

"That's where we're heading," he said to Pookey Bear. She looked over the distance and then nodded approval.

To get there they had to cross a few shallow streams. As the day warmed they would flow stronger, but at this early hour they were easy to traverse.

The sun was still struggling to climb over the mountain peaks around them and all but the island was in shadow; he hoped it would be warmer in the sun.

Louis carried Pookey Bear over the streams, hoping across easily on large stones.

A movement caught his eye and they stopped halfway, trying to make out several animals grazing a mile away.

"What are those?" asked Pookey Bear.

"Maybe deer — I can't tell from this distance."

They settled down on the island, nestled between several large boulders on the far side, where the wind was less. Pookey Bear tried repeatedly to talk Louis into starting the meal with the chocolate, but failed.

Finally, she sighed and said, "I miss our Missy dog."

Louis was silent for a moment, then said, "Do you remember what she looked like? How she snuggled with you in bed, and how much she liked to lay by the fire?"

The little girl's blue eyes blinked as she remembered the dog.

She closed her eyes for a moment and then said, "I can still see her."

Louis open a jug of water and handed it to her. "That's her spirit, and it will always stay with you."

*

In Kathmandu, Louis dragged himself up a flight of stairs, slowly, one at a time, until he got to the reception desk on the sixth floor.

"I am sorry about these stairs," said the clerk, "but the elevator, he is broken."

Louis leaned against the desk, drained of all energy, catching his breath.

Just then Dee walked into the reception. She wasn't moving too nimbly either. She didn't see Louis and addressed the clerk.

She said, "Can you make sure my fiancé finds my room when he gets here?"

Louis looked up and beamed. "Fiancé?"

She turned to him with a small cry and they flew into each other's arms. Louis held her with all of his remaining strength.

The next day they went to a Tibetan doctor who took their pulse in three different places and then prescribed a regiment of tea with little black pellets.

"No milk. No sugar."

The pellets tasted bitter.

"This is horrible," said Dee.

Louis grimaced as he swallowed some tea, but within twenty minutes they both started to feel better.

The next morning Louis stared at the pellets before dropping a few in his tea. He said, "These things look like goat turds. Do you think they feed the medicine to the goats and then harvest the turds?"

Dee sipped her tea. "I don't care. I do feel better now."

Over the next week they meandered through Kathmandu; always walking side by side, slowly. They still didn't talk much, and Louis couldn't shake the feeling that the big peaks were still over his shoulder, watching them.

*

Pookey Bear polished off the last of the chocolate bar with a grin, and they collected the wrappers to keep them from blowing off. An hour had passed and the sun was strong enough now to burn away the chill.

They lay in the sunshine on their backs, shoulder to shoulder, feeling the warm glow.

Louis let the gentle rays warm his weary bones. In that clear morning sunshine, he felt loved. And it charged him, and filled him with expectation, like something grand was about to happen.

As he shouldered his small daypack he heard the clickity-clack of hooves. He looked over one of the large rocks and saw at least fifty elk moving their way. They had been trotting through the moraine behind the small island.

Quickly he lifted Pookey Bear onto his shoulders.

Now the elk were passing them, less than twenty feet away. They snorted loudly, and a few rolled their eyes in surprise when they beheld Louis with Pookey Bear on his shoulders.

"Yeah!" she shouted as they began to move away.

Louis's heart was racing, and his exhilaration was fueled on by the look of excitement and bewilderment in his daughter's eyes. As he listened to her laughing and shouting, their grey, worry-burdened journey suddenly burst into an adventure bright with color.

The Magna, Hollis, New Hampshire

Chapter Three

Rocky Mountain National Park, Colorado
(April 2002)

After they returned from their hike, Louis made breakfast; using the propane stove he cooked scrambled eggs in tent's vestibule. His belly was already full of yogurt and granola bars, but they had a long way to drive and he craved something more substantial.

They had to wait for Pookey Bear trying to roll up her own sleeping bag. She angrily refused any help. The Shrimp watched it all with wonder as Dee got her dressed and then put away everyone else's sleeping bags.

They stopped at the park bathroom where Louis shaved with ice-cold water. Dee washed the pan, plates and cutlery, and then organized the cooler. After everyone had used the toilet they piled back into the Vinniman and were on the road by nine.

Dee heated a bottle for the Shrimp, and then put on a movie. Today's feature: Disney's *Tarzan*.

By dropping south to Kansas they had escaped some of the bad weather, but their goal was Seattle, so they now had to head northwest. As a parting gift, Louis's parents had prepaid the ferry passage from Seattle to Skagway, and even though they still had many miles to drive once they disembarked, Louis felt if they could just make the ferry he might be able to stretch their money far enough.

When they left the park they turned due north on route 87 toward Wyoming, and before noon had passed Cheyenne.

The girls were settled down, resigned to being strapped into their car seats for the day only because of the movie player. Tarzan was mimicking Clayton in the back...

"Oh, I see..."

Dee had fallen asleep in the passenger seat, a pillow between her head and the window.

Louis watched her, wondering if her luck had been good or bad when she'd fallen in with him. They'd both been younger, freer, and it could have happened differently. He wondered how his life would be if a different woman now sat in that seat.

*

Louis had first run into Jackie at a coffee shop. She'd been engaged at the time, but they'd established a friendship. She told him where she worked—a club in south Nashua—and on rainy days he would stop down and visit.

Back then Louis ran a painting crew in Hollis. They did mostly exteriors so when it rained work stopped. His partner, Satchmo, was also in his late twenties and didn't mind the shortened work weeks caused by storms; and the crew were a handful of younger guys who had few financial obligations.

Everyone had a nickname there, too: Big Wes, Pearl Fish, Seano, Gator, Pistol Pete. Louis they called Whip. He claimed he got the nickname from a habit of whipping his empty coffee cup at the slowest worker, but I've heard others state it was from a play on his last name that rhymed with mayonnaise, and that later turned into Miracle Whip, and then just Whip.

As soon as a couple of rain drops hit, one of the guys—usually Pearl Fish—would draw a circle on the ground. Louis would then declare how many drops were needed to call it a day; his choice usually depending on how badly he needed to finish the job.

Later it would be contingent on how long it had been since he'd last seen Jackie.

"Come on, Whip," Pearl Fish would plead, regardless of how low a number he set. "You know it's gonna rain. Why work if it's just gonna wash away. Let's go to the Big M."

The Big M, or Mathews, was a strip club that had opened a few months ago in southern Nashua. It was the only one in New Hampshire and had caused quite a stir.

The women in Nashua didn't think much of the guys that went there, but Louis didn't care. He found that most women his age — twenty-nine — didn't want to get involved with him because he traveled every winter. They were looking for something more solid.

At Martha's Exchange on Main Street he'd met a young woman once, and she'd soon steered the conversation to the cost of new homes in the area, and finally, professions and income.

"Why would anyone ever rent?" she'd asked him.

He'd wanted to retreat out of the conversation, which had begun to feel like an interview. Knowing Louis as I do now, I can vividly image him wanting to turn and run.

When he told her that he tried to make enough money in six months to travel the other half of the year she didn't look impressed.

He added, "But you can live in some of these countries for two or three hundred dollars a month — hotels and transportation included!"

She looked around the room uneasily. "But how will you ever pay for a house? Or save for retirement?"

"I'd rather collect experiences than possessions," said Louis.

She had smiled at him with a hint of pity and said, "I think you just don't want to grow up," then walked away.

The first time he went to visit Jackie at Mathews it was a rainy Monday afternoon. He went alone, and he didn't tell his crew where he was going because they would have all piled into his pickup to come along.

He entered the club, which was decorated with lots of brass railings and mirrors. In the middle of the room was a long stage with seating around it at floor level. The guys sitting there would place money on the stage, and the dancers would slowly circle from one customer to the next, grab the cash, and do a little dance for them.

Touching the ladies was strictly forbidden. They danced topless, in skimpy little thongs. They would bare all in a private dance, but only at a few feet's distance.

The DJ announced Jackie just as Louis walked into the club. Only a few other patrons were present in the back of the room getting private dances. "Fresh from a photo shoot for *Field and Stream* magazine..." the DJ was teasing, "our own star from Maine!"

She smirked and flipped him off as she stepped onto the stage wearing five-inch heels, a short skirt and a silky top. Soon the music began. The first song was Sarah McLaughlin's *Ice Cream* and Louis watched her dance to it from the doorway, unnoticed.

With no customers in front of her, Jackie danced like she really enjoyed it. She swung around the pole at one end of the stage, and it seemed to Louis that she didn't have a care in the world.

"Your love is better than ice cream,
better than anything else that I've tried."

She smiled when she saw him by the door, and motioned to a cushioned seat a few feet away from the stage. Louis sat there, watching her dance to the near-empty room, not wanting the music to end.

She eventually finished and came over, and they talked for the next two hours.

Before he left she also told him her real name.

*

They drove all day, passing Casper, and eventually Sheridan. The girls grew restless, and they stopped at a McDonald's with a playground. Pookey Bear climbed all over it and then put up a fit when they left after an hour.

Around sunset they reached Cody, Wyoming; for the last hour the baby had been screaming nonstop. Dee and Louis scanned the side of the road for both accommodation and a restaurant or grocery store.

Their cooler was just about empty; the few items left were sloshing around in melted ice water. It was off season, but the motels they passed all seemed to post outrageously high rates.

Finally, a diner with neon lights appeared. It looked warm inside, and not too fancy, and they decided to go in for a meal.

Louis's appetite left him at the prospect of spending money, but he put on a brave face. "I'm starving!" he shouted. "Who else is hungry?"

"Me!" yelled Pookey Bear.

"What do you say we get a big meal, and then crawl into the tent?"

Dee looked at him skeptically. The temperature had dropped sharply once the sun set, and they both knew it was going to be a cold night.

"Can't we get a room tonight?" she asked.

Louis looked at her. "Did you see the rates? A night in one of these motels will use up what could be groceries for a week."

She unhappily began to dig through the ice on the bottom of the cooler. "Okay, but if we're not getting a room I want to do some shopping tonight so we have food."

Louis agreed, and after a leisurely meal at the diner they drove to a grocery store where Louis pealed three twenties out of his wallet and gave them to her. Four more remained.

"Buy whatever we need to get us to Seattle. Can you do it with this?"

She looked over their remaining supplies. "Yup—sandwich meat, mac and cheese, bread, fruit, milk, eggs and cereal."

"Okay," he said, but then she added, "Oh, and diapers—it might be close."

He gave her another twenty, but said, "Try not to spend it if you can."

She looked at the money, then back at him. "I don't care if we sleep in the Vinniman tonight, but I'm not tenting it—it's too friggin' cold."

Around ten Louis parked the van in a lot by a local attraction billed as "The Real Wild West." They planned on being gone before it opened at eight in the morning, but it was a long night, with Louis starting the Vinniman up every thirty minutes and letting it run for five.

In the morning they continued west, heading toward Yellowstone National Park, with the sun winking in the rearview mirror.

*

Eventually Louis had started to look forward to getting rained out of work. He would watch the weather reports, and glance at the sky when the clouds began to thicken.

As soon as a few drops hit the circle he was gone.

He'd become friends with Jackie, and one of her girlfriends named Simone. They weren't allowed to just hang out with guys, so when he talked to Jackie, Simone would dance for the two of them, and after a while they would switch.

Both women were twenty years old, and they were focused on making money. There were at least fifty dancers who worked at Mathews, and Jackie and Simone shared some gossip about the ones that did coke or slept with customers. The two of them might smoke some weed or have a few drinks at work, but they had plans for the future.

Simone wanted to go to Alaska and run a restaurant. Her boyfriend was living there now, putting in the foundation. She was petite with long black hair and a sultry stare, and as she gyrated to the music, naked except for her heels, Louis noticed the smoldering looks she often gave Jackie.

Jackie just wanted to get out of Maine. She was on her way to California, and would go as soon as she'd saved a nest egg.

Other guys would see him in the corner, getting private dances from two girls for a full hour, and figure he was spending a fortune, but mostly he only paid for a few beers. Every now and then he'd buy a dance from one of their friends so she could join their conversation.

Most of the girls were from out of town, and he was a local, so he told them about local quarries they could swim in, or where to go in Nashua for a drink when they weren't working.

Jackie had hinted that she was having trouble with her fiancé, but Louis didn't ask further. He liked how uncomplicated their friendship was. He loved the liberal feel of the club; the sense that you were doing something a little bit wayward, but not that bad. What a great way to spend a Monday afternoon, he thought, while everyone else is doing their boring nine-to-five. He liked the dancers; he never felt like he was being judged when he spent time with them.

One rainy afternoon Louis drove to the club a little more anxious than usual. He'd heard that Jackie had broken up with her guy and wondered if that would change his relationship with her.

He entered the club and spotted her in the DJ booth, picking out her music.

She had her back to him and was chatting with the DJ, so he waited for her to turn around.

When she spotted him her eyes lit up and she screamed, "Hey!" unwittingly right into the microphone.

The thirty-odd patrons jumped in their seats.

The other dancers clapped and a few whistled at her.

The DJ shouted, "Settle down, Jackie!"

She laughed outrageously, put her arms in the air and did a sexy little move, and then danced in a circle.

When they had a moment alone he asked her if she wanted to go on a road trip with him to his family cabin in northern Maine. She said yes, and they excitedly decided to drive there on his motorcycle the following Monday.

*

At noon they skirted Yellowstone Lake, and shortly after Louis pulled over at the National Park headquarters. The park had just today opened for the season. Louis reserved a camping spot despite Dee's disapproval.

"They say it's gonna snow — are you crazy? We're gonna all freeze to death."

Pookey Bear had been wild all morning, squirming in her seat, because she thought they were going to a "park" – one with playgrounds, or at least a swing, but they found none. There wasn't even a field she could run around in, because winter still had a grip on the land and everything was frozen.

Louis hoped she might like to see Old Faithful and talked up the geyser while they drove to it.

"Wait till you see this thing — water is gonna shoot right out of the ground and up into the sky."

They parked the Vinniman a hundred feet away from the geyser. Dee looked out the window skeptically. A strong wind had picked up, one with a deep chill to it, and as she bundled both girls in multiple layers she asked, "When's it going to off again?"

Louis fidgeted. "Well, it erupts every ninety-one minutes — give or take a few — but I'll find out when it's gonna blow next so we don't have to stand out there waiting."

He exited the car, and ran to the group with his head down, trying to shelter it. When he returned his ears were red. He quickly shut the door and said, "Any minute!"

Soon they were standing roughly forty feet away from the geyser.

Pookey Bear eyed the hole in the ground suspiciously. "I don't see a geezer."

Louis knelt next to her. "Just wait. In a minute water is going to shoot out of that hole."

"How much water?"

"I don't really know — enough to fill a swimming pool."

She looked around at the frozen parking lot.

"I don't want to swim."

By the time it finally erupted Dee felt like an eternity had gone by. Her cheeks were flushed red and her toes numb. The Shrimp was in her arms, snuggling against her for warmth. What the hell are we doing here? she thought. We should be in a nice warm room somewhere all cuddled up and watching a movie.

A rumble brought her back to the present and she stepped back as water shot up almost a hundred feet in the air. The wind blew the mist in their direction and suddenly they weren't just freezing, but also wet.

"I'm cold," said Pookey Bear.

"Back to the Vinniman," said Dee with a glare.

They rushed back and Louis cranked up the heat. Before they buckled the girls up they changed them into dry clothes.

When Louis pulled into the campground Dee was livid. "We can't still camp. Look at that wind—you're insane."

Louis shrugged. "We're all warm and dry now. And it'll be nice inside the tent."

They both stared at the girls, who were indeed warm now, but their faces were red from windburn.

"It's too cold to set up a tent!" shouted Dee. "If you want to go camping, you set it up!"

This was the maddest he'd seen her in a long time, and he knew he'd get no help from her.

Louis loved to camp. And he loved weather, too—all kinds of weather. You couldn't get him to cancel a hike because of an impending storm or a chilly day; you had to find another excuse or he'd make you go. And he certainly wasn't going to bail on camping because of a cold wind. He'd tented in Patagonia, and almost lost his toes to frostbite on the highest mountain in the Andes, Aconcagua.

So as he prepared to set up their tent in icy gusts, I suspect there was a part of him that looked forward to the challenge. He probably would have preferred a little help, but wouldn't be stalled because he had to do it alone.

He exited the Vinniman and opened the Thule roof box where the camping gear was stored; the wind caught the lid and almost tore it off.

After a minute he had the tent and poles out; by that time his hands were numb. He didn't want to think about the wind chill, but as tears skidded off his cheeks he knew it was bad.

He assembled the poles and staked the tent corners down on the windward side so the breeze would help rather than hinder. Once he had the inner shell up he jumped inside, zipped it up, and tried to warm his hands by vigorously rubbing them together. But the wind was furiously tearing at the shell, and he had to climb back outside, add the outer fly and cinch everything down tightly. He hammered a few more stakes into the hard ground and tied two support ropes to nearby trees.

From inside the Vinniman Dee and the two girls watched his progress while eating macaroni and cheese. The engine was running and it looked comfy in there and Louis wanted to join them, but he was almost done so he kept at it.

He moved the sleeping bags and kitchen supplies into the tent, and had hot cocoa cooking in the side vestibule when the girls came in.

Dee was smiling, all traces of her annoyance gone. One thing he'd loved about her from the beginning was her ability to shake off anger and not hold a grudge. She might get real mad, real quick, but once she vented it was over.

"Give me some of that hot chocolate!" she said, rubbing her hands together like she'd helped set up the tent.

"Me too!" shouted Pookey Bear.

*

When Louis picked up Jackie for their trip to the cabin he was excited and anxious at the same time. They had not been intimate, not even kissed, and most of their time together had been at the club where they were constantly observed by the bouncers.

He sat in her kitchen, waiting while she got ready, and did his best to relax before the five-hour ride to the cabin. Jackie's roommate, Simone, had the day off and drifted around the apartment.

At one point Louis looked over and caught Simone watching him, stealthily, like a predator. He wondered if she was just protective of her roommate, or if there was something more going on there.

Jackie came down the stairs wearing a tight-fitting leather jacket, a short skirt, and black boots. I once asked Louis what she looked like back then, and he'd grinned and said, "She looked pretty damn hot."

They said goodbye to Simone, and again Louis felt her eyes on him.

He took Jackie outside and introduced her to his motorcycle, a maroon-colored 1985 *V65 Magna*. The bike was nine years old, but the previous owner had barely driven it and there were less than two thousand miles on the odometer.

With 1100 ccs it was fast even in comparison to newer bikes. Louis had been surprised by its quick takeoff and once almost lost his friend,

Bone, off the back when he popped the clutch and shot off like a rocket from a stoplight.

Bone had been the only person to ride on the back of his bike that summer — mostly for short rides to or from a bar. Jackie stuffed a few things into the black leather saddlebags, and he handed her a helmet.

She stared at him for a moment and then leaned forward and kissed him on the lips.

Then she pulled on her helmet and climbed onto the bike. The sun was shining but it wasn't that hot. Mid-seventies. And there were just enough clouds to create pockets of shade on the highway. They blasted through southern New Hampshire, crossed the Piscataqua River and entered Maine. Without a care, they cruised up the state turnpike and Louis was elated to have Jackie clinging to his back. He was smiling so widely that his cheeks were pressed oddly against the inside of his own helmet.

After an hour he noticed two cars trailing close behind him, like shadows. He was doing eighty and was surprised by their persistence. He reached behind with his left hand and felt Jackie's bare butt cheek, confirming his suspicion that her skirt was fluttering up in the wind. She usually wore a thong and from behind must have looked pretty naked.

Louis gripped the throttle and increased his speed to ninety, which made one of the vehicles lag behind, but the other kept right up. The driver flashed his lights a few times and Louis opened the throttle up to one hundred. The car finally fell back a ways.

A few miles down the road signs for a toll booth began to pop up and he slowly decelerated. He smelled smoke and wondered if there was a nearby fire.

By the time he pulled up to the toll both the pursuing vehicles had caught up again. He ignored them because he now smelled smoke strongly, and then he saw a wisp of it in the rearview mirror. He stopped at the booth and fumbled with his helmet.

The attendant shouted, "Hey, you're on fire!"

He glanced at his left saddlebag and saw smoke pouring out of it. He hopped off the bike and discovered that the heat from the exhaust pipes had burned a hole right through the leather and ignited a package of Pepperidge Farm cookies.

With Jackie's extra weight, the saddlebags hung lower — they were now actually resting on the exhaust pipes.

They walked the bike to the side of the road where Louis raised the bags so they wouldn't hang so low.

A pickup passed them, and Louis saw the passenger glance at Jackie and say to the driver something that ended with, "… smokin'."

His face broke into a wide grin when he realized the smoldering saddlebag had been out for five minutes now — he was describing Jackie.

*

The next morning Louis woke with Pookey Bear's face inches from his own. "I have to go to the bathroom," she whispered.

Shortly after they'd all climbed into the tent the temperature had plummeted, and then the snow had started. It made muffled puffs as it came down on the tent, and once an hour Louis shook the shell to keep too much weight from piling up on it.

But the wind had died completely, and as the snow covered the sides and slowly enclosed them their tent warmed up.

And so Louis was nice and toasty when Pookey woke him.

"Okay, give me a minute."

He backed out of the tent, carrying Pookey Bear, and was unprepared for the spectacle that awaited them. A foot of sparkling white snow covered the ground, and a herd of elk, at least sixty of them, stood silently watching them in the early morning sun. None of them moved — they barely blinked — as they observed the two humans.

A light breeze ruffled their fur, and the way their gaze followed the man and the little girl making their way to the restrooms gave the impression that they were one creature.

"Whoa," exclaimed Pookey Bear.

Louis paused for a moment to look at them. Pookey Bear wiggled out of his arm and crawled up onto his shoulders for a better view.

They began to walk through the herd.

Louis wasn't sure how close he should get and sidestepped cautiously around a big bull that stood between the tent and the bathroom.

Pookey Bear said, "Hi!" and its ears perked up.

As one the animals watched them. Pookey Bear was grinning, and waved excitedly as they passed each elk.

Just as they reached the restrooms Dee scrambled out of the tent with the Shrimp. She stood and looked around.

"Oh my!" she blurted out.

All the elk turned and looked at her at once.

Louis motioned for her to be quiet and said, "Settle down, Jackie."

Erawan Falls, Thailand - 1996

Chapter Four

Whidbey Island, State Park Campground, Washington
(April 2002)

Two days later they were camping in the state park on Whidbey Island, thirty miles north of Seattle. Douglas firs and western hemlocks towered around them, and a gentle breeze blew through the campground, carrying with it the salty scent of Puget Sound.

There were a half-dozen other campers spread out in a loop, but most of the sites were empty. A hundred yards away a public bathroom sat by the quiet road that led deeper into the park.

"The ferry doesn't leave until noon tomorrow," said Louis.

He glanced at the ferry timetable. "It's not that far away, but we should still get there by ten so they can load the Vinniman."

Dee pulled the cooler out of the back of the vehicle.

"I won't buy any more diapers—we'll have to wash out the cloth ones," said Dee. "But we're gonna need some more food."

Louis folded up the timetable and put it in the glovebox. He didn't mention that by his calculations there was no way they would have enough gas money to drive from Skagway to their destination in Healy, Alaska—even if they didn't spend any of their remaining money on food.

He said, "We have fifty bucks left. We'll stop at that grocery store we passed before we crossed the bridge and you can get what you need. I'll put any money left in the gas tank."

She tilted the cooler upside down to let the meltwater drain out and said, "Milk, bread, cheese and some more cereal should do — we'll be fine with that and what we've got."

She handed him half of the last granola bar, and placed her hand on his and said, "We're gonna take it one step at a time, okay?"

He smiled weakly and remembered that once he had said those very words to her.

*

On Thailand's west coast along the Andaman Sea, they'd decided to leave their quiet bungalow and hike to the next beach to cash a traveler's check.

Andaman Beach had no ATM or other cash resources, so when they needed more *baht* they would hike over a small hill that clung to the base of a prominent cliff to get to Railay Beach, a more populated area with tourist services.

Lush jungle covered the top of the cliffs and clung to the craggy terrain. The tall limestone precipices were perfect for rock climbing, and high above several pairs of climbers were slowly ascending.

The cliffs extended right to the water's edge, and many had deep, water-worn caves at their bases. When the tide was low you could walk around the hill at the base of the cliff by their bungalow, but at high tide the only option was to follow a short but steep path through the jungle-clad slope up and over it.

It usually took less than ten minutes to ascend the hill and then descend down the other side.

They got to Railay in the late afternoon, and after cashing a traveler's check, they had dinner at one of the restaurants that lined Sunset Beach. There were only a few bungalows on their beach, and it felt strange to be around all the people.

When they were ready to leave the night sky was dark, the stars obscured by a cloud front that had rolled in. There was no moon and they stepped carefully along the dark beach, trying not to stub their feet on the occasional piece of black coral protruding from the sand.

Dee was holding her sandals in her hand and promptly stubbed her toe. "I really should have worn my boots," she said as she rubbed her foot.

They reached several boulders that marked the beginning of the trail over the hill, and Louis flipped on his flashlight. Dee was wearing a small daypack, and retrieved her own flashlight from it. She didn't turn it on yet, but instead followed closely behind Louis.

They ducked under a large rock and entered the thick tropical forest that covered the hill. Creepers dangled across the path and they hunched forward. It was at least ten degrees warmer in the jungle.

Dee turned her flashlight on. Its beam was very dim.

"Just stay close," said Louis.

At first they made good progress, and soon they were halfway up the hill. Then Louis stumbled and the strap on his left Teva sandal broke. They stopped to examine a long scrape on his ankle. Dee's flashlight had faded to a dull glow.

"Do you have any more batteries in your pack?"

"No," she said, regretful now that she had put them in her Walkman earlier that day.

"I've got a lighter," she said, "but that's it."

Louis shook his head. "That won't do. Just walk right behind me and we'll get through this."

She stepped closer, resting a hand on the small of his back.

A few minutes later they reached the top of the hill. Dee´s light was dead. Louis was limping slightly. From the top they could just barely make out the lights of the one small restaurant on their side of the hill.

They began to descend and suddenly Louis's light died.

In the dark he banged it against the edge of his hand several times.

"Hold on," he said as he unscrewed the flashlight in the dark, carefully took out the batteries, wet their ends, and tried again.

Nothing.

In the black night, the jungle around them seemed to constrict, like a giant, green python.

Dee pulled out the lighter and handed it to Louis.

He flicked it on, but the jungle around them seemed to swallow the light. They could barely make out the creepers only a few feet in front of them. Crickets and other insects were chirping loudly.

In the gloom they crept down the trail toward the sea. They could sense a large drop-off; the tide had come in and the waves crashing on the rocks below them were deafening. Dee clung to him from behind, so close that he could feel her heart beating like a hummingbird's against his shirt which was now soaked with sweat.

He held the lighter in front of him and took small steps. The trail was difficult to make out, and a few times the crunch dead leaves under their feet indicated that they had veered off it. Dee thought of the scorpions and centipedes that moved over the jungle floor and once more chided herself for not wearing her boots.

The lighter grew hot in Louis´s fingers and every few steps he had to stop and change hands.

The trail descended steeply, over ancient black coral with sharp edges, and around limestone boulders that had broken off the towering cliffs they were skirting. A trickle of blood was oozing down Louis's ankle and made his Teva, which now hung on only by the toe strap, slippery.

After twenty long minutes of carefully maneuvering in the dark the trail flattened out and led inland, away from the water. The crashing of the waves receded.

Suddenly the lighter flared up and then with a "pop" it exploded.

Louis dropped it quickly and shook his hands.

"Fuck!" he yelled.

The dim lights of the restaurant were no longer visible. Louis peered through the dark, trying to glimpse them again, because they had seemed an obtainable goal.

In the darkness Dee started breathing rapidly.

Louis had always claimed that he wouldn't marry a woman he hadn't traveled with, partly because he wanted to know how they would handle stressful situations together. Well, here we are, he thought to himself.

"Now what?" asked Dee, panic rising in her voice.

Louis tried to peer through the dimness and glimpse her face.

He said, "We're gonna just take it one step at a time. It doesn't matter if it takes us all night, as long as we don't freak out we'll get through this."

Louis thought of his father, who always said, "The key to being brave is too pretend."

If they could both just pretend their way through this, they would be fine. He could just barely make out her nod, only inches away, but now he sensed a new steadiness in her that in turn relaxed him.

"Okay," she said.

The bamboo around them whispered in the wind.

And then, only a few feet away, they heard something move.

"What was that?" Dee whispered urgently, the calmness dispersing instantly. Suddenly she was up against him, her nails digging into his chest.

They stood still and listened, holding their breath. Whatever it was wasn't moving closer, but skirting them. Louis knew at night the jungle was thick with snakes—deadly cobras among them—but to mention that would only scare Dee more. And he was pretty sure they were as keen to avoid two people stumbling through the dark as Dee and Louis were keen to avoid snakes.

"Most likely a monitor lizard," he said, "just wait a minute and it'll move on."

Dee shivered. She had seen one of those by their bungalow that morning. It had been almost six feet long.

Time seemed to stop while they waited for it to move away.

"Wait!" Dee suddenly exclaimed. She took off her daypack and dug into a side pocket to produce another lighter.

"This one only sparks," she said. "I was going to throw it out, but it might give enough light for us to see something."

Louis flicked it, and barely made out the trail ahead of him. Dots formed in his vision, but for a brief second he'd seen the way. They took baby steps, clinging to each other, and moved forward a few feet.

He struck the lighter again.

Now he saw how the trail descended sharply, into the darkness. He remembered this section. They kept inching forward feeling the way with their feet. But the blinding flickers of light often made things appear unreal. Deceiving.

A few times they lost the trail and had to backtrack.

At one dead end he found himself on a narrow ledge, hovering above dark water smashing on rocks, with Dee clinging to the rocks above him.

He may have only been in that precarious position for a few minutes, but it scared him so much that years later he told me a part of him was still there, listening to the pounding of waves, the moist, salty air buffeting his face, and wondering if his evening would end by drowning after a sudden fall.

Through trial and error, they stayed on the path, clinging to each other, like one creature with four legs.

Louis yearned to move ahead and be done with the ordeal. But even at the snail's pace they had maintained he had banged his shins repeatedly in the dark, and he knew the important thing was to be slow and safe.

"I think we're about thirty feet above the beach," he said hopefully.

More endless minutes passed as they inched forward, descending at first, then climbing over and under a field of boulders, until they finally reached the end of the trail and stumbled onto the beach.

Louis limped to the water's edge, took off his damaged Teva, and soaked his foot in a pool of sea water.

The salt stung, but he hoped it would prevent infection.

Now that they were out of the shadows of the jungle the world seemed to have lit up. The clouds had blown away, and the stars twinkled brightly overhead to faintly illuminate the beach.

A cool breeze dried the sweat on their skin.

Dee was smiling broadly, fear and dread wiped away.

She took a few quick steps and began doing cartwheels in the direction of the restaurant. "Next time we do that hike I'm bringing five flashlights!" she yelled.

Louis grimaced. "Next time we're gonna do it when it's sunny out."

*

Pookey Bear and the Shrimp were crawling around in the tent, happy to no longer be confined to their car seats. Across the road a small path led to the beach, and the salty smell of the water was floating on the breeze, but the girls seemed content to just play on top of their sleeping bags, pretending they were on rafts on a wild river.

Louis restlessly unloaded the Vinniman, taking out the crates from the back and unpacking them. There was an endless battle for space in the vehicle, and even though they were constantly using supplies, it felt like they carried more than when they left.

He threw out the boxes the cereal came in, and consolidated the corn flakes and cheerios in plastic bags that he stored in one of the crates. His maps had become disorderly and he folded up a few and discarded some local maps he'd picked up along the way.

Dee lay on her back, a few feet away, watching the tops of the pines as they swayed in the wind.

He thought that one of the big differences between him and Dee was how they experienced time. Louis seemed to always exist in either the past or the future. He was continuously either reflecting on some former adventure, or planning what the next one would be.

These days he worried a lot about the road ahead, and digging through his supplies relaxed him.

Dee was always in the present. She couldn't tell you the names of half the places they had traveled to. The past was the past. But she had a way of enjoying the moment that Louis envied.

He watched her now, humming a tune, seemingly oblivious of the challenges ahead of them.

She noticed his gaze and winked at him, then reluctantly got up and walked over to the Vinniman. She hauled the car seats out and was about to turn one upside down and shake it when Pookey Bear walked up and stopped her.

"Let me see it," she said.

Dee set it down, and Pookey Bear reached her little hand into the crevices in the fabric and pulled out a half dozen M&M's.

She smirked. "Bummy treats," she said as she plopped them in her mouth.

Louis wouldn't rest until the entire vehicle was empty, so while he collected the odd pieces of trash and laundry in the back, Dee wiped down the dash and emptied the ash tray.

Stuck to a piece of gum in the back she found the remnants of a joint. She couldn't remember the last time they had smoked pot and figured it was pretty old.

Louis said, "I found about four dollars in change in the glove box. We'll save it in case we need to make a call."

She held up four quarters and said, "I found a buck! Let's use some of it to buy my Pookely Dukes a candy bar—that'll mean a lot to her."

Then she held up the roach and added, "And look what else I found."

He went to grab it, but she held it just out of his reach.

"I think we need clear heads right now—we should just throw it out."

For the first time in a while Louis smiled, just barely, and said, "Not unless there's a clear sign, right?"

Dee smirked, knowing he was referring to their first time in Thailand.

*

They were on their way to Nepal and had scheduled a two-month layover in Singapore. Louis's plan was to travel north, through Malaysia to Thailand, and celebrate New Year's Eve on an island called Koh Phangan.

"They have crazy full-moon parties there, and this month the full moon falls on December 31st, so it should be a good one."

After two flights and eighteen hours of air travel from America they landed in Singapore. They took a taxi across town, purchased a train ticket, and then lay on a bench for four hours while they waited for the train.

They had a berth on the overnight train, and the rocking motion should have set them to sleep, but the excitement and jet lag kept them up and instead they talked through the night.

"Koh Phangan is such an amazing place," said Louis. "The phosphorescence in the water makes it glow when you swim at night — it's pretty cool when you're stoned."

Dee held his stare for a moment.

"I promised my mom I wouldn't end up in a Thai prison. I don't think we should smoke."

"Oh, they're pretty relaxed about it on Koh Phangan. There weren't even any cops on the island when I was there ten years ago."

She teased him. "Ten years ago. Ten years ago. All your stories begin with ten years ago. But listen, I don't care what it was like then, unless I see a clear sign that it's really okay I don't want us to smoke."

Louis agreed.

They got off the train on Malaysia's west coast, but still had to go north and then cross the peninsula to get to the ferry terminal on the Gulf of Thailand.

The morning was cool as they walked the six blocks to the parking lot where they were told they could get a ride, and the people they met smiled and bowed at them as they passed. Dee loved Southeast Asia right away. The smells that filled the air were heavy and rich, and she stopped twice to sample food from street vendors.

"This is heavenly!" she said, rolling her eyes as she ate another bite of *Pad Thai*.

She wore a cotton dress that dangled on her shoulders from two small spaghetti straps, and her blond hair flowed over her shoulders as she bounced along. Louis noted that she hardly looked like someone who hadn't had a good night's sleep in almost three days.

They passed a construction site with a dozen workers, and the men gawked at her. When she looked their way they beamed, and then averted their eyes.

One of them came forward, his eyes always on Louis, not Dee. When he was a pace away he smiled shyly and extended his hand to Louis and with his forehead indicated ever so slightly in Dee's direction. "You are lucky man."

Louis looked back, proudly, and noticed the other men nodding at him as well. "Thank you," he said and was surprised to feel his face flush red.

They crossed Malaysia in a large sedan taxi, packed with a half-dozen other travelers, in three hours. Then they waited another three for the ferry to arrive.

When they sailed into the Gulf of Thailand Dee couldn't sit still. One minute she was pointing out the long-tail boats zipping by, the next she was transfixed by a few dolphins frolicking in the wake of the ferry, then she was counting the fish in the water by a small island they passed.

"It's so beautiful," she said. "I can't believe everyone doesn't come here. Why would you go to Fort Lauderdale for spring break when you could go to Thailand?"

This question had often been on Louis's mind when he traveled. Whether in Africa or Asia, he'd always encountered twenty Australians or Canadians for every one American even though based on populations it should have been the opposite.

He shrugged. "Well, the American media does make the rest of the world look scary."

They stopped briefly at Koh Samui and Louis refrained from mentioning he'd once lived here for seven weeks in a bungalow with two Thai women. It seemed a long time ago, and he'd been nowhere near as happy as he was now with Dee. For the first time in his life he felt completely free and content. In love.

When they docked the sun was setting. They walked along the beach and heard music and suddenly remembered it was New Year's Eve.

The party was going to take place on the long beach near the dock, and along the shore various bungalow complexes were blasting their own music, mostly techno. The booming bass followed Dee and Louis around like a lonely dog.

They tried half a dozen guest houses, but none had rooms available.

At the far end of the beach they hiked over a small knoll and found one with seven bungalows, run by a friendly family, and they still had rooms available.

They rented a bungalow by the water's edge at the end of a peninsula. A beautiful sunset had painted the horizon red and orange, and a cool breeze ruffled the fronds of the palm trees above them.

The man who ran the complex was in his thirties, and made them feel welcome.

"My name is Klahan," he said. "You need anything, just let me know. My wife runs the kitchen and she's an excellent cook."

He patted his stomach as proof.

He had the mellow misdemeanor that had kept Louis yearning to return to Thailand. A mix of trustworthiness and friendliness that made Klahan feel like family even though they'd just met.

"Would you like some soup?" he asked.

"We're pretty tired, and I think we'll just go to bed," said Louis, "but I'm sure we'll be up for a big breakfast."

The guy smiled and turned to back away but stopped and added, "If you want something to smoke, I have."

Dee gave Louis a worried glance.

"Not tonight," said Louis.

The proprietor gave them a stern look. "It is not a problem smoking here," he said as he gestured at the buildings around them, "but don't buy or smoke anything if you go to the rave — it always gets busted."

Dee looked nervous.

Louis asked, "But it's okay here you said?"

He laughed. "Sure. I smoke every day. If you want to smoke, then just find me and we will have a smoke — you don't have to buy."

He left and they lay down under the mosquito net on their simple bed and instantly fell asleep.

They woke from the fireworks at midnight.

"Happy New Year," said Dee as she snuggled against Louis.

For months their destination had been the big full moon party, but now that they were on the island, just a short walk away, neither made a move to go to it.

*

Louis was loading their camping gear into the Thule, while Dee cooked eggs on the propane stove. The kids were watching two squirrels chasing each other up and down a tall pine.

"You go first," said Dee with a nod at the bathrooms. They would be on the ferry for three nights, and they didn´t know if showers were on board.

Louis rubbed his stubbly chin. "I'm gonna have a shave, too."

"Can I go with you?" asked Pookey Bear.

"Sure, get a towel from mom."

They were halfway to the bathroom when Pookey Bear pointed excitedly at a tall hemlock on the other side of the road.

"Look! An eagle!"

Fifty feet up a bald eagle watched them.

"I want to show mom!" she shouted, the shower forgotten.

"Okay," said Louis. "Go get her. You can shower with her when I'm done."

He watched her skip back to the campsite, then turned and continued on to the bathroom.

Thirty minutes later he returned. Dee had buckled the Shrimp in her car seat and had *Peter Pan* playing on the portable DVD player.

"Did Pookey Bear show you the eagle?" he asked.

She gave him a puzzled look. "Not yet. Where is she?"

Louis looked around. "She went back to you. Isn't she here?"

Dee stood up straight, the color draining from her face.

"I haven't seen her since you left."

They began to search frantically, calling out for her as they each walked in a circle around the camping area.

Within a few minutes other campers were joining in the search.

Louis ran to the bathroom and checked all the stalls.

"She´s not there," he said, his voice tight in his throat.

They were both pale and shaking. Dee had to sit down. Louis wanted to scream in frustration.

"I've got to get to the park headquarters," he panted. "We have to call the police. Someone could have taken her."

Dee's eyes were unfocused as her mind raced, trying to guess where the girl could have gone.

"Leave the Shrimp with me," she said in a daze. "I'll stay in case she comes back." She began to sob.

Just as Louis put the Vinniman in gear to back up they saw Pookey Bear emerge from the trail across the road. He threw the vehicle in park and they both ran to her.

She pointed proudly at the path across the road. "The eagle flew that way and showed me where the beach was."

When her parents both burst into tears she suddenly got scared and started to cry as well. They hugged and sobbed together. For a moment, the tears of joy washed away all worries about gas money, employment and the future.

*

The twitter of birds and lapping of waves woke Louis the morning after the big New Year's Eve rave on Koh Phangan. It was early when he climbed into a hammock on the porch of his bungalow. The tide was retreating, and the sand was littered with pieces of plastic.

He hated to see the litter, and it made him glad they hadn't gone to the party. It looked like the partiers had just thrown all their trash into the surf.

Dee emerged wearing a sarong and a bikini top. She looked refreshed, all signs of the journey from America gone.

She walked to the water's edge and began picking up shells.

"I'm gonna make a necklace for my sister," she said.

She lifted one of the pieces of plastic and studied it for a minute.

Louis looked up from his hammock and could see there was something inside.

"What is it?" he asked.

Dee shook off the sand and sea water and he could see now it was a sealed zip lock bag. She opened it, sniffed the contents and smiled.

"It's weed," she said and laughed.

Louis jumped up and ran around picking up other bags. There were over twenty of them, and each held a quarter ounce of marijuana.

"I bet the party got busted like Klahan said, and somebody dumped their stash into the water."

Dee stuffed them all into her daypack. "I'm gonna give it all to him," she said.

Louis pleaded with her. "To Klahan? Come on, Dee."

She shook her head.

"Don't give me that—it's a lot of weed and we're not keeping it."

Then she looked at Louis and tossed him one of the bags. "Okay, you can keep one—but I'm giving him the rest."

He smiled back. "That's better. You can't deny a sign like this."

*

When they were finally all back in the Vinniman and ready to go the color had returned to Dee's face. Again Louis marveled at her ability to shrug things off and bounce back.

Now she sat in the front, preparing a bottle for the Shrimp.

Louis had just put the Vinniman in reverse when she told him to stop. With a mischievous grin, she grabbed the roach from the ash tray, and said, "Hold on a minute," and then slipped out of the vehicle.

He yelled after her. "What about me? That's not fair."

She stuck her head back in the window.

"Suck it up—one of us has to play adult, right?"

Robert Louis DeMayo

Skagway, Alaska with Tugboat Pete

Chapter Five

State Ferry, Alaska's Inside Passage
(May 2002)

Denali was still a long way off as they settled into their small cabin on the ferry, but at least for a few days they didn't have to worry about filling the gas tank or driving conditions. Dee hoped this would help Louis relax while they sailed north, but he had yet to take a deep breath. Since they'd driven the Vinniman onto the bottom deck of the ferry, he'd been making one trip after another between the vehicle and their room, hauling up whatever supplies they might need during the voyage.

"They sounded pretty strict about not wanting anyone to access their cars once we're underway," he said to her as she gave him a quizzical look.

Finally, he arrived from his last run, arms loaded with sleeping bags and pillows. When he stepped into the small cabin — only ten by fifteen feet — Pookey Bear was climbing the ladder to the top bunk.

"This is my bed! This is my bed!" she shouted.

The accommodations were clean, but as sparse as he could have imagined. One metal-framed bunk bed, a small bathroom with a toilet and sink but no shower, two chairs, and a shelf against the wall below a lone porthole.

It was all painted in battleship gray.

When the ferry began to move they all went up on deck and waved at the people on shore, and then Louis returned to the cabin and pawed through the maps and guide books he'd brought along.

Dee returned an hour later, her face glowing with excitement and wind burn. "You really should come up on deck!" she said. "We're skirting along Vancouver Island and it's sooooo beautiful."

In the hallway, the Shrimp lay bundled in a carrier while Pookey Bear ran back and forth down the hall.

"Come on, mom," she pleaded. "You said only a quick stop."

Her windblown hair gave her a wild look, and Louis wished he could shake off the serious demeanor the journey had brought on, and join her.

But he couldn't.

He looked up from a map and said, "Do you realize we have over eight hundred miles to drive still once we get to Skagway? I didn't think it was that far."

His face was pale and Dee knew better than to discuss the journey ahead. Instead, she said, "We're going back on deck. Could you make some mac & cheese?"

Reluctantly, Louis put away the map.

Later he joined them and they watched the sun set beyond Vancouver Island. A chilly wind picked up, and the girls all went below to eat, but he remained as the sky darkened.

An unshaven man in his fifties stood along the railing, watching the island pass by. He had straight blond hair and wore a heavy flannel shirt and a down vest that seemed to stem from the 70's.

Louis looked out to sea. He noticed that the island was tapering to a point and soon they would pass it.

"It'll be open water from now on," said the man. "At least until tomorrow when we pass Graham Island."

"And how much further beyond that until we reach Alaska?"

The man scratched his beard, then said, "Most likely late tomorrow."

"Do you know what time?" asked Louis.

The man smiled out the side of his mouth, leaned forward, and spat with the wind. He said, "You gotta lose that city mentality here. We'll be there soon enough."

"I suppose you're right," said Louis and went below to their cabin.

The next day a heavy wind blew over the water and the ship swayed from side to side as it plowed forward. They stayed in the cabin most of the day. Dee looked a little seasick, but Pookey Bear was restless and constantly climbed all over the bunk bed.

She begged all day to go up to the top deck, but Dee didn't think it was safe. "Maybe when the wind dies down."

Louis took a long nap with the Shrimp, and when they awoke he found the cabin empty. He wrapped the infant in a warm blanket and took her on the deck where he found the others, sitting in chairs, staring off over the bow of the ferry."

"Still open water," said Louis with a frown.

Dee took the baby from him. "No, we passed a big island on our left a few hours ago. And if you look to the right you can just barely make out British Columbia."

She rubbed her hands together and said, "The next land we reach will be Alaska — we're almost to the Inside Passage!"

Alaska! Whenever Louis even said the word his voice took on another tone — like it was a magical place where only some were allowed to venture — and I believe as he approached it again he must have felt his pulse quicken. For months they had been preparing for this adventure, and for weeks they had been crossing North America with Alaska as their heading.

Now, they were almost there. He inhaled the salty air and felt his lungs expanding. Finally, he could catch his breath.

We may arrive with no money, he thought, but we'll get there.

Pookey Bear must have sensed he was coming around, because she snuggled beside him, and then climbed onto his lap.

Dee leaned against him, the Shrimp bundled underneath her jacket. She took the blanket Louis had brought out and lay it over both their laps.

He exhaled deeply and thought, maybe all this stressing is a thing I can shake. He remembered the man he'd met on the deck the night before. He would most likely say that worrying about money was a city thing, too. And then spit over the railing again.

"What land is that?" asked Dee, pointing to the right shore where several deep fjords cut back into the mainland.

"This entire region is part of the Tongass National Forest," he answered, "And I would guess that's the Misty Fjords National Monument."

Dee nudged him. "You know, someday our Pookey Bear might have to do a report on this, why don't you tell her a little about it?"

Louis cleared his throat and lifted the little girl up on his lap. "Well, my little Bear, we are currently cruising through the biggest national forest in the United States — 17 million acres. My favorite president created it, Theodore Roosevelt."

Pookey Bear gave him a blank stare.

Dee tried to hide her smile.

The little girl asked, "Are there animals on those islands?"

Louis smiled. "Yes, there are."

He glanced ahead and noticed they were turning slightly toward the mainland: soon they would be passing islands covered with tall pines.

He pointed at one. "Even on a small island like that you might find an eagle nesting, and ducks and puffins along the water's edge. In the water are seals and otters."

Pookey Bear craned her neck to see closer.

The ship still rolled slightly, but the waves had died down over the last few hours, and as they entered the Inside Passage the wind ceased as well. From the number of smaller islands they passed it was clear that outside the main channels the water was much shallower.

Pookey Bear hopped off Louis's lap and staggered drunkenly to the railing. Dee gave him a panicked look and he quickly grabbed her hand.

They held onto the railing and she said, "I saw a dolphin, earlier."

"Really?" asked Louis. "I wanna see one."

She stared down at the water, trying to see beyond what was reflected on the surface. "What's down there?"

"Well, on the bottom there'd be clams and crabs and sea cucumbers."

The little girl raised her blue eyes and gave him a questioning look when he said "sea cucumbers" but then dropped it and glanced at a larger island they were passing.

"On the bigger islands you could find deer, and foxes, and probably squirrels and porcupines, too."

Talking about nature was relaxing him, and he focused on the water ahead of them. For the next five hundred miles they were going to be weaving between islands, and in the end ploughing straight up the glacially carved fjords that led to Skagway.

He loved the old-growth forest that he could see from the deck and yearned to walk amongst the red cedar and spruce trees that covered the islands. His desire to immerse himself in nature seemed to equal that which drove others to religion. For Louis, a walk through the woods was a prayer session, and every encounter with a creature was a sermon, be it an arctic tern, a mountain goat, or a great-gray owl.

It was all sacred.

He watched the islands in the thickening gloom, and tried to discern if the outcroppings were made of limestone or granite. He hoped to see an animal—maybe a deer, or if he was lucky, a bear—and he could take that as a sign that things were going to be okay. But from the deck of the boat the islands looked void of larger animals.

When the soft pastel colors faded from the darkening sky the others returned to the cabin, but he remained on deck, peering through the gloom. The smells floating over the water brought back memories from their last time in Alaska, and while the sky grew blacker he remembered a canoe trip he'd taken with Ryan, the man they were traveling to see.

*

Ryan was skidding his black pickup into the dirt lot and stopped in a cloud of dust. Louis sat in the cab, a small daypack on his lap. In the bed of the truck an aluminum canoe slid around; a length of rope tethered it to a metal ring so it wouldn't fly out, but it did nothing to hold it in place. I wish he would take it a bit slower, thought Louis. He wanted to say something; the canoe wasn't impervious to dents and he had no desire to do the journey in a leaky boat.

But he knew better. Instead he waited, letting his friend cool down.

Ryan had been in a foul mood when he'd picked him up, and seemed just itching to fight with someone. Louis had noticed his friend developing a more aggressive attitude since moving to Alaska, like the wilderness had turned him into something wilder.

Louis stepped out of the truck to the sound of rushing water. Thirty feet away he glimpsed the river through the trees. The water was a cloudy tan color and looked cold.

Above them, to the right, a bridge spanned the waterway, and the rush of cars and trucks on the George Parks Highway rivaled that of the river.

Louis walked to the water's edge and stared over the rapids, surprised at the shallow flow.

He tossed a rock into the river and listened to Ryan curse behind him. Gotta be Simone, he thought. They've been bickering lately.

Ryan untied the canoe, and with one violent jerk pulled it out of the truck. It came crashing down loudly in the dirt.

He walked up and stood beside Louis. After a moment Louis asked, "So what's got you so pissed off?"

"Everything!" he said, kicking a few rocks into the water.

Then he added, "And everyone! Did you hear Daniel got himself arrested?"

Louis cocked his head. "What happened?"

"That dumb-fuck! He's got a warrant out in Georgia, so when he cashed his paycheck last week his social security number sent out a red flag."

"They take him away?" asked Louis.

"They sure the fuck did," spat Ryan. "Cuffed him in the kitchen, then led him out right past all the customers."

"That must have been a scene," said Louis.

"You should have seen it," began Ryan. "When they first cuffed him the cop called Daniel a hippie, and he freaked out and shouted back, 'I'm no hippie—I worship Satan!'"

And then as they led him through the dining room, Daniel got angry and added, "May demons inhabit your soul and your corpse be spoiled!"

Louis chuckled at the image. Currently the restaurant had a surplus of cooks and Louis figured Ryan was madder about the spectacle of the arrest than losing Daniel.

Ryan walked back to the truck, grabbed a backpack out of the backseat and swung it over one shoulder, then snatched the canoe and dragged it over toward Louis.

He kept on ranting. "Shit, people come up here and act like they're in Timbuktu, like nobody will ever find them again."

Then he stepped away to relieve himself and Louis saw him shake his head and mutter, "What the fuck does she think I'm gonna do?"

Yup, thought Louis. I knew it wasn't just Daniel. He's mad at his wife, too.

Louis had hoped Simone would come along. The plan was to canoe down the Nenana River for fifty miles from Healy to Tanana. The trip would take three days, and they would sleep in the open. Originally Dee was supposed to come also. But then she got pregnant, and when the weather began to turn two weeks ago she'd caught a flight home to Maine to be with her family.

"I thought the river would be bigger," said Louis.

Ryan laughed loudly. "Shit, this is only the Teklanika. It's just a tributary to the Nenana. If you're scared of this little thing you're gonna be terrified when we get on the Nenana."

"I didn't say I was scared," Louis replied defensively.

He walked over to the truck, opened the back door and pulled out two sleeping bags, two sleeping mats, and a blue plastic tarp. Ryan was supposed to have picked up the food and other supplies, but Louis didn't see any, and all the guy carried now was his pack which looked empty.

Louis asked, "Did you get the supplies?"

Ryan grinned. "Oh, I've got supplies all right."

He dropped the pack, opened it, and lifted a bottle of Jack Daniels and a package of chewing tobacco.

"What do you have?"

Louis pulled a plastic sack out of his daypack. Inside were a dozen granola bars and six oranges. It wasn't much, but together with the steaks, potatoes, and bacon and eggs that Ryan was going to pick up it would have been fine.

"Is Simone gonna swing by with the rest of the food?" Louis asked.

Ryan snapped back. "Do you see her?"

He walked to the truck, grabbed two wooden paddles, and stuck his keys above the visor. Even though he was stomping around irritated, Louis sensed that once they took off he'd be fine. The two had known each other in New Hampshire, and although Ryan had always had a crazy streak, he also had a good heart, and generally had known when to start applying the brakes.

But that was before he'd come to Alaska.

Ryan reached into his backpack and produced two trash bags. He handed them to Louis and said, "Put the sleeping bags in these."

"Maybe we should just run to the store and get some more food," said Louis as he stuffed the sleeping bags into the plastic.

Ryan glared at him. "Don't be a fuckin' pussy! Get in."

Then he lifted his shirttail to expose a pistol, winked, and added, "Don't sweat it—I'll shoot us some dinner if it comes to that."

A few minutes later they passed under the bridge. The water moved quickly through the little channels, throwing them from side to side as they scurried along. After little more than a mile on the Teklanika they reached the confluence where the river poured into the Nenana, a much larger stream. Ryan was in the back, steering, and Louis sat in front of him, paddling as needed.

The water here was bluer, and Louis guessed it to be roughly fifty feet wide; there were a lot of sand bars which made that difficult to judge.

"Now we're on the Nenana," said Ryan. The anger had begun to leave him.

"What's this river rated?" asked Louis, and then instantly regretted to have opened his mouth.

"Rated?" sneered Ryan, his face twisted like the word disgusted him. He now had a mouth full of tobacco, and he spat over the side before he said, "It's rated do-able. How's that? And after the recent rains there might be a few sections that are now barely do-able."

Louis stared back defiantly. "You know what I'm talking about."

Ryan grinned. "Okay, most of it is I or II. With the rain there might be a grade III in there somewhere."

Louis shook his head. "We're gonna try to run a grade III rapid in an open canoe?"

Ryan's pack sat on the floor of the canoe, between his legs. He ignored the question and reached down, searched inside, and pulled out the bottle.

He smirked and said, "The locals call this section here the Drunken Upper."

While he took a long pull the canoe turned sideways. He re-stowed the bottle, straightened the canoe out, spat again, and then said, "Listen, the rapids won't kill you — you just get wet. What you do have to watch out for is overhanging trees or exposed roots on the shore. You don't want to get swept right out of the boat and held under."

He jabbed his finger ahead, where the river forked. "They call these rivers braided because they constantly divide and unite and if we don't stay in the main channels we'll spend half the trip portaging back to the main flow. So pay attention."

Louis stuck his hand in the water, which was ice cold.

He said, "Seems the real danger is the water — it's freezing."

Ryan chuckled. "Well fuck yeah! It comes right off a glacier."

He lifted his paddle in the air so the water dripped close to Louis and said, "My advice to you — try to stay dry, and whatever you do, don't fall in."

Back in New Hampshire, Louis had grown up next to a river and knew well the dangers of hypothermia but decided not to push the point.

They continued through the day. The river broadened, and at times looked almost a half mile wide. It flowed north, and a few times the George Parks Highway was visible on their left, but for the most part it felt like they'd left civilization behind.

The Alaska Range with Mt. Denali was behind them, and the Brooks Range was far to the north; the land they passed through tilted at times in long slopes, but otherwise seemed featureless, giving the impression that the entire world was built around the river.

Ryan was pretty competent at steering them through the channels and avoiding submerged rocks. He constantly shouted directions to Louis in the front, and together they battled their way through the torrents.

"Back paddle on your left! Harder! Now shoot for that gap between the boulders!"

Ryan had also continued to work on the bottle; he had a pretty good buzz going by lunch when they stopped on a sand bar for a quick break.

"Look what I got," he said, holding up a bag of weed.

He reached inside, grabbed a pinch of marijuana and dumped it in his palm, and while he talked he broke it up.

"When the cop searched Daniel he found his weed and he handed it to me. He said, 'This will only complicate things—he's in enough trouble already.'"

"Sounds like a pretty cool cop."

Ryan chuckled. "He should be—that was an easy arrest. Fuckin' Daniel all but handed himself in."

He pulled a rolling paper out of his wallet, dumped a palmful of the mulled-up weed into it, and rolled a joint.

He paused and licked the edge of the rolling paper before spinning it all closed.

They climbed back into the canoe and Ryan lit the joint and smoked it steadily for the next ten minutes. Louis was too nervous to try any when Ryan eventually offered him the roach.

"What?!" shouted Ryan. "This is Matanuska Thunderfuck—you have to have a toke."

Late in the day they passed under a large bridge, and five minutes later Ryan steered them to shore and got out. The bottle clunked against the side in the canoe, as he stepped off. It was almost half empty.

Louis climbed out as well, and took a few steps away to relieve himself.

Suddenly the report of a gun shattered the silence and Louis instinctively crouched low. He turned around to see Ryan pointing his pistol straight up and firing once more, and another time, and another, until it was empty.

"What the fuck?!" shouted Louis.

Ryan had a crazy look in his eyes as he grinned and said, "When in doubt, empty your magazine."

He let the spent shells drop on the gravel, then reached in his pocket for more ammunition and began to reload.

"You just wait," he added with a nod at the shore.

There was twenty feet of gravel between the water and the shore, and beyond that lay a clearing at least fifty feet wide before the woods closed in. Louis glanced in that direction and saw what he thought were two wolves bounding in their direction.

In seconds they were upon them, snarling and trying to nip their feet. Louis took a step backwards, closer to the boat, but Ryan just continued to load his gun.

Soon a tall, burly man appeared in the clearing, stomping towards them with an angry expression. He had a full beard that hung down over a thick flannel shirt, and he wore a floppy leather hat.

His eyes were red with rage as he approached.

"You should'a known better than that!" he shouted.

The man also held a pistol, and as he approached Ryan he raised his right hand and pointed the gun at him.

Louis backed up further, kneeing one of the canines out of the way— he was surprised it hadn't bit him—until he was standing by the canoe.

Ryan and the man bumped chests a few times, and then pressed their heads against each other and growled like they were grizzlies fighting over a dead caribou.

Ryan fired his gun at the clouds, and the large man did the same.

Louis stepped into the canoe and shouted, "Ryan, I'm leaving!"

A dozen shots rang out as Louis pushed off shore, and then both guns clicked empty.

Ryan turned and ran for the canoe.

The water was up to his knees when he dove and flopped into the boat. Louis paddled for all he was worth, and after a few strokes Ryan joined him.

They were nearly a hundred feet away by the time the man had reloaded his gun. He held it in front of him, pointed it at the canoe, and fired until it was empty.

Bullets hit the water on each side of the canoe.

Louis ducked and paddled like hell. His heart was racing. He imagined a bullet smashing into him from behind. Each time the gun went off he braced for the impact.

He didn't know whether the man was a lousy shot or just trying to scare them, but he kept his head down and dug frantically at the water until a bend in the river took them out of sight.

Soon thereafter they pulled over on a sandy island in the river.

Louis was still catching his breath. "What the fuck was that?" he demanded when he could speak again.

"That was awesome!" shouted Ryan. "That's what it was."

"You could have gotten us killed! Who was that?"

Ryan chuckled. "Just a disgruntled patron from the bar."

"We did this river run just to piss him off?"

Ryan shook his head earnestly. "Nope, but I figured as long as we were here, why the fuck not?"

"And what about those wolves?" asked Louis. "I thought they were gonna tear us apart."

Ryan laughed. "They're sled dogs. They get the shit beat out of them when they nip their owners so they just make a lot of noise and look scary."

"So that was all show?" asked Louis.

Ryan looked back in the direction they had come. "Well, they probably have a little wolf in 'em, and they're extremely loyal. I bet if I'd actually shot him they would have gone for us."

Ten minutes later they were sitting around a small fire. The driftwood they collected was damp and didn't burn well. A light rain began and Ryan opened the plastic tarp and lay it over their gear.

When Louis began to peal an orange Ryan stared at him for a minute before he said, "I got a trade for you — half the whiskey for an orange and a granola bar."

Louis handed over one of each and accepted the bottle with shaking hands when Ryan offered it. He choked down a few big swallows before Ryan snatched it back.

"Easy, killer, we got a long night ahead of us."

Louis sighed. "You really think we've got enough supplies for this trip?"

Ryan laughed. "No — fuck no. But I got in a fight with Simone at the grocery store and left it all in the cart."

The two munched down their granola bar, and Louis was relieved to see familiar traits of his old friend again. Ryan crumpled up the wrapper, looked at Louis and said: "We'll get there hungry and order a big meal at the restaurant. Don't sweat it, a little hunger never killed anyone."

They were on the river early the next day; without the chores of cooking or cleaning dishes there wasn't much else to do than pack up and leave. It was late August, and the days were starting to get shorter.

The rain had picked up in the night and they'd thrown the plastic tarp over their sleeping bags. The damp, cold earth beneath them had worked its chill into their bones and Louis felt stiff.

The river was swollen and rough, and on the first few rapids several waves came over the edge of the boat. They continued for a few miles with the water sloshing around.

"Wish you had a skirt for the canoe," said Louis.

Ryan laughed. "This is nothing. We should have started at McKinley Village and run the canyon before we set out."

Louis scoffed at the suggestion. "That's a grade IV. We'd never make it in this canoe."

Ryan scoffed. "You're such a pussy."

"I'm not afraid of running this river," replied Louis. "I just don't want to drown if I can help it."

At the next section of rapids, they were forced into a bottleneck and water poured over the sides and flooded the canoe. Only a few inches of the boat sat above the waterline, and their possessions floated around them. They pointed the craft at the shore and desperately paddled before they were swept into the next rapid.

They unloaded the boat and tipped it upside down. Louis hopped in place, trying to restore feeling to his legs that had gone numb from sitting in the frigid water.

A few hours later they rounded a curve and suddenly found themselves at the top of a long, slanted hill with the river flowing down the middle of it. Louis thought it had to be at least two miles down to where the river leveled out, and as he peered ahead he could see rapid after rapid piling up in front of them.

"We're never gonna make that," he said nervously.

"You just watch and see," said Ryan with a devilish grin.

For the next thirty minutes they worked together, paddling hard, to navigate the torrential waters. Water splashed in huge waves into the canoe, and twice they barely made it to shore with a heavily waterlogged vessel. The weight of their sleeping bags made it clear that they were sodden despite the trash bags they were stowed in.

Two thirds of the way down the hill, they briefly got hung up on a rock and the back of the canoe dipped underwater. As they left the rapid and paddled into an eddy their packs were floating around them in the canoe.

They paddled like heck towards the shore, and Louis fearfully watched the water pulling them into the next section of rapids, where the canoe would most likely go under and its contents would be swept away.

They went all-out to get the heavy vessel to shore and then climbed out, panting heavily with water pouring from their clothes.

"You see," wheezed Ryan. "All you gotta do is make it to shore and you're fine. When we get out of here we're gonna run the canyon."

"You're fucking crazy."

They slept that night on another sandy island. Their sleeping bags were sogging wet so they spread them out near the fire, lay on their sleeping mats, and used the plastic tarp as a blanket.

Louis shivered all night, and was ready to go at first light.

They set off on empty stomachs, the granola bars and oranges long gone.

"How much further do we have?" asked Louis.

Ryan looked around with a bewildered expression.

"Gee, I'm really not sure where we are."

Ryan was probably just messing with him, but suddenly Louis was worried by his lack of knowledge of the region. He hadn't seen the highway since crossing under the bridge the day before, and with a chill he realized if he lost Ryan the only sensible thing to do would be to just keep following the river until he saw a road or it passed by a town.

"Not a good river to get lost on," said Ryan. "If we miss the take-out at the town of Nenana we'll get swept right into the Tanana River and there's no gettin' off that until Manley Hot Springs ninety miles downstream."

"Well, are there some landmarks we should look for?" asked Louis.

Ryan was smirking out of the side of his mouth. "I shouldn't have said anything—I didn't mean to scare you."

"I'm not afraid—I just want to know what we're in for."

Ryan sneered. "Maybe you should have stayed in the lower forty-eight. Alaska isn't for everyone."

They were entering another section of rapids, and while they each paddled hard to keep from being swept into a side channel with lots of exposed rocks, Ryan was shouting over the water's roar.

"I can see now why you didn't want to run the canyon!" he yelled, "You seem afraid of the consequences if something went wrong!"

Ryan let out a howl and added, "Alaska isn't for pussies."

Ahead the water smoothed out for a stretch, and Louis set down his paddle and turned around.

"You know what, Ryan? You can go fuck yourself! Just because I don't want to drown doesn't mean I'm a pussy. And if you're so set on running the canyon when we get back—let's do it. I don't care anymore. You want to lose your canoe, that's fine. I'll just swim to shore."

Suddenly Ryan whooped and his face lit up with a smile.

"That's what I was waiting for!" he shouted. "I guess you do have a set of balls."

"I'm not a coward!" Louis yelled right back, "I'm just not suicidal. But fuck it, I'm tired of your crap—let's run the canyon."

Ryan looked into Louis's eyes and simply said, "Naw."

Louis looked confused. "You don't want to run the canyon?"

Ryan shook his head. "Fuck no, we'd never make it."

Over the next few hours Louis noticed Ryan looking for landmarks. He didn't seem worried and Louis figured he'd only been messing with him when he'd acted lost.

Soon they reached the town of Tanana and Ryan steered them to a landing in a parking lot behind what looked like a restaurant.

They stowed the canoe under a tree, went inside and sat on stools in front of a mirrored bar.

A waiter took their order, and Ryan frowned at the guy's New Jersey accent.

He set two glasses in front of them, added ice, and then poured some whiskey in each.

"You up here for the season?" asked Ryan. He was apparently unsatisfied with the drink.

"Sure am," said the man.

"Well," began Ryan, "how long do you think you'll have to be in Alaska before you know how to pour a decent drink?"

The man looked down at the glasses. "That's a regulation shot."

Ryan stared at him until he added a good splash in each glass.

As he walked away, Ryan mumbled, "Fuckin' pussy."

*

The ferry was now deep in the Inside Passage, and the walls of the fjord were only a few hundred feet apart. Tall trees leaned out over the water, and there was barely a trace of the wind. It felt like they were traveling back in time, to a wilder point in history before man had settled the land.

Sometime in the next twelve hours they would reach Skagway. I image he was nervous and excited at the same time, both looking forward to, and dreading, facing his fears.

Louis thought of the river trip on the Nenana, and of Ryan.

After that journey he'd felt more connected to Alaska, as if his friend's crude attempts to intimidate him had been a rite of passage. Personally, I think the fear and the cold and the adrenaline all combined to forever connect him with the place.

He'd come up on deck to clear his head. In Skagway the road to Healy lay ahead, and they didn't have enough gas money to complete it. Soon he would have to confront that fact.

The cabin had felt claustrophobic, but on deck with the wind in his face and the memory of his trip on the Nenana, he sensed a growing confidence taking over.

He had endured Alaska's harshness before, and he would do it again.

Together with Dee, he had camped for five months, dealt with grizzlies sniffing around the tent, shivered in the cold mornings, and hiked many miles through the beautiful landscape. And during those days he had felt more alive than he could ever remember.

He closed his eyes and his mind was flooded with the intoxicating smell of spruce, and the chirping of birds watching from the tilted trees that surrounded their camp. He remembered observing a full-grown grizzly amble right up to their van and stare at them, and a bald eagle that swooped down and snatched a monstrously large salmon from the Teklanika River, struggling to fly away with it.

A man stepped out onto the deck. It was the guy he'd talked to two nights before. The guy walked to the rail and stopped a few feet away.

Louis said, "I didn't catch your name last night."

The man shrugged. "I didn't throw it."

Louis stared him in the eye until he finally cracked a smile.

"Tim," he said and extended his hand.

Louis shook it. Everything was gonna be fine, he thought. We'll find a way to scrape up enough gas money — and we will make it to Healy. Once we get there we'll be working and things will be great.

The guy stared at the eastern side of the fjord, and after a long silence asked, "Where you guys heading?"

"Healy," said Louis.

Tim chuckled. "Really? That's where I'm going."

Louis grabbed the rail when a sudden wave lifted the ferry. "I've got some friends up there that own a bar and we're gonna work for the season."

The guy furrowed his eyebrows. "There aren't many bars in Healy. Which one?"

"The Denali Smoke Shack."

Tim stared at him for a minute without speaking.

Finally, he asked, "You're traveling with your wife and a couple young girls, right?"

Louis peered at the rugged man's face, which suddenly had grown serious. He said, "I am."

Tim pursed his lips and said, "You must be friends with Ryan and Simone."

"Yeah, you know them?" asked Louis, cheerfully.

Tim looked out over the water and scratched his stubbly chin.

Suddenly Louis sensed something was wrong.

"When's the last time you heard from them?" asked Tim.

The wind was rapidly sneaking out of Louis's lungs. He said, "Not for a while. I can't reach them by phone and they haven't responded to any of my letters. Why?"

Tim spit over the railing. "I don't know how to tell you this, but last I heard is your friends divorced and left the state."

Louis had to lean against the railing. He was gripping it with white knuckles. "Are you sure?"

Tim's eyes held a sympathetic look. "Unfortunately, I am" he said. "I was at the state auction where their belongings were sold."

Louis was having difficulty breathing. Tim gave him a brief look and said, "Good luck," then went inside.

In the gloom Louis watched the shore pass by. His stomach felt like it was filled with hot lead. He was gripped with uncertainty. Where should we go from here? He thought. How are we gonna find jobs?

He resolved to keep his mouth shut when he got back to the cabin so the girls could enjoy the last night on the ferry, but he knew Dee would read his panic right away.

Still he tried to look relaxed, pausing in the doorway and taking a deep breath of the salty air. His smile felt forced and frozen.

He took one last look at the dark forest they were passing.

This was the ancient land he had yearned to return to. Now he was here, with his girls, but he felt it was slipping away.

Pookey Bear and the Shrimp, Skagway, Alaska

Chapter Six

Skagway, Alaska
(June 2002)

The canvas door flap of the wall tent was fluttering in the wind, but Louis was too warm and cozy to get up and secure it. He guessed it to be around six in the morning. It was difficult to tell because every day was dramatically longer than the last. He'd been told by other campers that by the end of June there would be twenty hours of daylight.

Sunshine poured down on the snow outside with the promise that it would melt away soon. The bushes and trees that surrounded their campsite were devoid of leaves, but little buds on the branch tips hinted that they would one day provide shade.

They had found the wall tent in the back of the Mountain View Campground, right next to several old railroad track lines. There was a row of the tents, each twelve by twelve feet, on framed plywood platforms that lifted them off the frozen earth. A sparse framework of two-by-fours kept them rigid.

They had spent their first night in Skagway at a private campground next to the ferry terminal, but when the owner found out they were looking for work—and not passing through—he quickly turned nasty and told them they could only stay for two nights.

"That guy was an asshole," said Dee, when they left there.

"What's an asshole?" asked Pookey Bear.

Louis smirked, glad for once to be blameless for yet another swearword that the young girl learned.

"I think he was a drunk," said Louis. "At least he smelled like alcohol."

Soon after they found Mountain View. When the new camp host showed them the wall tent everyone loved it. Compared to regular camping or sleeping in the van it almost felt like a home, and the girls played happily on the dry plywood floor while Louis and Dee unloaded the Vinniman.

"What about the train tracks?" asked Dee, nodding at the nearest one, only thirty feet away.

Louis walked over and examined them. They were rusty, and sticks and half-rotten leaves covered the metal rails.

"I don't think they've been used in years," he said.

The first few days in the wall tent were quiet, but busy. After realizing that Ryan and Simone were no longer in Healy, the final push north seemed foolish. Louis could be stubborn when it came to changing a plan, but Dee pointed out the obvious.

"Look," she said, "we don't have gas money for another eight hundred miles, and who knows if we'd even find jobs up there."

Skagway, on the other hand, was busy; and there seemed to be lots of work.

Dee had also discovered that she had an aunt and uncle and several cousins living in Skagway, not in Juneau like she'd thought; so they decided to stay.

Winter was just loosening its grip on the town, which sat at the mouth of the Taiya Inlet, at the very end of the Inside Passage. Snow still covered the ground, but it was melting quickly; a stream ran along one side of the campground, and it flowed along the main street all the way to the inlet where the cruise ships docked.

Dee and Louis had zipped together their two flannel-lined sleeping bags, and as the early morning light filtered through the canvas, Pookey Bear and the Shrimp snored peacefully in the middle.

Louis sleepily watched the tent flap blow in the morning breeze and listened to what was going on outside.

A loud horn sounded by the docks. Then from further down the tracks there was a bang, followed by a large screech.

Pookey Bear sat up quickly, jumped to her feet and shouted, "My People!"

"Your what?" asked Louis. He tried to stop her, but was distracted by another loud bang outside the tent.

Pookey Bear wore a heavy cloth nightie, and while she stepped into her pink slippers she looked at Louis like he was dim-witted.

"My People," she said again and then stepped outside.

The screeching outside was getting louder, and Louis pulled his jeans on. Dee opened her eyes. "What's that?"

"I don't know," he replied.

He snatched a quick glance out the doorway, trying to locate his daughter, and then searched frantically for his shoes.

"Pookey Bear said she saw a train yesterday when I was at the bathroom sink washing dishes," said Dee.

"I doubt that," he said as he located the shoes and hopped into one. "Those tracks look abandoned."

Louis stood outside and squinted down the tracks, towards the inlet and the docks. Suddenly a whistle blew, and a large cloud of steam rose above the cottonwoods that bordered the campground.

A long steam engine came into view. Louis grabbed Pookey Bear, who was standing ten feet from the tracks, and moved her back a few paces.

They watched the train approach, and the young girl was so excited she was jumping in place. Behind the engine followed a dozen cars, filled with people. Below the windows, *White Pass Railroad* was painted in white letters.

Pookey Bear stepped forward slightly and began waving.

Flashes went off as the passengers took photo after photo of the young girl in the nightie standing in front of the wall tents.

The train pulled away and the little girl turned around, her face beaming. "My People love me," she said as she gave a final wave.

The first week in Skagway, Louis and Dee had taken turns watching the girls and searching for work. The town was as busy as a beehive. Everything seemed designed around the crowds of people that would soon parade off the cruise ships.

They had reached Skagway just before the season started, but Louis and Dee lacked qualifications for the jobs most strongly in demand: tour guides and jewelry salespeople.

Dee's aunt and uncle escorted them around the town and helped them get orientated, and the two cousins promised to visit the campground soon. Dee finally got herself a few shifts at The Alaskan Bread Company. The manager seemed friendly, the food was good, and her aunt told her it was where the locals ate. It wasn't one of the historic hotels where the women dressed like gold rush prostitutes, and I image that left Louis a little bit disappointed—and relieved—at the same time.

Tour guides were required to have a current health certificate and a Commercial Driver's License, or CDL, and Louis had neither. So he settled for a job at the town's small airport.

He worked days and Dee nights so one of them would always be with the kids. The first week crept along ever so slowly while they waited for their first checks. Dee brought home some tip money, and one night she showed up with a mistake from the kitchen—a rack of ribs—that they devoured with relish. Even Pookey Bear gnawed on a rib until no trace of flesh was left on it.

It rained almost constantly, and often, during a dreary afternoon, they climbed into the Vinniman and watched movies. Pookey Bear preferred *The Jungle Book,* and viewed it over and over on Uncle Bone's player. It must have insinuated itself into Louis's memory, too, because he was always quoting Mowgli, "Oh, I'd do anything to stay in the jungle."

Skagway looked bleak in the cold, damp weather. The naked trees and bushes made the campground seem desolate, and brooding drifts of clouds hung over the town, obscuring the glaciers.

By cuddling together, they stayed warm at night. The campground had a bathroom with showers and a sink to do dishes, but the hot water was intermittent and not to be counted on.

When someone called out that there was hot water, Louis would run across the campground, soak a facecloth in it, and then return quickly to the wall tent to give the Shrimp a sponge bath, or change her diaper if needed.

The desperate feeling that had clung to them as they drove across America was slowly lifting. Using tip money, Dee had bought two used bikes for ten dollars each, and now they were looking for a small bike trailer so they could tow the girls around town.

It seems to me they landed on their feet.

It also seems that I've been jumping around a little between the present and the past, but for the next few chapters in our tale I'm gonna mostly stick with the present, because for the first time in his life, that's where Louis was: in the moment.

Louis walked the seven blocks from the campground to the docks, following Broadway's wooden sidewalks past restored buildings with false fronts. A variety of characters were standing in the doorways, dressed as if it were still the Klondike Gold Rush of 1898, and if you didn't know better, you might think it was still going on.

At the end of town, the docks clung to the left wall of the inlet — also known as the Lynn Canal — and pulling up to the closest berth was a massive cruise ship. It looked ready to plow right up Broadway.

Louis had to laugh at its enormous size.

A man with short, light-blond hair and a scruffy beard was leaning against a piling, watching the ship. He heard Louis chuckle and looked his way.

"First time you seen one of them come in?" he asked.

Louis laughed. "Yup. Knew they were big, but that thing's huge."

The guy looked to be in his mid-thirties. His voice was deep, and there was something about him that reminded Louis of the ocean.

"You should see it from the water," he said, gruffly.

Louis gave him a questioning look and he gestured with his stubbly chin at a tugboat that was slowly coming into view.

They watched as it nudged the much larger boat into position.

The guy extended his hand. "Name's Pete," he said. "Normally I'm piloting one of those tugs, but my license lapsed, and now I gotta wait until July before it'll be straightened out."

"You miss the work?" asked Louis. "That why you're here?"

Pete shook his head. "Heck no! I don't mind taking some time off — there'll be more than two hundred cruise ships coming into Skagway over the next months. I'll be plenty busy before the summer is over."

Then he scratched his chin and added, "I just miss the smell of the water. I didn't even know this ship was coming in. How 'bout you?"

Louis looked back at Skagway and the coastal mountain range behind it. He said, "I like the view of the pass from here."

They both turned their gaze inland, beyond the town. Mountains loomed in the distance, glaciers clinging to their ridgelines, and in the distance beyond them they parted and faded into what Louis knew was the White Pass.

Here, at the termination of the Inside Passage, thought Louis, you've reached the end of the line. Unless you were willing to cross through the mountains you have no option other than to turn around. Not many of Skagway's visitors had time to go over the pass, but the locals did, and eventually many of the seasonal workers did too.

"You been over the pass yet?" asked Pete.

Louis scratched his own beard. He hadn't shaved since before the ferry.

"Almost," he said, "we drove to the U.S. border post about fifteen miles up the road, but then turned around."

Pete chuckled. "I haven't even gotten that far."

Beyond the border post, the Klondike Highway ascended to the White Pass; on the other side is British Columbia's Tormented Valley. Continue for forty more miles and you enter the Yukon Territory.

Louis stared at the distant pass and thought of the Yukon; everything he'd ever heard of it made it sound like a land of mystery and adventure.

He could feel it calling. And yes, according to Louis, the Yukon does beckon. The rational side of him said he needed to put in hours at his new job and take care of his family, but there was another side that urged him to venture beyond the pass.

He hated to turn away from a journey.

"I can see what drew the gold rush stampeders over the pass," he said. "I love the wilderness, and I can't wait to get up there."

Pete smirked. "Those guys were chasing gold, not nature—and most of the ones that did rush over that first year died. But if you like the outdoors so much you should get a job as a tour guide."

"Don't have my CDL," said Louis, "besides, I got a job." He told Pete about the work he did at the airport.

Pete lit a cigarette, took a long drag off it, and then exhaled.

"Listen," he said, "you're gonna hate that job. I know the boss, his employees call him the Dark Lord because he's angry all the time."

Defensively, Louis said, "But I get free flights throughout southeast Alaska when there's an open seat."

Pete smiled. "Perfect, get on one to Haines for your physical, and then another to Juneau to take your CDL. You can get it all sorted and be guiding tours in a few weeks—in tips alone you'll double your wage."

Louis's mind was spinning with the suggestion, but he'd never spoken publicly and didn't know how he'd do. Suddenly he felt his lack of knowledge of the area would stand in his way as well.

"I don't know, Pete," said Louis, "I don't know much about Alaska, or the gold rush. I can't even figure out why the Lynn Canal is called a canal."

Pete laughed. "It isn't a canal! It was carved by glaciers, not man, so it's a fjord. Those dumb fucks in the 1800s didn't know what they were doing when they named it."

He then slapped Louis's shoulder and said, "Shit, if I can do it, you can."

"You're a tour guide, too?" asked Louis.

Pete smiled shyly. "Well, until my papers come through I need some way to make beer and cigarette money."

That night, Louis made a fire. A former tenant of their wall tent had cleared a large, circular space, right next to it, and built a fire pit in the middle. Soon other campers started showing up with their chairs.

Most lived in tents, some in vehicles, and a few others were also in wall tents. Skagway normally had a population of approximately eight hundred, which dwindled to less than five hundred during the winter. But each spring the town experienced a boom when fifteen hundred seasonal workers joined the residents.

Most of the new arrivals were somewhere between eighteen and thirty. Dee and Louis were the only parents in the campground, and they suddenly felt old and domestic.

Roughly a third of the seasonal workers lived in the campground. There were so many new faces there that it was tough to keep names straight in the beginning, but once they began showing up at the fire it got easier.

The young people instantly took to Pookey Bear. In the wall tent on their left lived a pretty young woman named Zana. She sat in a chair by the fire now, reading a story to Pookey Bear, who perched on her lap. She'd made a friend for life when she took the young girl for a walk down the boardwalk and bought her an ice cream cone. Zana worked as a tour guide for an outfit called Southeast Tours, and always had her nose buried in a guidebook.

The Shrimp didn't fare as well initially. Whenever the baby crawled to the wall and leaned against the loosely hanging canvas, she fell right out of the tent.

Luckily, the first few times this happened she landed in a foot of snow, and although she was cold and angry, she didn't get hurt. At night there were always a few people sitting around the fire, and after her first few falls someone always volunteered to hold her.

"She reminds me of my baby sister," said Julie, who was currently holding the sleeping infant. Julie was twenty-one, traveling with her boyfriend from Minnesota, Adam, and lived behind the wall tents in a small popup tent. She had wavy brown hair and a warm smile and the little girls couldn't get enough of her.

The Shrimp seemed content to be held by strangers. Sometimes there would be fifteen or more people sitting around the fire, drinking and telling stories, and through the course of the evening the Shrimp would be passed from one person to the next until she'd travelled completely around the fire at least once.

In the wall tent to their right were two guys, Ben and Chris, who'd both gotten jobs with tour companies. Ben guided hikers on the Chilkoot Trail, one of the two ways the prospectors made it into the Yukon. And Chris worked for Skagway Street Car, a company that used yellow tour buses from 1927. Most of their guides were women, but Chris was a mechanic and had found a position in the garage.

Ben was at the fire, too, but ignored the conversations around him because he was reading. Since he first arrived he'd read every book on the gold rush that he could find, while Chris was climbing every peak around Skagway that was reachable without ropes or crampons.

A tall couple walked by and waved. Tom and Sasha lived in a modified school bus which they had parked on the far side of the campground. A wood stove in the back kept it warm and cozy inside. Tom was from Wisconsin, and Sasha had been born somewhere in Eastern Europe and had a thick accent.

A potbelly pig lived with them in the big, blue bus, and they let Pookey Bear walk it from time to time. Tom bartended at Moe's, and Sasha waitressed at the Golden North Hotel. They generally slept late which frustrated Pookey Bear to no end when she wanted to visit the pig.

"Please wake them up," she would plead. "I think they've slept long enough."

The bus had broken down just as they parked it, so Tom was searching for someone with mechanical experience, while saving tip money to repair it.

Another neighbor, Tristan, was also at the fire that night. He worked at the Golden North Hotel, too, but in the kitchen. Tristan seemed only interested in women—not just the women in Skagway, but those from the cruise ships as well.

"I saw you hitting on that dark-haired girl today—why do you bother with the passengers?" Ben asked him. "They're gonna be back on board before you could barely get their name."

Tristan just shrugged. "You never know."

He glanced over at Zana and asked, "Want to come over to my tent and listen to some music?"

Zana had lowered the children's book, covered Pookey Bear's ears, and said, "Kindly fuck off, won't you?"

Then she removed her hands from the girl's ears, and said in a pleasant voice, "Now, where were we?"

In the following days, the first few ships came and went and the town fell into a busy rhythm that continued through the summer. Suddenly everyone had pockets full of tip money which made the rain and cold a little more bearable.

At the end of the day the ships´ passengers all went back aboard and the shops closed, and it was then that two of Dee's cousins came around. The older one, Francis, was twenty and wanted to be a minister; his younger sister, Amanda, was eighteen with long, curly brown hair and a mischievous nature. She instantly got branded with a nickname by Pookey Bear.

"This is Amanda," said Dee.

Pookey Bear stared up at her, then asked, "Salamander?"

In an attempt to give her a little dignity, they shortened it to Sal.

Much of the conversations around the fire pit revolved around work. Now that most of the seasonal workers had put in a few shifts there was a flurry of activity from those who didn't like their jobs and wanted to switch before the season was in full swing.

Louis learned much about the seasonal jobs just by listening to the people at the fire. There was the city tour on 24-passenger shuttles, where the guides told the gold rush history while they visited the city overlook and the Stampeder Cemetery, and then continued up the Klondike Highway to the Canadian border post and back. There were horseback tours in the nearby town of Dyea or the Yukon, and there were guided hikes—even excursions up on the glacier where the tourists could fly via helicopter. And then there were the jewelry shops. It seemed more gold left Skagway in the pockets of the visiting tourists than ever made it out during the gold rush.

Ben wanted to work on the glacier, but passed when he found out about drug testing there. "I'm not giving up weed for a job," he said.

Louis considered working in one of the jewelry shops or as a timeshare salesman, since those jobs offered housing and he thought it might be better for the girls, but Dee stopped him.

"Hun," she said, "I don't think you have any idea how unhappy those jobs would make you. But I can see it—and I'd rather be cold at night, and happy, than see you go through that."

In the end, Louis settled on the job at the airport.

Pete, it turned out, was right about his assessment of the boss at the airport job, but the Dark Lord only swooped in every now and then. Most days Louis checked in the few passengers that were flying within Southeast Alaska, collected the freight to be loaded when a plane did come in, and didn't even see him.

It seemed to be a bad-luck day: someone had stolen Louis's bike, and his gortex jacket had been swept into a mud puddle by the wind and was a wet mess. So on this late afternoon, instead of riding, he walked the dozen blocks to the airport, wearing just a flannel-lined, button-up shirt, over a *Dreamtime Travellers* guest house t-shirt. It had been raining sporadically all day, and he was soaked by the time he got to the airport.

He settled down at his desk in the small airport, one of two. The other one was staffed by a red-faced woman who always looked dressed for church.

"Well, good day to you," she said when she looked at his dripping attire. "I would have thought you'd have an umbrella on a day like this."

Louis was already mad at himself for not preparing better, and her comment stung. He turned on the small heater under his desk, took off his soaked outer shirt and draped it over his chair, then pushed it closer to the heater before walking to a back room with a table, chairs and a coffee machine.

One of the pilots had already come in and now sat at the table, sipping a cup of black coffee.

Louis poured himself a coffee and said, "Hey Steve, how're the friendly skies?"

Steve was in his late thirties and a well-seasoned pilot. He'd been born in Alaska, and didn't get caught up in all the tourist activity after work. He didn't drink the night before he flew, and he didn't hit on the passengers, like some of the younger pilots. On Louis's day off, Steve had flown him to Haines with the mail so he could get a medical examination.

Steve took a long sip from his mug. "That nasty crosswind is blowin' again. Not bad once you're in the air, but taking off and landing is a bitch."

Louis went back out to his desk and sat down. The church lady, whose name was Violet, looked disdainfully at Steve. She leaned over toward Louis, and in a low voice said, "That one used to have some potential, but he's washed up now."

Louis liked Steve, and although he wanted to stay out of Violet's gossip — which was non-stop on some days — his curiosity was piqued and he had to ask, "Why's he washed up?"

Violet gave him a surprised look, like he should have already known the answer. "Well, he left our church. That's what he did."

Steve suddenly emerged from the back room.

He ignored Violet, whose face had turned even redder than before, and addressed Louis. "It was pissing down earlier so I didn't unload. Mind giving me a hand?"

Louis reluctantly put his wet shirt on over his t-shirt and walked out to the plane with Steve. On his way he seized the long handle of a wheeled cart and dragged it along behind him. Lying folded on the cart was a plastic tarp.

Steve opened the plane's cargo door, grabbed a few boxes, and handed them to Louis who piled them on the cart. Within a few minutes the cargo hold of the small plane was empty. It was still sprinkling, so Louis covered the cargo with the tarp and pulled the cart back into the building, unloaded it, and then piled a half dozen boxes to be delivered to Juneau onto the cart. This was where Steve was headed next.

He returned to the plane with the boxes just as Steve fired up the engines, and after loading the boxes in the hold Louis shut the cargo door and waved goodbye.

"Good luck!" he yelled.

Louis went back inside and watched the plane taxi inland, to the start of the one runway. There was only one air strip, and it ended right at the water's edge. There was a story in Skagway about someone once leaving the gate at the other end of the runway open, and an elderly couple in an RV had turned in thinking they were still on the Klondike Highway. They'd gone right off the end of the runway, doing fifty miles an hour, and shot straight into the Lynn Canal.

Violet was watching the plane as well. As Steve took off she said, "You know, if he'd stayed with the church he would have had faith, and not needed luck."

Louis didn't want to get into it with her, but the more he thought about it, the more her statement bothered him.

Finally, he said, "I think skill and a cool head are more important than luck or faith."

She stared at him, and for a moment her eyes simmered, but then she shrugged and said, "I guess I'll be praying for both of you."

Later, when the skies were black and stormy, Louis shut the office down. One night a week he worked late and Dee stayed home, in the wall tent, with the girls.

There was one more plane due in, and he watched it land, the wind tossing it all over the place as it approached the runway. It taxied to the airport building a few minutes later.

The Dark Lord came through the door, water dripping from his jacket. His hair was wet from the short walk, and there were beads of rainwater clinging to his face and eyebrows. He shouted, "I need that plane unloaded and loaded in five minutes!"

Louis jumped to his feet, grabbed his cart, and started walking quickly to the plane. The Dark Lord was right on his heels. From the west lightning flickered but there was no thunder.

"Am I the last one today?" he asked briskly.

"You are," replied Louis.

The Dark Lord grunted, opened the door to the cargo bay, and stood back.

Louis began unloading boxes, but stopped to cover them with a tarp in the rain. The pilot nudged him to the side.

"You're too slow," he said. "Get out of the way!"

He grabbed the remaining boxes and roughly tossed them onto the cart. The boxes were getting soaked now but he didn't seem to care.

"Get these out of here! You got any outgoing?" he shouted over a rumble of thunder that had finally reached them.

Louis shrugged. "There's nothing. Steve took it earlier."

"Good," he said. He jumped in the plane which he'd never turned off, shut the door, and within a few minutes he was gone. Louis watched the plane lift off, noting how the cross wind sent it sliding sideways in its ascent. That had to be scary, he thought.

It was around ten at night and the sun may have been hovering around the horizon, but the storm clouds obscured it, and soon the town was enveloped in a rare darkness for June; the temperature dropped ten degrees.

By the time Louis got back inside he was shivering. Violet was gone. He closed the office, locked the door, and began walking the twelve blocks back to the wall tent.

The wind came at him from the pass, and he turned his head away from it, towards the docks to his right. He folded his arms to protect his chest and leaned forward. He had begun studying to be a guide, and he pondered facts about Skagway's notorious wind to divert his mind from the sharp chill that pierced his bones.

The name Skagway was derived from a Tlingit idiom, *shgagei*, which refers to the rough seas in the Taiya Inlet, caused by the strong northerly winds pouring down through the White Pass. The town itself, he had read, was known as "The Home of the North Wind" and the locals claimed you never breathed the same air twice.

He'd shaved for work, and now his cheeks stung and flushed red.

He kept his head down while the wind bore down on him.

Louis had an uneasy relationship with the wind. Once it had smacked him sharply, and ever since he had respected it — maybe even feared it a little.

*

It had happened in New Hampshire. After a year of traveling together, Louis and Dee had returned home, only to end up separated. Maybe they'd just spent too much time together, and in the end they were shouting and screaming at each other in a heated fight on the side of Interstate 95, the Maine Turnpike, just as a rain storm rumbled in.

Louis had jumped on his motorcycle and accelerated south. In the distance dark clouds were stacking up. The air was moist.

He wore a black leather jacket and had a helmet on, but the half-windshield on the motorcycle wasn't ideal for rain.

He was doing eighty when he saw the wall of rain hitting the road ahead. His heart still racing from the fight with Dee, his blood pumping with adrenaline, he decided he would try to punch through the storm and pulled down on the throttle.

Throughout his life Louis would tell me it was one of the stupidest things he ever did.

Still thirty feet away from the sheet of water, he hit a cool wall that instantly slowed the bike down by twenty miles per hour, but he was still flying. Things seemed to happen in slow motion in that small buffer and he watched the rain creep closer as he covered the last twenty feet. A blast of cold air shot through his leather jacket, creeping in at the wrists and then flowing under his armpits and down his back.

The bike glided over the dark pavement.

He felt his forearms and shoulders tense, and then the force of the rain when he did finally hit the downpour almost knocked him off the motorcycle.

He fought to stay upright and somehow managed. He touched neither the gas nor the brake, just tried to steer, hoping the tires wouldn't hydroplane right out from under him.

The rain gripped his exposed flesh with fingers that hurt like nails.

The back tire fishtailed out to the left.

And then the force of the storm was coming from above, not ahead of him. He felt the momentum of the motorcycle lessen.

He slowed to thirty, and then twenty miles an hour. He tried to make it to the side of the highway, the rain pelting down all around him, the road flooding with a few inches of water.

A blaring horn followed by a blast of light in his mirror alerted him of an eighteen-wheeler and he barely got out of the way in time, bouncing roughly through a pot hole in the breakdown lane.

He turned off the machine, staggered off the bike, and stood in the rain, not sure why he hadn't crashed. He felt like he'd been slapped by a giant hand.

*

Ever since the wind had haunted him. And now, the walk to the Skagway campground seemed to take forever.

Behind every gust Louis could now sense an echo of his impact with the storm on the Maine Turnpike. And it wasn't just the craziness of hitting the wall of rain and what came after — in retrospect those unforgettable moments in the cool buffer before were just as scary.

A month later he had reunited with Dee, and the years following had been filled with love, and babies, and laughter, but none of that mattered in his memory of the impact. The wind pushing that storm had seemed like a conscious entity, one that had wanted to hurt him, as did this wind.

In the random gusts he felt it teasing him. Taunting. He knew its source was far off in the Yukon where the Tlingit Indians believed the old gods still ruled, and as it chilled his ears he would swear he heard it whisper, "You are insignificant."

He longed for his bicycle. Both his thick shirt and t-shirt were now dripping, and water ran from his hair onto his face, where it lingered as if waiting to freeze.

He thought of Violet. And Steve. And the Dark Lord.

Would praying keep those guys safe? He didn't think so.

And how about luck? A burst of wind hit him and his ears and cheeks went numb.

What saved me on the motorcycle that day? He asked himself. Was it my skill? He didn't believe that was it; he'd ridden for years, but he was no professional. Was someone praying for me? He didn't think that was the case either.

Dumb luck then?

He didn't like the idea of relying on luck, and didn't think the pilots would either. He thought the Dark Lord was a jerk, but as he imagined flying off into the black, stormy skies he had to acknowledge that the guy had balls.

He then had to admit to himself that if he'd been readying to take off before a storm hit he also would be impatient with someone casually unloading his plane.

Finally, the campground came into view. It looked sad with all the sagging tents lit up by the streetlights. The rain had melted the remaining snow and the small stream by the campground was swollen. The tent occupied by Adam and Julie was half caved-in and a large puddle had formed in front of it. It looked empty and he imagined they were in a bar somewhere.

At least his own wall tent beckoned, warm and inviting with the glow of a candle flickering inside. He exhaled and summoned the last of his energy to get there.

He sat in the threshold and took off his shoes, then hung his dripping shirt on a nail on one of the boards that framed the doorway.

The candle cast an orange glow on the girls. They were lying next to Dee; all three were deep in slumber.

They'd left a space for him on the nearby side of the sleeping bags.

He shivered uncontrollably as he undressed and left his socks and t-shirt in a wet pile by the door. His hands were pink and wrinkled as he slowly squeezed in next to the Shrimp.

She wore only a diaper and from even a few inches away he could feel heat radiating from her. He didn't want to touch her because he was so cold and numb, but even under the covers he found he couldn't get warm, and her heat was irresistible.

He paused a moment, then placed one finger on the little girl's back, trying to move her just a little so he could slide deeper into their bed.

She didn't budge so he touched her with two more fingers.

The heat flowing off her little body pulsed under his fingertips and he felt guilty, stealing it, but it seemed like a magic elixir that would bring him back to life.

He focused on the glow at his fingertips, feeling it warm his blood before flowing throughout his cold body. He couldn't remember the last time he'd actually been warm and dry in clean clothes.

Pins and needles began to surface on his numb hand.

He gently placed the palm of his hand against the child's back and for a moment was lost in the sensation of the warmth.

Again, he felt guilty. He thought of his exchange with Violet regarding faith and luck once more. The luck that had come to him over the years was mostly in the survival of accidents, and he wasn't sure that counted—does being scrappy count as luck? And he'd never had a big break, or won a lottery. Louis believed most of what he had in life he'd obtained through hard work and determination.

Still, luck had to be in there somewhere. He just didn't think it was something that could be counted on. It would be nice to have it on your side, but he could do without if he had to.

He began placing his other numb hand on the baby, one finger at a time, the thumb last. He didn't want to give her a chill or wake her up so it took almost five minutes before he had both hands fully on her.

"Thanks," he whispered. "I really needed that."

And I imagine he did. Whenever I heard Louis talk about that night he always stressed that the cold had bored its way deep into his bones.

He stared at the little baby and whispered, "You can have any luck that I have left in this lifetime. We'll trade."

Dee sensed his presence, smiled briefly and turned around to drift off to sleep again.

Louis was ready for sleep now that he had stopped shivering. He snuggled against the Shrimp and said, "Thanks sweetie, I'll do fine without luck. I'm surrounded by love."

One week later Louis and Dee walked down Broadway, following the little trickle of a stream that ran along the road. Cousin Sal was watching the girls so they could get a drink.

Dee's bike had also gone missing and they scanned the bike racks along the road as they passed them, looking for their stolen bicycles. The bike guy was sold out or they would've just bought two more.

It was past nine o'clock at night, but an eerie, creeping light still hovered over the town, making it seem like ten or eleven in the morning.

They reached the boardwalk and found it strangely empty. All the cruise ship passengers had gone back aboard. Dee and Louis´s footsteps echoed off the wooden slats as they passed the storefronts.

"Sometimes this place feels like a ghost town," said Dee.

It had been a busy day. Around ten thousand passengers off four cruise ships had spilled through town. But now, at this late hour, you could shoot an arrow down the sidewalk without hitting anyone.

They entered one of the hundred-year-old establishments called: The Red Onion Saloon.

In the corner a scruffy guy with an acoustic guitar sat on a stool and belted out a tune. His name was Steven Pile, and Louis knew him from the campground.

In fact, the twenty-odd patrons in the place were all from the campground. They had that messy-hair, damp-clothing look that easily set them apart from the well-groomed cruise ship passengers. The guys were unshaven or bearded, and most of the women wore cloth hats.

Steven began a song called, *On our Way*. The song was about leaving Skagway after putting in a full season. Most of the patrons had temporarily abandoned the lower forty-eight for Alaska, and although this season was still young, the words must've rang true because the crowd shouted encouragement, whooping and cheering.

Well it's like my time has finally run up in this crazy place.
And I'm leaving tomorrow but you won't see my sorrow in my face.
Cause I spent too much time working, not enough time getting paid,
And I spent too much time drinking, not enough time getting laid.

As one, everyone hollered at the last line. Before Steven could begin the chorus, Dee turned to the bartender, a guy named Trevor, and quickly ordered a few Alaskan Ambers.

Steve sang the next few lines, and those in the bar that knew the words sang along.

And now I'm back on the road, paid all the debts that I owed,
And we're setting our course, one quick stop in Whitehorse,
And we'll be on our way.

Again, everyone cheered when Steven mentioned Whitehorse. Louis had yet to make it there, but the folks who had driven to Skagway had — and he would soon.

Louis looked at the walls of the saloon while he listened, noting a few historical items. He had flown to Juneau and obtained his commercial driver's license — on one of his friend, Steve's shifts — and he was researching the gold rush days to qualify as a tour guide, becoming a walking encyclopedia.

In a corner, Pete was talking to a couple rafting guides, and Adam and Julie were in the crowd watching the musician. Sasha was leaning against the bar, waiting for a drink. She was still dressed like a gold rush show girl from her shift at the Golden North Hotel.

Steve finished his set. In the silence that followed Chris stumbled through the door in mud-covered hiking clothes, and shouted, "Made it to Upper Dewey Lake!" and half the bar cheered him on.

"I just love it when we have the town to ourselves," said Dee.

Even better were the "no ship" days. Then most of the businesses shut down and everyone set out on one of the local hikes, or to go fishing. The white-water company often opened their boats on these "no ship" days so locals and seasonal workers could ride for free, hoping they would in turn talk tourists into those tours.

Dee noticed a row of dolls on a shelf above the bar.

"What's up with those?" she asked.

"Well, this place used to be a brothel as well as a saloon," said Louis, "and you could tell which woman was available based on whether a certain doll was standing up or laying down."

"That's typical," she said with a frown.

"What d'ya mean by that?"

"Half of those women came here with men who got themselves killed and left them with nothing," she said, the color rising to her face.

"Their husbands got gold fever—what good did any of this Klondike stuff do for them?"

Louis looked around. "Nothin' good, I guess," he said.

It was stuffy in the bar, and after Dee and Louis finished their beers they stepped outside, next to an old building with a distinctive façade made from thousands of pieces of driftwood.

"This is the Arctic Brotherhood's main headquarters," said Louis. "It's one of the most photographed buildings in Alaska."

Dee looked at the strange structure.

Louis nodded at it and said, "These guys pooled their resources and helped each other get to the Yukon."

Dee stared at it. "More dumb-asses chasing gold. If I ever did a tour, it would be about some of the strong women who survived this whole cluster fuck."

Louis shrugged," Okay, point taken."

They casually began walking back to the campground. It was a rare treat to have a baby sitter, and they'd also gotten a break at the state daycare they'd checked the girls into. The state of Alaska offered discounted care for kids if both parents worked the same shift—the idea was to keep families together.

Dee would have to work days, and Louis had to give up his one, night shift at the airport, but that worked fine as he planned on quitting soon to guide tours anyway. The first month the state covered ninety-five percent of the cost of the day care, the next month it was eighty-five, and so on; on their last month in town they would only have to pay half the cost. Also, the kids already knew Julie from the campground, who had gotten a job at the daycare and was now known as Miss Julie.

Dee suddenly spotted her bike in front of the Golden North Hotel. "Hey, that's mine!" she shouted. "What do I do now?"

Louis smiled. "Steal it back!"

She climbed on the bike and slowly coasted with Louis walking beside her. She was grinning from ear to ear. Halfway to the campground a pickup truck with New Hampshire plates pulled up alongside them and slowly cruised at their side with Dee in the middle.

"You the folks from New Hampshire?" asked a striking woman with piercing brown eyes and short black hair.

"Well, I am," said Louis. "She's a Maniac."

The woman stared at Dee, and let her gaze linger for a moment.

Louis felt a bit uncomfortable at the way she stared and asked, "You're from New Hampshire, too?"

The woman leaned over and extended her hand out the window to Dee.

"I'm Lucy," she said. "I've been here a few years now — I own a home. But I finally flew back to my parents´ place last winter to get my truck."

They reached the campground, and Dee pointed at their wall tent.

"That's our place," she said.

Lucy looked at Dee and said, "I'm having a dinner party at my place, you should come by — I just stepped out to get some more wine."

The fire pit was coming into view and Louis realized there was a guy sitting there that looked familiar. He peered closer and recognized a friend, Dinty.

"Hey!" he called to Lucy. "That's one of our friends from New Hampshire. Can I bring him to the party?"

Lucy smiled coyly and said, "Actually it's ladies only."

Dee hoped off her bike. "Why don't you take Dinty out for a beer and I'll go hang with the ladies?"

"I can give you a ride," offered Lucy.

"Sure," said Dee, "just give me a minute."

Louis approached the fire pit and found Sal sitting with the Shrimp on her lap, and Dinty helping Pookey Bear add some small sticks to the fire.

"Hey guys!" yelled Dinty, "I was just getting to know your cousin."

Dee hugged him and whispered in his ear. "Love you Dinty, but stay away from my cousin."

He blushed slightly and smirked. "I'm too old for her anyway."

Dinty was thirty-five with a heavy five o'clock shadow and a devil-may-care look in his eyes. He seemed younger than his age, and Louis knew him well enough to know he definitely didn't think he was too old for her.

"Sorry I didn't tell you I'd be coming in," he said. "Wasn't really sure until last minute—and even then I almost missed the ferry."

Louis was glad to have him in town. He'd met over a hundred people in the last few weeks, but the oldest friend he had in Skagway had been a stranger three weeks before.

Pookey Bear stood in her nightie and pink slippers and staggered drunkenly. "Hi," she said in a sleepy voice.

"What are you doing up?" asked Dee. "It's way past bedtime."

The little girl shook her head and yawned while glancing around at the gloomy midsummer night sky.

"No," she said, "it's daytime."

Sal ran up and lovingly grabbed her from behind. "I can get this one down no problem, you guys go back to the bar—the first ship doesn't dock tomorrow until two o'clock."

On the street, Lucy lightly tapped her horn.

"They'll be at the bar," said Dee. "I'm going to a dinner party."

"At Lucy's?" asked Sal who then tried her best to cover a smile.

"Sure, she seemed nice enough." She kissed Pookey Bear goodnight, jogged back to the street, and climbed into Lucy's truck.

Ten minutes later Dinty and Louis were belly-up at Moe's, one of the few bars in town that wasn't once a gold rush saloon. There was a pool game going on in the back, and a jukebox was playing Hank Williams. A bumper sticker on the mirrored wall in front of them read:

"If assholes could fly, this place would be an airport."

Tom was bartending, but he was currently deep in conversation with Chris regarding the broken down bus.

"I don't think it's your drive shaft," said Chris, "you might be up and running with a new universal joint."

"Really?" asked Tom as he refilled Chris' beer.

"Won't know until we take it out and see if the shaft is bent, but I can order the part cheap through Streetcar."

Tom leaned forward and whispered, "You get me fixed up and you can drink free for a month."

Dinty looked at a few seasonal workers still dressed in gold rush era clothing. "This town cracks me up," he said. "What's up with the obsession over the gold rush?"

Louis laughed. "Finally, someone who wants to hear about the gold rush — Dee's had enough already."

He cleared his throat and began. "In August of 1897, the *S.S. Portland* pulled into Seattle and men began to unload sacks and crates filled with gold. The newspaper ran the headline, *A Ton of Gold*, and the rush was on. Down in the lower forty-eight, a million people prepared to set out for the Yukon goldfields. A hundred thousand made it as far as Skagway."

"Wow!" exclaimed Dinty. "Never heard of it. How much gold did they find?"

Louis blushed. "Well, not as much as you'd think. And most of the guys who got rich were up there in '96 when the gold was first discovered."

He held up his finger. "There were definitely more lucrative gold rushes, but what was unique here was the variety of people involved. Americans were suffering especially hard from a worldwide depression in the 1890's. That's why, when word of gold in Alaska hit, so many people from all different walks of life, dropped everything and headed north."

Louis gestured the bartender for another beer.

"And these guys had no clue what they were getting into. They were bankers, and doctors, and lawyers, and clerks, and factory workers, and unemployed men, too. All wanting to strike it rich. They didn't know prospecting, or how to survive in extreme weather conditions, or even how to work pack horses, but they were determined to escape the despair borne by the slumping economy. The word Klondike was on everyone's lips."

"Holy shit!" Dinty exclaimed. "Sorry, didn't know I was gonna get a lecture."

Louis looked over at Tom who was still in conversation.

"Hey barkeep!" he shouted, "How 'bout a couple Alaskan Ambers?"

Tom motioned for Chris to stay put and quickly grabbed the beers. "Here you go, sir," he said with a grin.

Louis took a sip and Dinty said, "I don't know. It sounds a bit crazy."

Louis stared at his friend. Throughout their childhood Dinty had been the guy who was not afraid to take a leap. Literally. Once he'd been on a motorcycle and an old lady's *Cadillac* had slammed into him from the side. Luckily, the car had its passenger windows open and right before the impact, Dinty had jumped off the bike and clung to the metal divider between the windows. The bike went down, and the old woman didn't even know she'd been in an accident until she turned and saw him suspended there, grinning.

"Mind pulling over?" he'd asked casually.

"All kidding aside," said Louis, "you're one of the few guys that I could have seen heading to the Klondike if you'd been alive then."

Dinty took a big gulp of his beer and asked, "How's that?"

Louis said, "Well, imagine you were on the verge of losing everything. Couldn't pay your mortgage, the cupboards are bare, and there's no work."

Dinty grinned. "Heck, I don't have to image nothing—I've been there already."

They laughed and clinked their bottles together. Louis said, "So now you hear about this place called the Yukon where gold nuggets the size of your fist are just lying around waiting to be picked up. Would you leave them there for someone else?"

Dinty smiled. "Fuck no! I guess you do know me. I'd be on the first boat or train headed this way to get me some gold."

"So would I," said Louis.

On the stool next to Dinty, Louis saw Adam from the campground, and shouted hello.

"Hey Adam—where's Miss Julie?" asked Louis.

Adam shook his head and lowered it to take a long swig off his beer. He was clean-shaven and wore a button-up shirt.

"It's not good, boys," he said, "she's being swayed by the dark side."

"What does that mean?" asked Dinty.

Adam sighed. "There's this group of women in town that have dinner parties every few weeks. They got a nice warm house with a fireplace, and after dinner they all climb into a wood-heated hot tub."

"What's wrong with that?" asked Louis.

Adam looked up. "I'll tell you what's wrong: they're all lesbians and they're looking for recruits."

Dinty tried to contain a smirk as he jabbed his thumb at Louis and said, "His wife just went to one of their parties."

Adam whistled for the bartender, Tom, and ordered a round of tequila shots. "That's not cool, man," he said. "You better keep an eye on her."

Louis chuckled. "It all seemed pretty harmless."

The shots arrived. There was an extra and Tom hoisted it up with them. Adam paused and stared at Louis and asked, "Did your wife bring a bathing suit with her tonight?"

Brow creased, Louis said, "I don't think she did."

Adam downed his shot and motioned for Tom to bring him another beer.

"Not cool at all," he lamented. "All them drunk, naked ladies in a witch's brew. It's not fair either."

Midsummer eve came and went and it seemed the sun never set. If you woke in the middle of the night it looked a little dusky, but it was always light out.

Louis sat by the fire pit, sipping a Heineken, and thinking on their prospects. Zana had set up an interview that afternoon for him with Dave, the owner of Southeast Tours, and his dispatcher, a guy named Brian. It hadn't gone smoothly. Dave, it turned out, was very skeptical.

Dave was a Vietnam vet, and always wore a cowboy hat and a jean jacket with the sleeves torn off. He stared at Louis with an expression of calculated appraisal.

"I don't know," he'd said, squinting one eye like he was sighting a gun, "I can't see it—you just don't look like a guide."

Brian sat beside Dave, listening while he answered emails on a computer. Brian was tall with short, dark hair and had come from Montana with his fiancé. Zana claimed he kept the show running smoothly.

Louis pleaded with him. "Look, I really need this job. I can do it."

Dave shook his head and was about to speak when Brian interrupted him, "We really could use another guide—if anyone gets sick we're screwed."

Finally, Dave cracked an uncomfortable smile and said, "Looks like this is your lucky day—don't screw up."

So far Louis had only done the city tour, but as it turned out he enjoyed talking history with the tourists and it came naturally to him.

He'd finished his tours for the day, washed down the twenty-four-passenger shuttle he'd driven, and now he waited by the fire for Dee and the girls to show up.

Zana had reluctantly got Tristan a job at Southeast Tours, too. He'd been fired from the Golden North because a manager caught him having sex with a waitress in the cooler.

"You won't be pulling that shit at Southeast Tours," Zana had told Tristan.

"How can you be so sure?" asked Tristan with a confident smile.

She stared him down. "Because I'm the only girl and I think you're a scumbag."

He had held up his hands defensively. "Hey, I'm just a guy lookin' for love."

Next door, Ben was sweeping out his wall tent. He'd met a woman who guided up on the glacier, and his desire to work up there was suddenly stronger than ever. He had shaved off his beard the day before, and then surprised everyone by stating he was giving up weed.

"She must be some woman," said Louis as he watched him shake his sleeping bag out and hang it on a clothesline.

Ben grinned. "She gets a couple days off every few weeks. You'll meet her when she's in town next."

Adam had found a job at a jewelry store. He had retail experience, and didn't want to work out in the cold. He didn't like camping, and his little tent wasn't holding up well.

"How much are the wall tents?" he'd asked Louis, but was discouraged when he found out that they were twice the cost of a tent site.

Dinty stayed in a small tent in the campground for a week, then accompanied Louis, Dee and the girls to the Haines fair. There was a free ferry from Skagway to Haines and it seemed like everyone was on it: Dee's relatives, Southeast Tours guides, and what looked like half the campground population.

At the fair, Pookey Bear won a guinea pig, and together with Dee, had convinced Louis that they couldn't live without a pet. Meanwhile, Dinty was making one trip after another to the beer tent.

At eleven at night, they took the last ferry back, and Dinty wasn't on it.

That was now over a week ago and Louis still had no clue what had happened to him.

On the street, Dee came into view, riding her recovered bicycle and towing a two-wheeled cart behind her. Her aunt had lent it to her for the summer.

The girls were bundled inside, buckled underneath a blanket. A plastic flap protected them from the eternal rain in Skagway.

Since it was always warm and toasty at school, both girls looked forward to leaving the damp wall tent for daycare. Their best friends there had colorful names: Cricket, Sahara and Magellan.

Dee pulled up to the fire pit and said, "I want to take Pookey Bear to the store."

Louis opened the cart's flap and unbuckled his youngest.

"Okay, I'll take the Shrimp," he said, but Pookey Bear shook her head.

"She's called Say Say now," she said.

"Who calls her that?" asked Louis.

Pookey Bear gave him a frustrated look and said, "Everyone."

He lifted up the baby and waved goodbye as Dee pedaled off with Pookey Bear.

The flow of the stream that followed the road had diminished a bit since the snow had thawed, but it still gushed along, three feet wide in some places.

A metal fence shadowed it. It had smooth, vertical poles that were far enough apart to see through, but not wide enough that the baby could fit through.

Louis set her on the ground next to the fence and she peered through at the stream that flowed from left to right, toward the docks. The Shrimp, now Say-Say, had turned one that month, but showed no inclination to stand. Part of the reason could have been that the campground was often muddy, and she was safest and driest when she was being held, so she didn't get many chances to practice.

An ancient white tour bus came around the corner and slowly cruised by the campground. A muffler leak gave the vehicle an obnoxiously loud roar as it drifted by in a cloud of exhaust.

Pete was driving it.

Louis saw him now, red-eyed and pale. He was looking hung over once again. He had connected with a girlfriend from back home. Her name was Marnie, and judging from Pete's appearance, she liked to party.

"How can you do a tour in that condition?" Louis had asked him a few days ago.

Pete had grinned guiltily. "I just turn off the mike and do a silent tour—can you believe people still tip me?"

Now, as Louis stared at the passing vehicle, Pete winked, an unlit cigarette hanging in his mouth. His window was open and Louis watched him flip on his mike and heard him say, "On the left, Skagway campground and assorted riffraff."

Louis smiled, happy to be included, and feeling proudly riffraffish.

Pete smiled again, hit the gas, and disappeared in a cloud of smoke.

Louis turned to check on Say Say. She had a firm grip of two of the vertical poles and was pulling herself up to a stand so she could see the water better. She stood there, shaky for a moment until she got her legs under her, and then she let go and stood freely for the first time.

The Tormented Valley, British Columbia

Chapter Seven

The Tormented Valley, British Columbia
(July 2002)

The 24-passenger shuttle left Skagway with every seat filled. Louis had driven the tour to the White Pass several times before, but this was the first day none of the other guides was accompanying him to listen to his spiel and critique his performance.

Now that he was alone with his passengers he tried to think of the best way to explain what had happened here a little over one hundred years ago. He'd read much on the Klondike Gold Rush, but felt the tour he had been giving under observation was too stiff and overstuffed with numbers.

He had plenty of time; they wouldn't reach the U.S. customs checkpoint for ten minutes. Now, absent the pressure of another guide riding along, he began to relax.

A few miles outside of town they passed the road that led to the Stampeder Cemetery but he decided not to mention it yet, as they'd be stopping at the cemetery on their return in ninety minutes.

They also passed the turnoff to Dyea, where the famous Chilkoot Trail departed. The Chilkoot was one of two ways in which men traveled from Skagway to the Yukon—the other was the pass they were currently ascending. Not as many men used the Chilkoot because the prospectors had to haul all of their gear up the steep pass on their own

133

backs, and most of the guys were in a rush and didn't want to be delayed by making multiple trips. On the White Pass they could use horses.

He remained silent again, not wanting to get ahead of himself by focusing on different ways some took to the Yukon. Instead he flipped on the microphone that extended from the dash and started at the beginning.

"In 1887, Captain William Moore landed on the muddy tidal flats of Skagway," he began. "The Captain had heard rumors of the mineral wealth of the Yukon, and hoped to find a way there."

A quick glance in the rearview mirror showed his passengers staring out the window with no indication that they were actually listening to him.

He continued, "Upon arriving, the Captain got lucky when he met Skookum Jim, a native of Tagish, Yukon, who claimed to know a way through the Coastal Range."

A couple behind him opened a paper bag and began to noisily unwrap their lunch. Others in the back were talking and didn't appear to hear him at all.

Louis sat back, frustrated. They weren't interested.

He turned off the microphone. They were approaching U.S. customs and a guard in a glass booth motioned him forward. On the dash he had twenty-four passports rubber-banded together, and he now set the bundle in his lap and placed his own on top.

He called over his shoulder. "Okay everyone, we'll be through this in just a minute. No photographs please and stay in your seats."

The guard looked relaxed as Louis rolled down his window and handed over the passports.

"All U.S. citizens?" he asked.

"Yes, sir."

"And you're just going up to the valley and back right? Nobody is passing through Canadian customs?"

Louis nodded. "Correct, we'll be heading back to Skagway in about forty minutes."

The guard quickly flipped through the passports then handed them back. "Enjoy the drive," he said.

"I plan on it," said Louis with a smile as he put the vehicle in gear.

The highway continued, always sloping upward. Since they left town, the Skagway River had flowed on their right, but now the mountains soared around them and they could barely glimpse the blue-white line as it flowed towards the town and the Taiya Inlet.

A mile up the road Pitchfork Falls came into view on the right, far across the gorge. The shuttle leaned slightly as everyone took out their cameras and moved to that side.

"Easy back there" said Louis, "We're gonna stop ahead so you can get out and take photos."

He pulled over and his passengers rushed outside with cameras pointed. A few moved behind the vehicle for a quick cigarette. Louis took a few minutes to scan his notes.

After five minutes he fired up the engine, the signal for his guests to get back on board. Then they continued up the highway.

Two miles up the road he pulled over against the right guardrail. There wasn't enough room to open the door and the passengers stared at him through his mirror, slightly confused.

He pushed the microphone out of his way and stood up and turned to face them. Some were glancing out the windows on the right, craning their necks to see down into the gorge.

Louis took a breath and said, "I'm sure that you've been bombarded with information on the gold rush since you set foot in Skagway, but I want to paint a picture here to show you that it wasn't just a matter of hiking to the Yukon and back. It was actually very dangerous, and for many of the stampeders it was terrifying."

He gestured across the gorge, slightly ahead of them.

"That's Dead Horse Gulch," he said. "It might look harmless now, lying there empty in the summer, but imagine it in the 1890s. There were roughly six thousand horses used on this trail during a two-year period and barely a dozen survived."

The passengers stared down into the gulch silently until one man raised his arm.

"Excuse me," he said, "but I've worked with horses all my life and I think I could get one of mine up that section without any problems."

"Well, I'm sure your horses were in better condition, and it sounds like you know how to work them," said Louis. "Most of the horses that died in the gulch were bought from glue factories in Seattle. They were purchased by greenhorn prospectors for five or ten dollars each, and then sold to the stampeders for up to six hundred."

The man nodded somberly and Louis continued. "And this pass had to be crossed in the middle of winter if you wanted to be in the Yukon, on Lake Bennett, when the ice broke up—which you did—so you'd be dealing with temperatures of fifty below zero, violent winds and almost complete darkness."

A gust of wind rocked the shuttle and whistled through the windows that some passengers had cracked open, only an inch. Even in summer the pass was a chilly place. The heat was blasting.

"Jack London came through here during one bad winter and wrote, 'The horses died like mosquitoes in the first frost.'"

A woman in the front had a horrified look on her face as she asked, "What would drive people to be so cruel?"

Louis paused. This was the crux of it. Why so much cruelty and death? "Well, most of the men that rushed up here after gold had no knowledge of how to work pack animals. They didn't know anything about prospecting either—they just wanted to be the first to the Yukon because the newspapers had made it sound like the gold was just laying on the ground, waiting to be picked up."

Louis took a sip of water. He was nervous and his mouth had gone dry. He said, "These people were desperate—they'd invested everything they had into this dream and were hell-bent to reap a reward. It wasn't uncommon to hear of someone being killed for moving too slowly along the trail. Many viewed this trail as a weeding ground that sorted out those who weren't cut out for the harshness of the Yukon."

Louis's tale had apparently made the gold rush desperation tangible. His passengers silently stared into the gorge. Even the occasional click of a camera had stopped.

"Imagine yourself in this line of prospectors, which was moving along the trail at a snail's pace and was sometimes stopped for hours," said Louis, "the freezing temperatures slowly numbing animals and men alike — then, every so often it would lurch forward. If a horse went lame, it was left behind. If a sled froze in place the owner had just a few minutes to free it before the men behind him pulled their guns in frustration."

In the silence that followed Louis started up the vehicle, put it in gear, and continued up the Klondike Highway. Soon they passed an old suspension bridge.

"That bridge was named after Captain Moore. Not much of a tribute for the guy who discovered the White Pass *and* was also Skagway's first settler."

He pointed above the bridge, "And that's the Cleveland Glacier — named for President Cleveland for reasons no one in Skagway can remember."

Louis loved this part of the tour. The spruce trees around them were becoming stunted, surrounded by sprawling alders and rounded, lichen-covered boulders, and as they ascended higher on the highway enormous, snow-covered peaks appeared all around them.

The group behind him gave a collective gasp as a new range showed itself on their left and he said, "Those are the Sawtooth Mountains."

A sign appeared by the side of the road: *White Pass Summit, 3,292 feet.* Just beyond it he pulled into a parking lot where a billboard read: *Welcome to Alaska.*

"We're now on the Fraser Plateau," said Louis. "Almost all of it lies in British Columbia — if we drove another eight miles up this road, I'd have to check you through Canadian customs, but we'll turn around before then." He opened the door to let out the guests for a photo break.

"This is the Tormented Valley," he said, "Most prospectors preferred to cross it in winter because the mosquitos were so bad in summer that they drove some guys mad."

Someone whispered, "It's so beautiful," and he nodded silently. The stunning scenery up here continued to move him.

The valley was lined with snow-capped mountains, their flanks white with glaciers that spilled down, dwindling into streams that filled hundreds of small lakes. It took a moment for it to come into focus for most visitors because the scale of things was immense.

At first, the valley looked desolate, like a landscape from the moon, but then the vast tundra and distant patches of stunted forest took shape, as did the deep ravines that cut into the surrounding mountains.

The numerous alpine lakes stretched away from them, reaching toward the Yukon, only forty-odd miles away. Louis had yet to go that far, but the few times he'd made it here had changed him. It was because of this view that he looked forward to going to work, and he was always ready to go way before departure time.

A woman with a New Jersey accent came forward, pointed at one of the lakes and asked, "Young man, is that lake tidally fed?"

Louis bit back a smirk, wanting to remind her they were at over three thousand feet above sea level, but instead he just said, "No ma'am, it's fed by rain and snowmelt."

He'd noticed that his guests were often a bit out of it: they staggered out of the vehicle like they were drunk, and some had a hard time grasping where they were and what they were seeing.

He figured the cross between living on a cruise ship, and then suddenly going up in elevation, was to blame.

It didn't bother him. Louis loved this job. Most people were in awe of the landscape, some seemed to have a once-in-a-lifetime experience on this tour, and he was happy to be part of it.

The next pullout had several outhouses, and Louis got on the mike to advertise them: "I'd highly recommend using the outhouse if you want to have an authentic Klondike experience."

When they arrived at the parking lot an old, tan tour vehicle was already stopped—Dee was there. She'd quit her waitressing job and also picked up a position as a tour guide when she understood how much money could be made; sometimes Louis collected over two hundred dollars in tips from one, two-and-a-half-hour tour!

Louis loved the fact that she now had to study history, and looked forward to hearing her spiel. He helped a few stragglers out of his vehicle and crept around Dee's tour bus.

He almost laughed out loud at what he saw.

Standing in a wide arc around her were ten European-looking men, each with one hand high in the air. In the other they were holding a cigarette. The men were filming with video recorders, and were slowly spinning in circles trying to take in the entire valley.

Dee stood in the middle, grinning.

She saw Louis and waved, then walked over.

"What's up with those guys?" he asked.

She shrugged. "They're all Germans, they don't speak much English and didn't want a lecture. They just asked to be driven to scenic spots so they could do this."

One of the Germans walked over to her, grinned proudly at Louis and said, "We have the best tour guide in Skagway."

The man walked back to their tour bus, and Dee turned and stuck her tongue out at Louis.

Louis pulled the shuttle into the parking lot for the Stampeder Cemetery that they'd passed earlier. A short trail led to the graveyard, where several groups were listening to their guides telling stories of some of the departed.

On their way down from the Tormented Valley Louis had told the tale of Soapy Smith and Frank Reid and their famous shootout. Soapy was a con man, and for a while he ran Skagway. Eventually a group of vigilantes confronted him and a town engineer named Frank Reid shot him dead. But before Soapy died, he managed to also put a bullet into Frank Reid, who died twelve days later. They were each buried in the cemetery, a short distance from each other.

Louis preferred to tell the story on the often cloudy or rainy descent from the Tormented Valley instead of at Reid's grave like other tour guides, because he felt it gave his passengers something else to ponder besides a foggy crash.

Therefore, they only stopped briefly at Frank Reid's grave, where Louis offered an interesting side trip. "I'd like to show you a waterfall that's located up an easy trail," he said, and when his guests agreed, he led them to Lower Reid Falls, a quarter mile beyond the northern end of the graveyard.

They passed a small crowd and Louis glimpsed Tristan on a stump addressing a group of women. Zana was there too, and she let her people listen to Tristan´s story of the shootout—which, by the wide grin on her face, was apparently hilarious.

She grabbed Louis's arm as he passed and whispered, "You really have to see this—it's priceless."

"Go on ahead," he said to his passengers. "I'll catch right up."

Tristan´s dragged out the story of the shootout, as this was the last stop of the tour and would hopefully inspire a good tip. He hammed it up, but there was a sense of resistance in his crowd and Tristan, usually over-confident, seemed strangely unsure of himself.

Zana whispered, "Tristan has a group from the Norwegian `Ladies Only` cruise and he hasn't figured out that most of them are lesbians. I watched them arrive—he kept hitting on a few of the younger women and it's really got the group mad at him."

Louis chuckled. He'd had several tours with similar groups. Normally, he'd tell them he was married, and that he had two daughters, and then just do the best tour he could.

He never had any problems. But then again, Louis didn't hit on his tour guests.

Tristan finished and walked past Louis and Zana, and Zana giggled and said, "Tough crowd, eh Tristan?"

He shrugged. "What the fuck?"

Louis was chuckling as he turned and hustled to catch up with his people.

The fourth of July arrived and the girls got dressed up for the parade. It seemed half the town was riding the floats, Dee included. The girls waved at her as she passed on a truck filled with women that worked at the Golden North Hotel.

I have an old photo of the girls; Pookey Bear had blue hair and kitty-cat whiskers painted on her face, and Say Say wore a one-piece cow costume.

Pookey Bear cheered her mom on, and then looked down at Say Say, bundled next to her, and said, "See, momma got people, too."

That evening the young girls anxiously waited for the fireworks, but even at nine that night the sun was still high in the sky.

They returned to the wall tent, read a few stories and collectively drifted off to sleep. Dee awoke with a start at midnight when she heard explosions down the street. It was finally dusky out, and Louis tried to wake up his oldest, but couldn't.

"Maybe next year," he said and tucked her in.

Pete no longer guided tours. He'd sorted out his lapped license and was back to piloting the tugboat that escorted the cruise liners to their berths. He now lived on the tug, which was docked alongside the pier. And he had a new girlfriend, too—one who didn't party as much as Marnie. He looked good.

Marnie, on the other hand, hadn't taken their breakup well, and from time to time she got raging drunk and roamed around searching for him to pick a fight.

Pete stayed on his tugboat a lot, trying to avoid her.

Once a week Pete was tasked with cleaning out the fridge and restocking it. Because the boat and its crew might have to ship out at a moment's notice for several weeks at sea, there were strict rules for the supplies on board and their expiration dates. So Pete often invited a bunch of the guys from the campground over, and cooked up bacon, toast, and omelets from stuff that had to go.

In mid-July Pete invited the boys over for a late night feast. Ben was back in town, off the glacier for a few days, and Adam came along too.

"How're things up on the glacier?" Pete asked Ben. Ben had finally been hired—after passing his drug test.

"It's fuckin' cold," he replied. "And I wish I could figure out Gina. I think she really likes me—we've even made out a few times. But she won't share a tent with me."

Pete handed him a beer and asked, "What do you mean, won't share a tent?"

"They put us in two-man tents," said Ben, "And I somehow ended with a tent to myself. I've asked her repeatedly to move in, but she won't."

Pete held up a hand of caution. "Take it slow! Women like to be romanced — and I bet there's little time for romance up on a glacier."

"Fuck women!" blurted Adam. He'd arrived drunk and was in a foul mood. Miss Julie now spent a few nights a week with Lucy and her girlfriends, and when Louis had last seen Adam at Moe's he'd been playing B-16 on the jukebox over and over again – Ben Harper's song, *Mama's Got a New Girlfriend*:

Papa he left home today
Said he ain't comin' back again
Said he ain't gonna be nobody's second best
Just cause mama's got a special kind of friend

"Easy there," said Ben. "They're not all bad. And I don't think all the woman that hang at Lucy's dinner parties are lesbians."

"I wouldn't know — she won't tell me anything. And whenever I ask her friends they just smirk at me and it really pisses me off. I have no idea what goes on there."

He looked at Louis and asked, "Zana's a regular at Lucy's get-togethers — what does she say happens?"

Louis shrugged. "I haven't asked her. Tristan asks all the time but she just tells him to fuck off."

"Well, what do you think?" he asked desperately.

Louis shrugged. "Zana is tough to figure. She's the only person I know here who isn't constantly trying to find a partner. I don't even know which way she goes."

"Probably both ways," said Adam as he pulled out a joint and grinned at it grimly. "This will make things better."

Pete held up his hands. "Not inside — and next time I don't even want to know about it."

"Okay, okay," said Adam, defensively. "I'll go up on deck."

He left and Pete turned to Louis.

"Hey, what happened to your friend, Dinty? Haven't seen him around."

Louis raised his eyebrows. "Hell if I know. We took the ferry over to the Haines Fair ten days ago and he disappeared. Wasn't on the last ferry home, and I haven't heard from him since."

"Maybe he...," Pete started when a scream from outside on the dock interrupted him.

"I know you're in there, you cocksucker!" came the shrill voice of a woman. She sounded drunk.

"Shit," mumbled Pete. "It's Marnie."

He ducked low, then went to the hatch and urgently whispered to Adam who was smoking his joint on deck.

"Get your ass in here before she sees you!"

Adam returned with a cloud of smoke lingering around him.

"That chick is angry," he said as he sat down.

"Fuck me," said Pete as he turned off the lights. "You know, when I dated her I didn't even think she liked me — now she's obsessed."

He cracked a beer and sat down. "I just don't get women."

"Me either," said Ben, and by his side Adam silently bobbed his head in agreement.

Later that night Louis stumbled back to his wall tent feeling buzzed and stuffed. He'd brought along a twelve-pack of beer as his contribution and with Pete's help had drunk all of it.

He was floating away, on the verge of sleep, when he heard someone singing Bob Marley's *Jammin'*, although with altered lyrics.

> *"Ooh, yeah! All right! We're salmon:*
> *I want some salmon wid you.*
> *We're salmon, salmon,*
> *And I hope you like salmon, too."*

The singer got closer, and Louis realized it was Dinty. He jumped up and put his pants on. It made him happy to hear his voice. Having a friend from New Hampshire around had made him feel connected to home, and when he'd disappeared there had been an emptiness — as well as some worry.

He glanced out the flap of the wall tent and saw him approaching, swinging two five-gallon buckets. They seemed heavy, and Dinty was swaying slightly.

Dinty grinned and kept singing,

*"We're salmon, we're salmon, we're salmon, we're salmon,
we're salmon, we're salmon, we're salmon, we're salmon."*

He hefted the buckets. *"And we hope you like salmon, too."*

Louis slipped back into his jeans and went outside. Dinty's buckets were indeed overflowing with salmon fillets.

They stepped to the fire pit so they wouldn't be talking right over the sleeping girls.

"I'd just about given up on you," he said to Dinty.

Dinty waved away his concern. "You know you don't ever have to worry about me — I'm a survivor."

"Well, what happened to you?"

Dinty had a daypack on, and after setting down the salmon-filled buckets he slipped it off, opened it, and took out a bottle of Jack Daniels.

He sat down heavily, unscrewed the cap, and then took a long pull off the bottle before handing it to Louis.

"I got pretty lit at the fair," he began, "and in the beer tent — while you were off getting a Guinea pig of all things — I met a fisherman who was looking to replace an incapacitated crew member."

Louis handed the bottle back. "You don't even know how to fish!"

"That's what I told him," said Dinty, "but I said if he'd teach me I'd work for free."

"I bet he jumped at that offer."

Dinty gave a smirk. "He sure did. I worked my ass off for ten days, he taught me how to fish, and today he dropped me at the Skagway dock with as much salmon as I could carry."

He hefted the bottle. "And a bottle of Jack!"

He stretched his arms and said, "I honestly don't think I could have carried another fillet."

Two weeks later tourism in Skagway was at its peak. There were no longer any "no ship" days, and often there were five cruise ships docked at the end of Broadway all at once. Louis and Dee made enough money to move out of the wall tent and into a small apartment across the street. It was located above a restaurant which had failed to open that season.

There were two bedrooms and two large eaves, and Pookey Bear claimed one as her room. The slanted ceiling was just high enough for her to stand, and she thought it must have been designed for kids.

The eaves stayed warm, a nice change from the chill in the wall tent; even though in the middle of summer temperatures usually reached the upper sixties in the day, they often dropped to freezing at night.

Cousin Francis obtained several mattresses from a church. He gave one to Pookey Bear, and helped her move it into her eave, and asked if he could use the remaining mattress in the other eave until he had lined up a place of his own.

He joked as he bent to enter. "This will be my monastic cell."

His sister Sal often babysat and became a regular at the apartment, too.

Dinty had become friends with Ben and Chris, and when Ben was up on the glacier—often for a week at a time—he stayed in their wall tent.

Louis and Dee continued to guide, driving up to the pass and back and reciting the old gold rush stories to the tourists, and they always had stories to tell about their guests.

One time, Louis had a family of four whose quiet disposition caught his attention.

They all looked pretty somber, and it seemed they'd suffered a tragedy. The parents and the son were pale and gaunt, and the daughter appeared disoriented.

The shuttle carried twenty passengers that day, and Louis was telling gold rush stories and pointing out features in the landscape as they made their way up to the Tormented Valley.

At the viewpoint the father walked up to him.

"Hi," the guy said awkwardly. "I've got a request."

"Anything. What can I do for you?"

The man stared at his feet for a few moments.

Finally, he said, "My oldest son passed on last month, and we would like to spread his ashes here. He always loved Alaska."

His wife came up and took her husband's arm, and they both looked expectantly at Louis.

Louis fidgeted for a few seconds, then said, "I'm sorry for your loss."

He looked over the viewpoint and counted a dozen other tour vehicles. There was nowhere to discreetly spread the ashes, and if someone saw and reported this, he would be in trouble. Technically, the authorities would consider this disposing of a body, which could cost Louis his bonus, maybe even his job.

Hesitantly, he said, "I think we could get in trouble if we did it here. We're actually in British Columbia right now, not Alaska."

Before they could speak he quickly added, "But let me show you a really nice place on our way back."

The mother gave a weak smile and said, "Thank you."

Ten minutes later he steered his shuttle back onto the Klondike Highway, heading for Skagway.

Louis flipped on his microphone and said, "If you look up through the trees on our right we are beginning to get a glimpse of spectacular Bridal Veil Falls. The source of the fall is the Carmack Glacier. Falls and cascades mark its entire length as the water drops over five thousand feet to meet the Skagway River below."

He parked the shuttle in front of the falls, which splashed into a pond, overflowing into a culvert that diverted the water under the highway. People sluggishly shuffled out of the bus, and then slowly raised their cameras in an attempt to photograph the top of the falls, far above them.

Louis gestured for the grieving family to follow him across the street. They climbed over the guardrail on the far side and continued through some alders for a few feet to a flat rock that overlooked the gorge and Skagway River far below.

"Careful," said Louis as they all crowed together on the rock. The son was carrying an urn.

Majestic mountains rose all around, and their flanks were glittering with waterfalls that trickled their way down to the river.

Below them a breeze ruffled the tree tops.

The dad looked around. "Sean would have liked this."

The daughter's eyes followed the urn as the son handed it to his parents. They cried silently as they opened it together.

Then they turned to the chasm and the dad tipped the urn upside down—just when a gust of wind swept up from the depths. It caught the ashes and blew them over the five people standing on the flat rock, covering them like ghosts.

After a moment of utter silence, the daughter burst out laughing.

She looked at her arms, and then at the urn which her dad was holding, and then at her parents and her brother. She laughed and laughed, and her parents watched her, a bit worried.

Finally, her laugh died down to a giggle, and color had returned to her cheeks, visible despite the ash coating. A single tear found its way down her powdered face as she looked at her family and said, "That was so Sean! That was him. He was always a jokester."

The others began to laugh, and then sob a little, and then they hugged, pulling Louis into their family embrace.

Suddenly, Louis missed his own family, and he couldn't help wondering if this might have been his own parents and siblings, had he met his fate on one of his countless and often dangerous journeys.

Some touring experience were deeply moving, others were bewildering. Once Louis was driving up the pass in a van that fit fifteen passengers. Dave of Southeast Tours wanted Louis to get familiar with the vehicles used for excursions to the Yukon, as he knew Louis was yearning to do those tours

He had recently made several runs into the Yukon Territory, to Carcross, roughly sixty-five miles away, and he couldn't wait to go further.

That day he was giving a private tour, organized by a guy named Joe who sat up front. The itinerary wasn't that different from the normal city tour that visited the Tormented Valley, but the guy had paid more and the office dispatcher, Brian, used two-way radios to check in with Louis from time to time just to make sure everything was running smoothly.

The van felt more personal than the shuttle. Altogether, he had eight other people in the van—four couples, and Louis chatted with them during the drive.

"So what ship are you guys on?"

"Believe it or not," said Joe with a grin, "we're on the Princess 'Star Trek' cruise."

Louis smiled. "Really? I'm a huge Star Trek fan. And my wife claims she had a crush on Wil Wheaton when she was young."

One of the women in the back giggled and said, "You're in trouble then, because he's on our cruise."

Louis and his brother, Diggy, had been obsessed with the science-fiction-series when it aired in the sixties. It had only run for three seasons, but they had watched the reruns for years. The series told the story of the starship *Enterprise* and its crew, led by captain James T. Kirk, on its explorations of various solar systems throughout the universe in the 23rd century.

Louis was sure this story had helped foster his desire to travel.

He raised his voice in the van and quoted the starship's mission:

To explore strange new worlds,
to seek out new life and civilizations,
to boldly go where no man has gone before.

Her husband asked, "Did you like The Next Generation as well?"

The Next Generation was a spin-off series from the late eighties, staring Patrick Stewart. Louis found him in the mirror.

"Definitely!" he said. "You guys are all fans, too?"

At once they all laughed. Joe said, "I guess we'd have to be, we're all writers for the show—and a few of the spin offs."

"Wow," exclaimed Louis. "I liked all those shows. In a lot of ways they changed my life. I've traveled all over the world to experience new cultures, and Star Trek was the first thing I remember watching where people did that. Literally travelling through space."

Joe chuckled. "Do you know that the line you quoted from the opening credits actually gave the producers some trouble."

Louis thought a moment. "I noticed in *The Next Generation* the wording was changed from 'to boldly go where *no man* had gone before' to 'where *no one* had gone before'."

Joe nodded. "It was. The original line actually came from a pamphlet called *Outer Space*, issued in 1958 by the White House when Eisenhower was president. In it he said 'no one' so we changed it back."

The lady directly behind him leaned forward and said, "I think you boys were just under pressure to be more politically correct."

Louis pulled over at the observation point for Pitchfork Falls, which tumbled down the opposite side of the gorge. When they were standing on the platform Joe asked, "Do you have a favorite *Next Generation* episode?"

Louis thought for a minute. "Probably the one when the *Enterprise* was called back to Earth in the 19th century and they find a buried box that contains the android Data's head."

They all laughed and looked at Joe who said proudly, "That was one of mine."

Louis knew he'd made the man's day—and his own as well. He stepped up his game a notch and brought them to a few extra places he normally didn't visit on tour. When he shook Joe's hand at the end the man gave him a hundred-dollar bill.

He drove to the car wash to clean up the van, thinking how much he loved his job. I would have paid to drive those guys around! he thought; instead, I've got my hourly check plus a crisp hundred-dollar bill in my pocket.

And when he thought back to their desperate drive across America, and how much a hundred dollars would have meant to him then, he felt they'd come a long way.

With the apartment came a feeling of domesticity, but also one of security. No longer was their sleep interrupted by anyone that walked by their wall tent, no longer did they have to worry that squirrels or raccoons would steal their food. They now had a fridge and stove, as well as access to a washing machine and dryer.

Most of all Louis enjoyed washing dishes in warm water.

Nobody had moved into their old wall tent, and every now and then he would return to it and sit outside by the fire pit. The campground was emptier now. Many people had left Alaska, tired of the cold, wet conditions.

Zana had moved into a friend's place and her wall tent was empty as well.

It made Louis sad to see the empty tent sites. When they'd first arrived there had been a buzz of excitement in the air, now there was only the wind rustling the cottonwoods.

Dinty sat at the fire when Louis walked into the campground one evening after a busy day of tours. A few feet away Tom and Chris were trying to install a new universal joint in the bus.

"I'm fuckin' ready for a beer," said Louis. "What a long day."

Dinty nudged him lightly and indicated some bushes a few feet away.

"Watch your language," he whispered.

When they lived in the wall tent there had been only barren shrubs around the fire pit. But during the summer the vegetation had filled in. You could no longer see the train tracks, only thirty feet away.

He noticed a flicker of movement, deep in the bushes. Then it stopped.

He leaned closer to peek inside the bush and suddenly heard a soft giggle. It was Pookey Bear. Over the last few months she'd become a listener, and he'd often seen her subtly eaves-dropping on some of the young folks that they knew from the campground.

Dinty reached to his side and grabbed two bottles of beer from a six-pack by his feet. He opened one and gave it to Louis, and then popped the second one for himself.

As Louis took a swig he noticed a motorcycle parked by the edge of the fire pit.

"Whose bike?" he asked as he lowered his beer.

"Oh, that's mine," said Dinty. "Just picked it up."

Louis stared at it for a minute. "You're gonna ride that back to New Hampshire?"

Dinty sipped his beer. "That's the plan. Heading out in a few days."

Louis frowned. "I was hoping you'd stay 'till the end of the season."

Dinty shrugged. "Didn't mean to stay this long—but I love it here."

"Then stay," said Louis. "There's only a month or so left in the season."

Dinty glanced at the motorcycle. "Wish I could. My mom needs caring and I should get back. It'll take me a few days to prepare—I'll see the girls before then and say goodbye."

Louis thought of his own parents, and his siblings, and a part of him yearned to be heading back as well. They'd made it to Alaska, they'd worked all summer and had stashed some money away, but there was still some to be made—and if he left early he'd lose his bonus.

"You gonna be in Hollis this fall?" asked Louis.

"Yup," Dinty replied. "I told my mom I'd help her paint her house."

"Well, I guess I'll see you then," said Louis, "We should be there in October."

"Can't wait!" said Dinty. "And the first Heineken is on me."

Soon it became apparent that they needed more provisions than could be found in Skagway's small grocery store. Their supplies of diapers and wipes was just about exhausted, and Dee had a growing list of other things they'd gone without that had to be filled.

When the next "no ship" day came around they piled into the Vinniman and started the long drive to the closest big store, which happened to be a Wal-Mart in Whitehorse, one-hundred-and-ten miles away.

"Alright girls!" shouted Louis as he put the van in gear, "Let's go to the Yukon!"

Pookey Bear's skeptical eyes watched him from her car seat, in the back. "What's a Yukon?" she asked.

He turned to Pookey Bear and said, "The Yukon is a magical land with trout the size of beluga whales, and mosquitos the as big as hummingbirds."

The little girl frowned. "I don't want to see a mosquito as big as a bird that hums."

Louis let up on the gas and stopped the Vinniman.

He turned and stared at Pookey Bear. "What do you want?"

She clenched her eyebrows together and said, "I need a cage for Lotion."

"You're Guinea pig? He needs a new home? Got it."

She nodded seriously. "Okay, you can keep driving."

They passed through customs quickly and left the pass summit behind them. It was strange to cruise across the Tormented Valley as a family, not as tour guides.

They reached Fraser Lake and Louis pointed at an expanse covered with stunted, twisted trees. He called back to Pookey Bear, "Those are *krummholz* trees — they can be three hundred years old."

The little girl lifted her eyes from the movie player for only a minute, but then Robin Hood and Little John drew her back.

Dee grabbed a Heineken from a little cooler between the front seats and handed it to him. "Settle down, daddy, we're not on tour anymore."

The chorus came along on the movie, and they all sang with it.

> *"Robin Hood and Little John walkin' through the forest,*
> *Laughin' back and forth at what the other'ne has to say,*
> *Reminiscin', this-'n'-thattin', havin' such a good time,*
> *Oo-de-lally, oo-de-lally, golly, what a day."*

Soon they were across the valley, at the Canadian Customs post in Fraser. Next to the red building stood a large water tower from the days of the steam locomotives, and a dilapidated old carriage was parked by its base.

Pookey Bear pleaded desperately to be allowed to climb on it, but Louis was afraid it would fall apart.

Twenty-five miles down the road they stopped at a *Welcome to the Yukon* sign, and Pookey Bear saw mountain goats on a high peak to the left.

A man with binoculars had also pulled over, and he let the young girl take a look.

"Most of the animals up there are goats," he said to her, "but the two on the left appear to be Dall sheep."

Pookey Bear found them with the binoculars and nodded seriously. She looked at Dee and said, "They're good climbers."

Watching her observe the animals made him wish she had been on tour with him. Over the last weeks he'd seen so many bear and deer that he'd lost some of the wonder he'd initially experienced.

But seeing her now made the wilderness and its inhabitants seem fresh and magical again.

They got back on the highway, heading inland.

They were passing Tagish Lake on their right. The highway here was a hundred feet above the water and gave them a great view of Bove Island.

Suddenly, a black bear ran across the road, not fifty feet ahead of them.

"Dad! Look!" shouted Pookey Bear. Louis slowed and pulled up to the bear as it ambled along the side of the road. It found a patch of berries and stopped to forage, unconcerned with the vehicle which came to a stop less than fifteen feet away.

"Is it gonna get us?" asked Pookey Bear as she shrunk into her car seat. Say Say perked up and looked around, alarmed by the tone in her sister's voice.

"No," said Louis, and she immediately asked, "Then can we get out?"

Dee laughed and again said, "No," and after a few minutes Louis put the car in gear. Before they were even up to speed they passed several deer on the other side of the road.

The girls abandoned their movie and made a contest to see who could count the most animals. Say Say sat on the driver's side of the Vinniman and anything on the left counted for her and Louis; animals on the right belonged to Dee and Pookey Bear.

Bennett Lake came into view on their left, and Louis couldn't help make the connection with the Gold Rush.

"Seven thousand boats sailed across this lake in May of 1896, after the winter ice had broken up — can you imagine that? All those men and women on their way to the Klondike."

Dee said, "Isn't this where they all wintered over?"

"Yup," said Louis, "the gold fields are still almost six hundred miles away."

Dee grabbed another Heineken and popped off the top and said, "Well, Walmart is only fifty so let's haul ass."

The Walmart in Whitehorse felt like Disneyland in comparison to Skagway's little convenience store. There was so much stuff! Dee had shown Louis her list, and the number of things she needed made him nervous.

"Let's not go crazy here," said Louis.

She stared him down. "It's a two hundred and twenty-mile drive — we're getting whatever we need, now."

The shopping carts required a dollar coin to be freed from their dispenser, and Louis was stunned.

"They're making us pay for the carts now?" he asked out loud.

Dee read over the sign on the machine and said, "Chill out, Scrooge, it says you get the coin back when you return it."

"We should start with the guinea pig cage!" shouted Pookey Bear.

"Just calm down for a little while," said Louis and scanned the list.

They began by stocking up on food, then moved on to kitchen and bathroom supplies, and finally ended in the camping section to get propane and batteries. In a month they would begin the long drive back to New Hampshire and they planned on camping the entire way to save their hard-earned money.

Pookey Bear dragged Louis to the pet section where he bought a small plastic cage and some cedar shavings.

By the time they left the store their cart was piled high. Just looking at it made Louis nervous. "That's a lot of stuff," he said.

In the parking lot a ragged Indian approached them and asked if he could return their cart and collect the dollar deposit.

"Sure," Louis said good-naturedly and regretted it when the guy kept mumbling drunkenly and checking out their bags while they loaded them into the Vinniman.

Out of the corner of his eye, Louis saw two other men heading their way, apparently to also claim the cart. One staggered and fell over before he reached the van, but the other one started a heated discussion with the guy already waiting for the cart.

Dee quickly put the kids in the car, Louis finished unloading the cart and pushed it away. These guys could have it out over the cart on their own.

"Phew!" said Dee when Louis closed the door and started the car.

"That was scarier than the bears," she said, and Pookey Bear agreed with a big, "Uh-huh!"

Louis found his daughter's eyes in the rearview mirror.

He said, "Generally, men are far more dangerous than animals."

The hour-long shopping spree under Walmart's fluorescent lighting had worn them down so they nixed their plans to get a meal in Whitehorse. Instead they got on the Klondike Highway and headed back to Skagway.

It was past nine when they stopped at Tagish Lake, just south of Carcross. The lake extended to the left and right of them, and from guide books Louis knew it to be over sixty miles long. The rocky shore was lined with spruce, and once they had turned off the engine the only sound was that of the gentle waves lapping the shore with a small hiss.

A soft glow hovered over the water.

Louis wished he'd brought the tent so they could camp. It was such a lovely night that they decided to stay for a little while and have dinner. These days they always kept a few collapsible chairs and the cooking gear in the Thule.

He broke out a metal table and the propane stove and began making hamburgers from meat they had just bought.

Dee sat in a camp chair and watched Pookey Bear walk to the water's edge and try to skip rocks. Say Say squirmed on a blanket by her feet.

There were no other people within sight. Hardly a car passed.

The far shore of the lake lay faded, over a mile away, and beyond it a mountain shot up out of the forest. Louis didn't know its name, but watched it while the meat sizzled, wondering how he might ascend it if he ever had a chance.

He had just taken the burgers off the stove when he heard Dee shout his name.

Not a hundred feet away a large brown bear plodded along the lake's shore, heading in their direction.

"Everyone in the Vinniman!" he shouted.

Dee scooped up Say Say and hopped in the passenger seat, and Pookey Bear came running up and climbed right over both of them. Louis took a moment longer while he threw the burgers and buns on a plate, then closed the Coleman stove and set it on the ground.

"He's getting closer!" shouted Dee.

The stove was too hot to put inside the vehicle so he kicked it under, and then quickly hopped into the driver's seat.

The bear approached, unafraid, and sniffed the metal table the stove had sat on. He greedily licked at several drops of grease and eventually knocked the table over with a crash.

"You're sure he can't get us?" asked Pookey Bear in a whisper. She'd climbed up front and Louis was holding her on his lap. He ruffled up her hair and said, "No, we're perfectly safe here."

"Then can I put the window down?" she asked.

Both Dee and Louis quickly said, "No!"

The bear was kicking around the table in the hopes of finding more to lick. Then he walked along the Vinniman, sniffing the ground.

He stopped by the passenger door and looked right up at Dee and Pookey Bear. At first, Louis had been uncertain what type of bear it was. There were a lot of brownish-colored black bears in the region — cinnamon blacks they were called — but now he could see the hump between this bear's shoulders, and the dished-in face, and knew it to be a grizzly.

"We are okay—right?" Dee asked quietly.

Louis smiled. "Yes, I've never heard of a bear smashing a window."

The bear was large, nearly four hundred pounds, Louis guessed, and a female.

It watched them, curiously, and then reached under the vehicle, attempting to get the stove.

"I really don't want to drive back to Whitehorse to get another stove," said Louis. The sound of the bear scratching the undercarriage had his nerves on edge so he started the vehicle and suddenly the bear backed away, but lingered near the van.

After five long minutes it finally drifted off.

Louis had just cracked the door to get out and retrieve the stove when two more bears appeared. They were smaller, but just as curious.

"I bet those are her cubs," said Louis.

"Oh, I wish I could cuddle with them," Pookey Bear called out.

One of them began messing with the left front tire and Louis feared he might puncture it so he reluctantly hit the horn.

Both bears jumped, but it was another few minutes before they continued along the shore, in the direction their mother had gone.

Louis opened the door and grabbed the stove from underneath the van.

He had just put the Vinniman in reverse when Dee gazed at a motorcycle coming their way.

It was Dinty. His saddlebags were so full they looked ready to burst, and a huge backpack was strapped behind him as he sped past.

"Looks like he managed to fit his salmon fillets in the saddlebags," said Louis. Dinty had spent his remaining days in town drying and smoking the fish.

"Do you think he'll have trouble getting the salmon through customs?" Dee asked.

Louis smiled widely, "I'm just gonna hope *they like salmon, too.*"

Dinty didn't see them. They had all said good-by that morning, and Louis felt a pang of sorrow as his one old friend in town departed.

"I'm gonna miss Uncle Dinty," said Pookey Bear as she watched him speed past.

In an old Alaska guidebook, I later found a postcard from Dinty. He'd sent it from some remote town in Manitoba.

It read:

"Broke down with a flat here, luckily I found a junkyard where they fitted an old Volkswagen tire onto my motorcycle. See you all back in New Hampshire!"

Robert Louis DeMayo

Klondike Highway, the Yukon

Chapter Eight

Carcross, Yukon Territory
(August 2002)

"Tristan! What the fuck!" shouted Louis as he opened the door of the 15-passenger van and found him unconscious, sprawled across the driver's seat. Tristan had no pants on and didn't seem aware of where he was as he opened his eyes and blinked repeatedly.

"Huh?"

The seat was tilted all the way back and when Louis leaned in to pull Tristan forward he got a whiff of the reeking van. A glance at the floor revealed a pile of empty beer bottles and orange peels. He stepped back to get a breath of fresh air.

"What the hell did you do in here?"

Tristan sat up and rubbed his head.

"I don't know — how did I end up in the van?" he asked.

"I don't care!" yelled Louis and glanced at his watch. "I've got a tour departing in ten minutes and this thing smells like a brewery."

"Stop shouting," pleaded Tristan as he searched the back seat for his clothes. "And where are my pants?"

Louis ran to the passenger door and quickly began collecting the trash. "Just get out! I'm gonna have to wash down the whole interior. Jesus!"

Tristan limped toward the campground in his tighty-whiteys and his pale upper thighs almost matched their color. It was still early, but there were ships in port so people were busy getting ready for the day.

Sasha, on her way to the Golden North, gave him a loud whistle from across the street.

Louis jumped into the driver's seat and sped off to the car wash.

An hour later he was in line at the U.S. customs checkpoint on the Klondike Highway. The van was now clean, although still wet in a few corners where the water had pooled. He had cranked up the heat, hoping to dry it for his customers, but it still smelled musty.

He'd been doing the Yukon tours for a few weeks now, and was on his way to his first horseback tour. Dave had started him on guided hikes up Montana Mountain, which took four hours and passed through a forest of Balsam Fir. Their airy scent made him dizzy. It was a beautiful hike; before they reached the summit the trail rose above the tree line, into a world of orange tundra and lichen covered rocks. Spectacular views of Tagish Lake extended directly below them and countless mountains faded to the horizon.

Louis and his fellow guides often saw bears on these hikes, but so far none had come closer to them than one hundred feet. Still, it was exciting to know they were this near, and it was hard to believe he was getting paid to do this.

A white guy named Wayne usually accompanied him on his guided hikes, along with an Indian from Carcross named Charlie. Charlie was descended from Skookum Jim, one of the co-discoverers of both the White Pass and the Klondike Gold Fields.

Like Skookum Jim, Charlie was from the Tagish tribe, although, like most of the Indians Louis had met in the Yukon, when first asked what tribe he belonged to he just said, "First Nation" - a term which encompassed eight hundred and fifty thousand people in over six hundred tribes all across Canada.

Before every hike, Wayne gave a talk to his guests on how to use bear spray and what to do if one charged the group. "Don't look the bear directly in the eye," he'd say, "just make a lot of noise and try to look big. If the bear does charge, hold the canister directly in front of you and aim for his face."

Charlie never liked that part, and would just shake his head and say, "The bear isn't gonna like that."

When Louis asked him how he dealt with bears, he paused, scratched his stubble, and then said, "I just tell the bear that I'm finally retired, I have my first grandchild living with me, and if he wants a fight I'll give him one because I'm not ready to die."

According to Charlie the bears never bothered him once he clearly laid this down.

Soon Louis was also driving to Carcross for the dog-sled tours. In the summer the sleds were mounted on bicycle tires. It was good exercise for the dogs. Only one guest could ride the dog sled with the trainer at a time, and in the meantime Louis would walk the rest of the group to a nearby stream and show them how to pan for gold.

There were traces of gold in the stream, and Louis got a kick out of seeing people—usually guys—get gold fever. Some of them didn't want to stop panning when it was their turn to ride the sled, and a few got so into it that Louis had a hard time getting them into the van when it was time to go.

Zana, Tristan, and two new guys named Michael and Nigel, all enjoyed the Yukon tours as well. At the end of the day the tour guides met for drinks and talked about the animals they saw on tour, compared their tips, moaned about the technical issues of certain vehicles, and recounted stories about difficult guests.

Today Louis was a little nervous, anxious about the outing. He knew how to ride, having grown up on a farm with a pony, and he'd ridden horses during his travels, but for the last three years he'd had an office job in New Hampshire and felt a bit rusty.

As they inched towards the customs officer's window, he looked into the rearview mirror and addressed his guests.

"Please pass your passports up to me," he said.

A moment later a man tapped his shoulder. "I'm really sorry, but I think I left mine at the Southeast Tours office."

Louis radioed Brian, who confirmed it was there, and they turned around and headed back the whole fifteen miles. The return trip set them back a half-hour.

A light drizzle escorted them over the pass, and dark, wispy clouds drifted over the highway. They slowly crossed the Tormented Valley and Louis tried to mask his growing anxiety with casual storytelling while nervously peering ahead in the fog for animals in the road.

He tried to make up for the time lost, but the weather didn't allow for great speeds. If they started the ride late, they would most likely finish late, which would put his passengers at the risk of missing their ship. The other guides had already warned him that there was no rushing the tough Yukon boys who worked as wranglers.

"They're a bunch of juvenile delinquents," Tristan said. "Don't trust 'em—half the crew just got out of jail. Always lock the van."

But if they missed their ship, Louis would be in a jam. One-quarter of Louis's pay was in the form of an end-of-the-year bonus. And if you were responsible for a guest missing their boat, the cost of flying them to the next port would come out of your bonus.

"Bonus is a bullshit name for it," complained Tristan one night. "It's part of our wage. He doesn't add anything—he just keeps some of it if we fuck up."

Today Louis had a family of five in the back, along with three big brothers from South Dakota. If all eight missed their cruise ship it would cost him a couple thousand dollars.

He stepped up the speed a little, but didn't dare go much faster until they shook the weather. Beyond the Tormented Valley the forest closed in and once or twice before he'd had to swerve around deer or bear crossing the road.

Fifty miles from Skagway they officially entered the Yukon and the clouds disappeared. The highway skirted Tutshi and Tagish lakes, and under sunny skies he made up some time.

"What a nice surprise!" one of his guests said, "We've had four days of straight rain coming up from Juneau."

Louis turned off the wipers. "We're in the rain shadow of the coastal range," he told his guests, "for much of the year it's drought conditions here."

Tristan had told him that sometimes on a rainy day in Skagway he would guarantee his passengers a sunny day in the Yukon; some of them he even talked into a bet.

A guaranteed tip, he called it.

They passed Carcross ten minutes later.

A mile beyond the town, the Carcross Desert appeared on their right; an odd expanse of sand in the midst of all the pines trees.

"According to the Guinness Book of Records, this is the smallest desert in the world — less than a mile across. It was created when the glacier here melted twelve thousand years ago."

Soon after they pulled over onto a rough driveway that wound its way through a grove of lodgepole pines. It opened up to a gravel lot where several vehicles could park. There was a porta-potty on one side, and beyond that a corral held a bunch of horses.

A wall tent had been erected fifty feet away, and a steady stream of smoke trailed from its smoke pipe. This was where the guests were served apple pie and ice cream after their ride.

He was still twenty minutes behind schedule when he put the van in park.

A young Indian, maybe eighteen, sat on the upper log of the corral and watched him. He didn't seem in any rush to hop off the fence and greet the guests.

Standing next to him was Joni, the woman who ran the operation. She glanced at her watch and frowned.

Behind her Louis could see the horses had been saddled. At least they're ready for us, he thought.

"Expected you a little while ago," said Joni.

She was around forty and wore tight-fitting jeans, a flannel shirt and a cowboy hat. Behind the scowl she was pretty — but the scowl was formidable and Louis figured she had to radiate toughness to keep her wranglers in line.

"Dave said you can ride. That true?" she asked, her gaze unwavering as Louis's passengers crowded behind him."

"Yeah, I can ride."

She gestured ahead. "Good. Danny will take the lead and you ride drag."

The Indian on the fence — Danny — stared at Louis but didn't acknowledge him. His gaze paused only a moment on Louis's gortex jacket before he turned, swung his leg over the other side of the fence, and dropped into the corral.

Joni turned to the guests and her face broke into an easy, relaxed smile. "Howdy folks, we're running a little late, so why don't you line up and one by one I'll match you with a horse."

Joni put the three brothers on the biggest horses. She put the father of the family on a big mare named Shelly, and his wife on a gentle brown horse.

"This is Bullet," Joni said to the woman, and when she blanched Joni smiled and cocked her head. "I'm just kidding. Her name is Lil' Bit and she's very sweet."

She pulled Louis aside and said, "Next time you got big men like that radio ahead — we barely have enough good-sized horses here today."

Louis nodded. "Got it."

Joni added, "I'm gonna put you on my horse, Shirley. She's a gentle old gal, almost twenty years old. I don't let tourists ride her so she might be a bit grumpy having a stranger in the saddle. Can you handle that?"

A warning bell went off in Louis's head, but he ignored it.

Zana had given him some advice the day before. "Make sure you ride with your guests," she'd said. "If you don't they'll give half the tip to the wrangler and treat you like a chauffeur."

"How do I know where to go?" he asked Joni.

"Don't worry, the horses know the way — and you'll be riding drag, behind the group. You're gonna do a loop out to the Watson River, and then along Emerald Lake and back."

Louis nodded again and then turned to help the guests get up on their horses.

A battered old pickup pulled into the lot, and a rugged looking guy in worn jeans, boots and a faded t-shirt, hopped out.

"That's Corey," said Joni. "I gotta go. Radio me if you need help."

Joni walked toward Corey, yelling over her shoulder, "And don't let the horses run for it when you hit the break point by the river — or when they smell the corral on the way back!"

"I got this," mumbled Danny.

Soon after Joni disappeared, Danny walked over to Louis leading a young colt.

"Joni said I'd be riding an older mare," said Louis.

Danny's eyes twinkled mischievously as he said, "Naw, she's down. I'm gonna put you on Timber."

Everyone was up on their horses, and ready, when the mother in Louis's party announced that she needed the bathroom. Now they were waiting for her to return from the porta-potty.

"So you're the new guy?" asked Danny, his eyes skeptically drifting over Louis. Danny didn't seem happy to be babysitting a new guide.

"Guess so."

Danny glanced at the van in the parking lot.

"You lock the van?" he asked.

Louis looked over at the vehicle. "I did."

Timber stepped uneasily beneath him.

"You ridden much?" asked Danny.

Louis shrugged. "Enough. We had a pony growing up."

Danny suppressed a smirk and muttered, "We'll see."

The woman returned and Danny hopped down to help her get up onto her horse, then climbed back on his own horse.

"How about you?" asked Louis as Danny rode past him, taking the lead. "You ridden much?"

Danny cracked a slight smile. "Just 'bout every day since I got out of juvie, six months ago."

Timber was dancing nervously. He glanced around, snorting with flared nostrils, then suddenly charged full-speed at an old pine with a low cluster of dead branches ten feet off the trail.

Louis was tossed backwards against the cantle, but narrowly kept his bearings and was on the verge of regaining his balance when he slammed into the branches and was knocked clean out of the saddle.

He thumped onto the damp forest floor, and he lay there for a moment trying to catch his breath. Twigs and sticks were sticking from his hair when he sat up, and he gingerly felt a long scratch under his left eye.

"Please don't make me need a hospital," he whispered to himself. He had no insurance and the adrenaline coursing through his veins was spilling over into panic.

Timber, whose reins had gotten tangled in the branches, stood a few feet away and stared down at him curiously.

The guests had been watching the spectacle from horseback, not sure yet whether they should laugh or be terrified.

Danny rode up, grinning like a devil.

He jumped off his horse, grabbed Timber's lead, and handed it to Louis who still sat on the ground.

"Wanna try that again?" he asked.

Louis stood up, brushed himself off and said, "Okay."

His legs were quivering as he swung up into the saddle again, but he was also mad at himself for not paying better attention.

He gripped the reins tightly, squeezed his legs into Timber's sides without nudging the horse with his heels, and in a stern voice warned Timber. "You settle down."

The trail wound through the lodgepole pine forest, and they ambled west until they emerged on a rise with a splendid view of the Watson River. From here the trail descended steeply, and ahead Louis could make out an open space by a bend in the river where he figured they would stop.

The last half mile angled down a long, grassy ridge, clinging to the steep slope as it descended. Louis took in the scenery with awe: the river winding its way around several low hills, the dark forest spreading out all around him, the long, yellow grass dancing in the wind.

The Yukon, he said to himself. Now that he was here he understood how it had pulled on the stampeders a hundred years earlier. He now knew the gold rush history so well that it came to him casually, and he easily entertained his guests with tales from yore. Enjoying it. Still enchanted by the dramatic epic that had unfolded on the very pass he drove through almost daily. He figured he could talk for ten hours without repeating himself.

In fact, guiding became easier with each day. The route they took to get to the Yukon encountered many breathtaking vistas whose geographical features lushly illustrated the gold rush history.

And then there were the animals. Black bears and grizzlies almost always came into view on the drive, and they frequently saw wolves, caribou, deer, mountain goats, Dall sheep and moose.

They even spotted a wolverine once.

As they approached the river, he sucked the sweet air into his lungs, no longer concerned with gas money or depleting groceries, no longer afraid the wood wouldn't last or the oil could run out.

He felt alive, and sensed deep inside that everything leading to this point had been necessary preparation.

Timber slowly stepped downhill, then began to pick up his pace, anxious to get to the halfway mark. Just as he began the decline, the rider behind him commented on the view and Louis looked over his shoulder and said, "The Yukon is..."

It was at that moment that Timber bolted forward and unseated Louis again. This time there was just a fast whoosh of air as he toppled backwards, and then when he landed, relief that he hadn't broken his neck in the fall.

Timber shot right past the front of the horse train.

Danny let him go. He rode back and looked down at Louis. "Maybe you should stay behind next time. You know, help with the pie and ice cream after the ride."

Louis stood and brushed himself off.

"He won't get me like that again," he said.

Danny stared at him, that skeptical look in his eyes.

"We'll see," he said again.

Danny nodded in the direction of the river and said, "He'll wait below by the willows."

Louis peered ahead and saw Timber standing down near the water by the fire pit, throwing his head around and snorting.

"You wanna ride?" asked Danny.

Louis waved him away, knowing that he'd never hear the end of it if he climbed up and sat behind him. He had the feeling that his trouble with Timber was the best thing that had happened to Danny all day.

He followed to the break point on foot and helped the guests off their horses. Danny pulled a thermos full of coffee out of his saddlebag, along with a half-dozen metal coffee cups.

After the break, it took thirty minutes to reach Emerald Lake. The center of the lake was deep blue, but the shallows were an intense light-green color, brighter than the pines that surrounded it. The lake resembled a tropical beach, weirdly out of place, surrounded by the tall pines of the forest.

Danny addressed the guests: "The lighter green near the shore comes from light reflecting off calcium carbonate that was laid down by glaciers fourteen thousand years ago."

Danny had been so quiet for most of the ride that his comments surprised Louis and he raised an eyebrow. Danny blushed and in a soft voice said, "Joni taught me that stuff."

They rode along the stunning lake for a few minutes and then turned back north, toward the ranch. Louis was finally feeling confident in the saddle, and Timber seemed to sense this. Soon they could smell smoke from the wall tent's stove by the corral.

After two hours on horseback everyone here was ready to take a break and eat some pie. The guides usually ate with their guests, but Zana had warned him not to drag things out.

"Get them seated and eating as fast as you can," she warned. "Ten minutes, no more — especially if you're running late."

Before Joni had erected the wall tent the horse rides had stopped a mile down the road at the Spirit Lake Lodge for pie and ice cream. But to reach the Lodge, the riders had to cross the Klondike Highway, and Louis had heard a few horror stories about doing this with a group.

He figured if he could smell the fire they had to be close. He stood in the stirrups to get a look ahead, and that's when Timber tried to break out from under him again.

This time Louis managed to grab the reins and pull him in.

Danny smirked, but held his tongue.

They reached the wall tent and Louis helped his guests dismount, and then led them inside for pie and ice cream.

Louis tried his best to get his guests moving, but when they were all back in the van they were still running twenty minutes late. He was able to catch up some time on the long, sunny stretch along the lakes before they hit the Tormented Valley and the rain again.

But then they stalled out at the U.S. customs office. The government had issued an alert and everyone had to get out and individually go through customs.

This and the thorough interrogation of two guests ahead of them from Eastern Europe set him back another fifty minutes.

Louis radioed Brian, and told him they were running late. "Then you better step on it," he said. "They won't hold the boat for you."

When they pulled up to the ship the gates were just being closed.

For a brief moment Louis felt his heart stop. He hit the horn and a man stepped out of the shadows and slid the gate back open again.

He exhaled and hopped out to help everyone out of the van. After a quick round of hugs, handshakes and discrete tipping, he headed back up Broadway to wash his van and call it a day.

A few days later Louis was slowly ascending the Klondike Highway, peering through a dense fog that obscured all but twenty feet of road directly in front of him.

He had three couples riding with him, and one of the husbands—a guy named Edward—had hopped up front to ride shotgun.

At first Louis was glad to have company in the front, but Edward turned out to be a terrible bore who wouldn't stop complaining about their cruise ship. He wasn't interested in the gold rush at all and barely glanced out the window, even when there was a break in the fog. Every few minutes he would switch from whining about the cruise to bickering with his wife who sat behind him.

They were midway through the Tormented Valley when Edward looked around and said, "When I bought my ticket for this tour they said it would be beautiful."

Louis nodded at the road ahead of them. "Bear with me. I'll bet we'll lose this fog soon."

The guy acted like he hadn't heard him.

"I don't know what they were talking about—you call this beautiful?"

Louis smiled and said, "Well, it isn't for everyone."

They rolled through the valley, and after a mile they dropped beneath the clouds. A dark band hovered over the landscape, ghostlike and never quite touching the ground. In fact, you could still see all the way across the valley to the base of two glaciers below the clouds.

Edward sat up straight and looked around.

A mile away the sun made a rare appearance: long, golden rays of sunshine broke through the clouds and sparkled off Summit Lake.

Edward looked a bit confused as he said, "Would you mind stopping for a minute?"

"Certainly," said Louis. He pulled over at a viewpoint and put the van in park.

Edward opened his door and stood. He slowly spun in a circle, taking it all in. The other guests joined him, his wife standing by his side. "What is this place?" he asked.

"This is the Tormented Valley," said Louis. He nodded at the lake in front of them. "And that's Summit Lake."

The clouds had blocked out all but one long, slanted ray of sunshine that lit up a small island in the lake, the water around it rippling with golden sunbeams. Ducks cruised around in the water, and on the island in the middle of the lake an eagle was perched in a stunted pine.

"That image right there is one of the most beautiful things I've ever seen," said Edward, his earlier remarks forgotten. He hugged his wife and pulled her closer.

After five minutes Louis glanced at his watch.

"We really should keep moving."

Reluctantly, Edward climbed back in the van, followed by the others. As they continued he kept his eyes on the landscape with a new sense of wonder. Every so often he remarked on the beauty of this place.

But Louis's mind was elsewhere. His outing with Timber was playing in his head again and again. It even haunted his dreams: in them he felt a caressing wind, speckled sunshine, and the smell of pines. But just as he smiled at this beauty there was a sudden jolt, followed by a violent fall that woke him.

Last night such a dream had made him sit straight up in his bed in the apartment above the restaurant. Well, on the queen mattress on the floor which they had scored at a yard sale.

He seemed to be the only one in the family that reminisced about the wall tent. He missed the light breeze that always accompanied a night in the tent, and the sound of the crickets. A few times he'd awoken in the night and heard some animal sniff around outside, and in the dark he'd try to guess if it was a bear, raccoon or porcupine.

The apartment, by comparison, was all very civilized. He had snuggled up against Dee on the soft mattress and tried to get back to sleep, but the ride on Timber wouldn't stop playing.

At some point, he finally dozed off.

The following day at the Southeast Tours office he talked with Brian, and requested the next horseback tour. Dave sat in the corner listening.

Word about his ride had of course long reached the office. "You sure you want to do that again?" Brian asked.

He did. Without a doubt.

He wanted another chance to prove himself.

And not to Danny, or even Joni for that matter. He just wanted to see if he could stay on that horse.

"Definitely," said Louis.

Dave looked at the scratch below his eye and asked, "What horse did they put you on?"

"Timber," Louis said, and Dave burst out laughing.

"Joni put you on Timber?" he asked.

Louis shook his head. "No, Danny did."

Dave couldn't stop laughing for a full minute.

"Well, he sandbagged you," he said as he wiped his eyes. "Here's the problem with Timber: for his first two years Joni didn't put a saddle on him, just let him follow the others, tethered to whoever rode drag. His second year she should have saddled him, and probably tied a bag of grain to the saddle so he got used to carrying a load, too. But she didn't do any of that—so he's got some bad habits."

"He's never been broken?" asked Louis.

"He's been ridden a few times. I know last week Corey took him out and he got bucked off halfway to Emerald Lake."

"Well," said Louis, taking a breath. "I'm going to ride him."

Dave shook his head. "You should be more careful—you only have shovel insurance."

Brian chuckled and Louis asked, "Shovel insurance?"

Dave put on a stern face and said, "Basically: if you get injured bad enough you'll be buried in the Yukon somewhere, in an unmarked grave, after being clubbed with a shovel."

"Still want that horseback tour?" asked Brian.

Dave held up his palms. "It's nothing personal, I just don't have insurance that covers you when you ride outside of the US. If you get on a horse it's up to you. And if you get hurt, you're on your own."

Louis nodded. Until he'd met Dee, Louis was sometimes overcome with an exhilarating feeling of immortality, and when he ventured into the Yukon a part of him tingled with this feeling still.

And not just immortality. Vibrantly alive was more like. Radiating a great joy to live life to its fullest, which rendered all risk irrelevant.

I've seen it in his eyes many times when he told his stories. If you looked into them you would swear you were there, feeling the wind blowing over a high ridge, throwing your hair around. The hair on your forearms would stand on end when he described the look in the eyes of a bear as it approached, or the swelling rumble of rapids churning when he was approaching them in a canoe.

I'm sure he felt it that day as he parked the van by the stables and walked his guests to the corral.

Joni was nowhere in sight, but Danny was there, and he had the horses ready.

"Got Timber for you right here," he said to Louis. "Unless you got too scared after last time."

"I'm ready for him," said Louis as he hoisted himself into the saddle.

In contrast to his teasing attitude on their last ride together, this time Danny grew serious as he rode up next to him, close enough that he could whisper and not be heard by the guests.

"Listen," he said, "a bear's been following us lately. I'd guess he's a thousand pounds, and that's large for these parts where they don't have a lot of salmon to feed on."

"How do you know he's following you?"

"You'll see," said Danny, "just look at the trail. I see his tracks overlapping the horse tracks from the last ride all the time."

Louis looked back at his guests as they all prepared, strapping down their water bottles and looping their cameras around their necks.

He wondered if they were leading them into danger.

"What do you think he wants?" asked Louis.

"The bear? Oh, it's probably not the horses—I'd say he's just curious. The bears come around this time of year because the caribou have all gone into the thickets to have their young. He can smell 'em—he's using our trails to get around."

Danny saw the concern in Louis's eyes and waved it off.

"Just don't let the horses run. That could trigger the bear's predatory instincts and he might chase you—and you'll never outrun him in this terrain. The horses stay on the trail but a bear will crash right through the woods. He'll catch you way before you reach the stables."

Timber stepped nervously, like he knew what they were talking about.

"Seriously?" asked Louis.

"Sure, these Yukon bears take down caribou or elk when they're hungry—and if a horse gets loose they'll kill it within a few days."

Danny stared him down. "This ain't Kansas."

"I'm not from Kansas," said Louis, but Danny had already moved ahead.

Normally Joni would be there to send the riders off, but today she was absent. Danny looked toward the parking lot and said, "I don't know where she is, but we have to get moving. Why don't you ride drag again and I'll take lead."

Louis said, "Sure," and pulled back on the reins until all the other riders had passed.

Timber seemed jumpy and Louis paid close attention to him. They stopped for the coffee break by the Watson River and he gave him an apple he'd stowed in his jacket. When they headed out to Emerald Lake he settled back comfortably in the saddle.

One of the riders dropped his hat twice, and Louis had to jump down and grab it.

On one long, straight stretch Timber suddenly grew anxious; his ears pricked up and he looked around. Louis wasn't sure what made the horse nervous, so he scanned the forest carefully.

The rider ahead of them—it was Edward—dropped his lens cap. After the stop in the Tormented Valley Edward had become the most enthusiastic person in the van and Louis enjoyed in the transformation the landscape had had on him.

He jumped down once more, picked up the lens cap, and handed it to Edward. "Hope you're getting some good shots," he said.

"What a day!" Edward said, "I can't thank you enough."

Edward nudged his horse forward and caught up with the others, and Louis turned to climb back into the saddle. But Timber was jittery and side-stepped, and Louis couldn't get his foot in the stirrup.

Within a minute, the other riders were out of sight. Louis grabbed the reins tighter, and finally pulled himself up by the saddle horn.

Timber whirled in a circle, making the pines around them spin, but Louis managed to stay in the saddle and straighten him out.

Timber was anxious to catch up with the group, but suddenly some primal sense in both of them gripped their attention.

Timber's ears went up, he stiffened and snorted.

Louis looked in the direction they'd come from—there was a brown bear coming down the trail toward them.

It was big. The biggest one he'd seen all season, and Danny was right—it seemed close to a thousand pounds.

Fifty feet away, thought Louis. Because it was directly behind them, Timber hadn't seen it. But he sensed it.

The bear lifted its nose and sniffed the air while peering at them.

They were upwind, so Timber neither smelled nor heard it.

But the bear could definitely smell and see them.

Louis watched the bear in awe—it seemed like a mythical animal.

Then he nudged the horse forward and Timber went around the bend, slowly, still sensing the bear but unaware how close it had been.

He wanted to kick his heels and ride like hell, but he remembered Danny's advice and kept Timber at a swift walk until he saw the others up ahead. Then Louis allowed him to canter to catch up.

Just before they reached the group, Timber stopped short and Louis crashed into the back of his head, frantically trying to grab a handful of mane, but managed to stay in the saddle.

Danny came riding back and said, "You did better this time."

"I saw your bear back there," said Louis.

Danny glanced down the trail. "Then we best keep moving."

After the pie and ice cream they were on the road.

Two and a half hours later Louis and his guests were back in Skagway, parked by the ramp leading to the cruise ship.

His people unloaded from the van. Most shook his hand goodbye and tipped him.

Edward was the last one, and his wife stood a few feet away waiting.

"That was incredible," he said. "I'm gonna have to come back here someday."

Louis shook his hand. This wasn't the first person he'd seen transformed by the Tormented Valley and the Yukon, and he felt more than a little pride in the fact that he'd showed it to him.

"You come back anytime!"

In Skagway the seasons were changing. The days began to shorten and there was now a cold bite to the air that rushed down from the pass. Suddenly the mountain slopes were alive with gold, orange and red.

Ben had given up on Gina — his love interest up on the glacier — and the job there as well. Now he was back to guiding hikes on the Chilkoot Trail. On the Sundays when they were off, Ben and Louis watched football together.

There was a small joint called Skagway Pizza that showed live coverage of the games. Because of the time difference, if you wanted to watch a game that started at noon on the east coast, you had to be at Skagway Pizza at eight in the morning.

The owner didn't mind opening early and turning on the TV, as long as his patrons were willing to eat pizza and drink beer for breakfast, which they were.

Having grown up in New England, Louis was a dedicated Patriots fan, and it somehow seemed like most of the young people in the campground were from either Minnesota or Wisconsin so things got a bit heated when the Patriots played either the Vikings or the Green Bay Packers.

"You're lucky you'll be gone in October," taunted Ben one Sunday morning, "my Packers are going to crush you guys."

Louis laughed. There was no way he'd be around in October. The bold wind that buffeted him wherever he went insured that; with the coming of fall it had grown more intense, more intrusive, and he couldn't image experiencing a full Skagway winter.

But still, he had unfinished business and couldn't leave yet.

The little brook that flowed up Broadway was now filled with salmon that slowly pushed upstream, unconcerned with the fact that there wasn't much stream left. Some of the salmon were three feet long, and seeing them try to move through six inches of water, propelling themselves forward with the last of their energy, was quite a spectacle.

They'd spawned in a small pond closer to the bay, and now they were just pushing on, driven by instinct, until they died.

One morning Ben stopped by Louis's tent while he was watching Say Say. "Got time for a walk?" he asked.

They sauntered through the campground to the stream and Louis set the little one down by the fence while they talked. Say Say, now a one-year-old, gripped the smooth, vertical poles and stood, watching the fish swim upstream.

Ben looked depressed and nervous. He had to leave soon to guide a group up the Chilkoot. Louis asked what was wrong.

"You know," he said, "I really liked Gina. I don't know why things were so weird up on the glacier. I really thought she liked me, too — but she was so cold to me up there."

"Maybe it was just the wrong environment," said Louis.

He shrugged. "I don't know. I just want to tear up the Chilkoot. Forget her. God, I can't wait to get out of here!"

"Not much left in the season," said Louis. "We'll all be out of here in less than a month."

Ben walked away, kicking a few rocks, and Louis turned back to Say Say who surprised him by being a few feet away.

"Whoa!" he said. "How did you get over there?"

The toddler was side-stepping to the left, holding the poles of the fence with one hand, cautiously reaching ahead for the next one to shimmy upstream with the salmon. Louis watched her in fascination.

She paused and looked through the poles at the salmon, her eyes filled with wonder, and her hands floated down to her sides, the mystery in the water obliterating her fear of walking unassisted.

The fish moved on, and so did she — without using the poles.

She took two tentative footsteps, moving at the same slow speed as the salmon. She was a bit wobbly at first, but grew more confident with each step, and only after three more steps did she reach out again to support herself.

Her first steps, thought Louis, and they're following the salmon as they migrate. He wondered about the symbolism of this. Would she one day feel compelled to complete a migration, or to return to this spot like the salmon did at the end of their life?

He liked the thought that his daughters would be somehow connected to this land — to Alaska. Pookey Bear was conceived near Denali, and now his youngest daughter was taking her first steps here.

On his next trip to the Yukon, Louis was passing Montana Mountain. Wayne, the guide who led the hikes up the mountain, was one of the toughest men he'd ever met.

Not only did he hike in a t-shirt regardless of weather, but he also carried a forty-pound pack which contained warm gear, a blanket, radio, two gallons of water and a whole banquet of snacks: dried salmon, trail mix, dried fruit, chocolate and nuts, plus a few waterproof ponchos and an emergency medical kit.

Sometimes Wayne did the hike twice in a day, but his reputation for toughness came from another source: Wayne was an avid sky diver, and a few years ago he'd had an accident. His parachute didn't open.

"You mean it only partially opened?" Louis had asked him once when the topic came up.

"Nope, it didn't open at all, just trailed behind me."

"Well — did you land in a lake or something?"

He shook his head. "I hit the yellow line on the airport runway. One guy who saw the whole thing said I bounced three feet."

Louis was quiet for a minute while he thought how improbable it would be to survive that. "How bad did you get hurt?" he finally asked.

Wayne sighed. "A year in the hospital, dozens of broken bones, but I'm fine now."

Suddenly Wayne's face broke into a grin. "The worst part of it is there's a Christian community in Whitehorse that heard about it — they think it's a miracle so they keep pestering me to join their flock."

"What'd you tell them?" asked Louis.

"Same thing every time," he grinned. "Get the flock out of here."

Louis chuckled under his breath as they skirted Tagish Lake. They would momentarily pass the lot where they parked when they were guiding hikes up Montana Mountain.

"What's that?" asked one of the passengers in the back.

Ahead, and to the right of the van, two caribou hopped over the guardrail onto the highway. One was an adult, the other was smaller and must have been born that spring.

The highway had been built on a narrow shelf of land between Montana Mountain and the lake. To the left, rock was exposed from the blasting, and the lake was only fifty feet beyond the guardrail on the right.

The caribou lumbered in the road, running right down the middle of it. Louis slowed down. They were fifty feet ahead. He hoped no vehicle would come from the other direction.

"Please don't run over the little one," pleaded a woman behind him.

And then three wolves appeared, hopping easily over the guardrail. The woman sharply drew her breath in.

The wolves were thirty feet behind the caribou, but from their van Louis and his passengers watched the wolves slowly close the distance.

"Do something," said the woman, panic rising in her voice.

The lead wolf was ten feet away from the young caribou, jaws extended, when suddenly its mother turned right down the ramp that led to a parking lot at the lake. The youngster followed close behind.

The sudden move bought the caribou an extra stride and they charged across the lot and straight into the lake.

The wolves stopped on the shore and stared at them.

Louis pulled into the lot and parked the van forty feet away from the wolves to watch with his guests.

"My goodness," said one of the women in the back. "This is all too much for me—that little caribou is gonna die out there."

Louis shook his head. "Caribou are actually good swimmers—he won't have any trouble at all as long as he stays in the water."

The woman gave him a questioning glance and he said, "The hairs of their fur are hollow so they float—they're much better swimmers than the wolves."

As they watched the three wolves stood completely still, and then without any indication that they'd communicated, two of them broke away to the right, running.

"Where are they going?" asked one of the men.

Louis stared in the direction they were heading. "I'd guess they're trying to get to the other side to be there waiting."

"Do you think they'll get there in time?"

"Well, it's less than a mile across, and it has to be seven or eight miles around, so they might. But as least there will be fewer wolves to deal with for the caribou when they get to shore — and they might wait until dark and lose them."

Twenty minutes later the excitement had died down a bit as they pulled up next to the corral and parked. While a few of the guests lined up to use the porta-potty, Louis walked over to the corral, where Danny was raking up manure.

"Timber's run off," said Danny when he noticed him looking around. "Most likely dead by now."

"What?" asked Louis.

"Well, that big bear is still out there, and he got one of our horses last month."

Louis sighed.

"Timber's scrappy," Danny said, suddenly softening. "He's smart, too, so maybe he'll keep moving. Joni has a few guys out there right now looking for him."

As if on cue, Joni skidded into the parking lot with her truck.

She shut the door and walked over to the corral. She introduced herself to Louis's group, then turned to Danny and said, "I'll take this ride. You head over to the stable by the Spirit Lake Lodge and clean things up for the big group we have coming in later."

Danny walked to the truck, not looking too excited about mucking up horse manure from another corral.

Joni smiled after him, indulgently, then turned to Louis and said, "When the big busses come in, I can't park them here so we base out of the lodge."

As soon as they had matched the guests to the horses, she led a big mare over to Louis and said, "You can ride Shelley today — I heard Danny put you on Timber. I hope you're okay."

Louis laughed. "I rather like Timber—I hope that bear doesn't get him."

She chuckled. "We'll find him. He's a good horse, just not ready for trail rides. When we get him back I'll have to spend some time with him. I should have straightened him out last year but I was too busy."

For the first twenty minutes of the ride Joni told stories, turning in her saddle so everyone behind could hear her. Louis followed along in the rear.

One of the riders kept searching his pockets, and finally said, "I think I left my passport in the van—it's not really important is it?"

She smiled patiently, "No, it's fine." But a few minutes later she rode back to Louis and whispered, "If he hadn't said anything I'd be okay, but now that he's mentioned it one of us has to ride back and get it. The Yukon is strict about guests having identification on them at all times, and if I get caught right now I'll endanger my permit."

"No problem," said Louis, "I'll meet you by the Watson River."

Shelly didn't like leaving the group and it took a big exertion to turn her around. On the way back she was jittery and kept looking around. Louis wondered whether she smelled the bear, and the further they got from the others the more he sensed the bear had its eyes on them.

She was a large horse, and she didn't take his commands well. Twice she tried to bolt ahead and he had to work hard to keep her to a fast walk.

But then a large branch snapped behind them and she shot off like a rocket. Louis tried as hard as he could to stop her, pulling back on the reins so much that her head was sideways and she could only see forward with one eye, but she still kept charging down the trail.

The path zig-zagged through the pines and Louis held on for dear life, leaning left and right to avoid low branches and shrubs.

Suddenly Danny's warning about triggering a bear's predatory instincts by running a horse entered his mind.

He looked ahead of them, trying to stay on the horse, but at the same time he feared that at any moment that damn bear could jump out of the bush and attack.

Then the horse turned sharply to the right and Louis realized Shelly was heading for the Spirit Lake Lodge, not the corral.

With a cold chill, it dawned on him that the Klondike Highway lay between them and the lodge.

Normally the highway was fairly empty, but he thought he could hear a truck engine.

They burst out of the forest and Shelly tore across the forty feet of grass lining the highway. To the left Louis saw an eighteen-wheeler hauling a load of logs. He turned to see the other way, where a camper was approaching.

"Just my luck," he muttered.

The big truck was closer, bearing down on them.

Louis pulled back on the reins as hard as he could, just as the driver wailed his horn. Right on the edge of the highway Shelly reared back onto her hind legs, almost toppling backwards.

Her front hooves clawed through the air, mere feet from the truck as it whooshed by with a sand-laden blast of wind.

He wanted to let out a sigh of relief, but as she lowered her front legs he remembered the camper.

The second Shelly's front hooves touched the ground she burst across the highway, racing right in front of it. The old man in the driver's seat was leaning back, half-expecting Louis and Shelley to smash right through his windshield.

His eyes met Louis's for a split second.

Then they were across. The camper sped on, and as Shelly came to a snorting stop in an open corral the guy in the camper finally found his horn and honked it long and loud.

Louis slid out of the saddle, his legs shaking so badly he could barely stand.

"What the fuck!" shouted Danny, whom Louis now saw standing by a wheel barrow a few feet away.

Danny grabbed the gate and closed the corral. Louis stumbled a few steps and then leaned against the gate. "One of the guests left their passport and Joni sent me for it."

Danny nodded. "I'll take care of this. You take a break."

Louis sat down with his back against a large pine. He could still hear the truck engine in the distance.

Back in Skagway, the pier was hopping with locals because Captain Erik got a toothache. He had pulled his shrimp boat as close as he could to the pier at the end of Broadway, and then hung a sign on the rail that read:

Fresh Jumbo Shrimp – $1 a pound!
(3 days only)

The Captain drank his fill at the Red Onion that night, biding his time before the scheduled extraction in the morning. But his pockets were full of cash, and with a little luck he thought he might even sell enough shrimp to pay the dentist while the hole in his mouth healed.

And during those three days nearly everyone at the campground got their fill of shrimp. When the gates closed on the cruise ships, and only the locals were filling the old saloons, the talk revolved around shrimp. It felt like a scene from Forrest Gump.

The smell of cooking shrimp filled the campground, and pot luck dinners where the campers could try each other's shrimp recipes were all the rage.

"I can't eat another shrimp," complained Adam as he set his paper plate into Louis's old fire pit. "I wouldn't if you paid me. I've had fried shrimp, shrimp kabob, pasta and shrimp, shrimp and steamed vegetables, stir fried shrimp. I'm done with shrimp!"

Chris tilted his beer can back. He burped loudly and said, "Me too! I never thought I'd say no more shrimp, but it's all I've eaten for days."

Ben had moved back into Chris' wall tent. Chris had been dating one of the Street Car guides and spent most nights at her apartment, so Ben mostly had the tent to himself.

"I thought that was against Street Car regulations," said Louis.

Chris shrugged. "End of the season, nobody cares."

He'd finally finished repairing Tom's bus, and once Sasha completed a few odd shifts they would be on their way to Michigan where they had winter work lined up. "I hope they get that bus beyond Whitehorse before the first snows hit," said Chris.

Louis sat in a seat next to him. "I hear that. I'd love to leave now and escape the bad weather," he said. But he knew he couldn't leave until the last cruise ship had sailed off — it was yet another thing that was tied to his bonus.

"Seen Adam around?" he asked.

"Nope," replied Chris as he cracked open another beer.

Suddenly, a little voice from the bushes said, "Adam has a new girlfriend."

Chris spat a mouthful of beer into the fire and laughed.

Louis recognized the voice of Pookey Bear.

"Where'd you hear that?" he asked the bushes but the girl had gone quiet again. Chris was still laughing.

It didn't surprise Louis that Adam had found a new girlfriend. Over the last few months he'd watched his friend transform from a pretty mellow, clean-cut guy, to a fairly rugged young man with a new look of confidence in his eyes.

Adam usually needed a shave, and his hair had grown out.

He was tan, too, and his legs rippled with muscles from all the hiking he did.

But it was more than that. There was a determination in his movements now, and in the expressions he wore. Even his tone of his voice seemed to have matured during the long, cold summer in the tent.

Louis pondered if family and friends in New Hampshire would see anything different in his eyes when he returned.

"You ready to go back for dinner?" Louis asked the bushes.

A short silence was followed by a small "okay" from behind the foliage.

Louis stood and waited for her to climb out of the bushes. They turned to leave when a fit young woman with curly black hair approached the fire pit.

"Do you know where I can find Ben?" she asked.

Louis stared at her for a moment, then said, "You must be Gina."

She blushed slightly. "I am."

"Well, Ben's on the Chilkoot for another day or two."

She looked over at his wall tent.

"I'm done for the season. Do you think he would mind if I stayed in his tent until he gets back?"

Before Louis could say anything Chris blurted out, "Fuck no! It's all yours — I'll be at my girlfriend's place for the rest of the season."

She smiled and blushed again, then walked to the street to grab her things from a friend's car.

Chris laughed. "That's exactly what he's gonna want to see when he gets off the trail — I knew that wasn't over."

The tourist season trickled to an end, with only one or two ships pulling in a day, and more no-ship days between. The few inhabitants of Skagway who would winter over began to settle in. For the next four months the ferries wouldn't run and the only link to civilization then would be the hundred-mile highway leading to Whitehorse — so long as it wasn't snowed in.

Sal watched everyone depart with a sad face. The winters here seemed endless, she said. Cousin Francis had plans to go to Canada's far north, to Yellow Knife, where he hoped to find work preaching.

Miss Julie was let go by the daycare now that there were fewer kids. She sailed off on the ferry, leaving Adam to his new romance. Zana left, too. She had somehow negotiated an early leave with Dave of Southeast Tours that included her bonus.

She had confided in Louis that she was missing her boyfriend.

Louis raised an eyebrow in surprise. "Didn't know you had one."

"Well, he's doing an internship in Vermont and I knew I'd barely see him this summer. I would have said something, but it was fun toying with Tristan — he seemed obsessed with my status."

Ironically, the most surprising transformation was Tristan. He'd begun dating a woman who sold jewelry at Adam's shop, and almost instantly he became a different guy. Everywhere he went, he was with her, holding hands and looking happy. When she worked he sometimes stopped by the campground.

"We're gonna go to Florida together," he told Louis. "She's got a nice place in the Keys and has some leads on work for me."

Tristan had finally found his girl it seemed, and his eyes no longer wandered over every woman he passed. He seemed more genuine to Louis.

Louis changed the oil in the Vinniman and began preparing for the long drive home. Instead of taking the ferry, they would drive inland to Whitehorse this time, and then cross Canada all the way to Montréal before dropping down into New Hampshire.

Every night now there was a party at Moe's, or the Red Onion, to see off someone else who was headed out of here. The crowds kept getting thinner, and there were no longer enough people to fill both bars.

The weather turned another notch colder, too. Dense, dark clouds drifted overhead and anyone who planned on driving over the pass and into the Yukon eyed the weather carefully.

Brian assigned Louis the last horseback ride of the season, and he drove to Joni's corral with four guests in the back of the van.

The peaks he passed were now thickly snow-covered, and the snow level had been descending lower and lower over the last few weeks.

As Louis pulled the van up to the corral, Joni, Danny and Corey were standing by a pickup in the parking lot. Louis pointed out the porta-potty to his guests and walked over to the truck.

"Howdy," said Joni. She wore a tight smile; there was something wrong.

"Everything good?" he asked.

Her face softened and she said, "Oh, it's all fine. Danny is gonna ride with you, Corey and I have some chores."

Corey shifted uneasily on his feet. His eyes were red-rimmed and he looked hungover.

Joni turned to Corey and the seriousness returned to her expression. "Let's go," she said.

"Come with me," Danny said to Louis. "I got a surprise for you."

Danny led the way to the corral. He was grinning.

"Look who we found," he said and pointed at Timber. The horse was saddled, and standing by the rail with his lead tied to it.

"I'd almost given him up for dead," said Louis.

"Us too!"

Joni´s pickup tore out of the driveway, the back tire spinning and kicking up gravel.

"What's up with those guys?" asked Louis.

Danny chuckled. "Joni sent Corey out with a few other guys to see if they could find Timber. They got lucky, and stumbled on him the first day, on the backside of Emerald Lake."

"So why's Joni pissed?"

"Well, the boys had figured they'd be gone a few days anyway, and they'd packed supplies. When they didn't radio in Joni went out lookin' for them and found them passed out drunk."

"So now she's gonna make him sweat out the alcohol?"

Danny whistled. "She may look like just another pretty face, but Joni's tough—I wouldn't want her that mad at me. Did you know she bow-hunts brown bears? That takes balls."

The four guests walked up and Louis helped Danny get them on their horses.

A light rain was picking up and Danny eyed Louis's gortex jacket. "You feel like selling that?"

Louis zipped it up. "Nope."

The jacket had a fleece lining. It had kept Louis warm on a few cold occasions—like when he climbed Aconcagua in the Andes to over twenty-two thousand feet.

Danny smiled out of the side of his mouth. "Better keep it close or I might steal it."

The rain came down steadily over the next hour. Luckily, the guests also had good rain coats and weren't concerned much with the weather; they'd seen plenty of rain over the last few days of cruising up the Inside Passage.

"That's Labrador tea," said Danny as he pointed to a plant, three feet tall with white flowers. "You can boil it to make a medicinal tea, or use it to flavor meat."

Louis had to suppress a chuckle as he listened to Danny. Through the course of the summer the young Indian had learned that if he played the part of a tour guide he'd occasionally get tipped, and he was beginning to get good at it.

Timber followed the others obediently, but Louis sensed a jumpiness to his movements and kept a strong grip on the reins. The horse had only been back a few days, and his time alone in the wilderness had clearly shaken him up a little.

Danny had even suggested Louis choose another horse for this ride. "Might want to pass on Timber today."

But Louis hadn't heeded the advice. It was the last ride of the year and he wanted to end his adventures with Timber on a good note.

They paused on the big hill that overlooked the Watson River. The willows and buckbrush lined the water in a yellow band, and dried leaves were blowing in a rising breeze.

Suddenly there was a distant crack of lightning, and soon the dark clouds unloaded a torrent of rain. Timber began to step nervously.

Louis gently nudged the horse's ribs with his heals, and they began to walk down the long hill, the rain pelting the wet grass. Louis was riding drag, and he watched the guests ahead of him following Danny.

They were still descending toward the river when another bolt of lightning hit and Timber jumped forward, trying to pass the horse directly in front of him.

Louis pulled hard on the reins, turning Timber up the hill to steer him away from the steeply dropping slope to the left. He was afraid Timber might nudge one of the other riders off the trail and down the hill. Timber wasn't as big as Shelley, and Louis managed to pull his head right around so he had no option but to continue up the hill.

But the colt wasn't willing to be reined in, and instead began charging up the hill. It was a long way to the top, and very steep, and Louis doubted Timber could make it in a sprint.

He leaned forward in the saddle, making sure his feet were solidly placed in the stirrups. Timber soon began to tire, but when Louis started to rein him in again he bucked into the air and they were falling backwards.

The next seconds seemed to pass in slow motion, very much like those moments just before he hit the thunderstorm on his motorcycle.

Louis felt strangely detached, like an observer, as the horse twisted in the air, and they were falling, falling. He glanced over his shoulder at the steep slope of wet grass angling down.

He felt Timber stiffen, bracing for the impact. Louis briefly pictured landing underneath the horse, his body broken in a dozen places. Time seemed to stop, and the church lady at the airport appeared in his mind's eye, saying, "If he had faith he wouldn't need luck."

In a flash, he remembered gifting Say Say his remaining luck that cold night in the wall tent.

He wondered if his little skill could save him.

He thought of Dave's shovel insurance, and realized that Timber would have it little better if *he* broke a leg.

And then they slammed into the wet, slippery earth.

Timber somehow landed on his feet, and amazingly Louis was still in the saddle, but as the momentum carried them forward Timber bucked into the air again.

Louis held on like a barnacle; luck, skill, and faith all forgotten.

He squeezed his legs as tight as he could, gripped the reins with his right hand, and grabbed the saddle horn with his left.

They reached the trail twenty feet ahead of Danny, and Timber turned right, onto it, and then bucked three more times on the way down to the Watson River.

Somehow Louis remained in the saddle.

When they reached the river Louis slumped to the ground.

Danny rode up next to him and grabbed Timber's reins.

Louis groaned, panting.

After a few minutes Danny said, "We can switch horses for the ride back if you want."

Louis slowly stood, looked at Timber, and said, "No thanks. I can handle him."

He watched the river while he caught his breath

Danny smiled wide, his expression tinged with a little guilt as he said, "Well, nobody else wants to ride him—that horse is crazy."

Tugboat Pete was going to sail out of town the next day. He'd gotten a job piloting a tug in New York City Harbor.

"That's not too far from New Hampshire," he said, "so you might see me again someday."

Louis thought of the quiet little house on the lake that he'd left over six months ago. At the time it had seemed like everything to him, but now he didn't know if he wanted to go back to it.

On one of his last tours someone had asked him what he'd planned on doing for the winter and he'd been stumped for an answer.

For most of his life he'd planned and planned, but now more often he found himself daydreaming about the rides on Timber, or the hike up Montana Mountain.

Suddenly, the house by the lake seemed boring.

"Any suggestions?" he'd asked his guests that day.

A woman in the back said, "You should go down to Sedona and drive jeep tours."

Louis had chuckled at her suggestion, but it had planted a seed.

He turned to Pete and said, "I might just head to Arizona."

Pete cracked a fresh beer and handed it to Louis, and then grabbed another for himself.

"Well," he said, "I might see you there as well—I've got a daughter in Tucson."

The next day they headed out of Skagway. The Vinniman was loaded, and they planned to stock up on more supplies when they passed the Walmart in Whitehorse.

"Lotion is ready," said Pookey Bear as she cradled the plastic cage. The guinea pig looked a bit alarmed: maybe it was as anxious as Louis about being snuck past customs.

"Just keep him low when I'm talking to the border guards."

A snow storm was set to hit Skagway the next day, so they were determined to leave soon, but between packing, saying goodbye to friends and relatives, and loading the Vinniman, they didn't hit the road until early evening.

"Once we're beyond Whitehorse we'll be heading south so we won't have to worry about the weather," said Louis.

When they crossed the Tormented Valley it was already coated by a dusting of snow; but the road was clear.

It was getting dark when they passed Tagish Lake and Dee suggested they stop.

"Let's cook something up and get the girls into their pajamas," she said. "You and I can drive into the night."

They made hot dogs and mac and cheese for dinner, and then Dee washed the dishes in the lake while Louis put away the stove. Further down the shore of the big lake they noticed several bears, but none came near.

Suddenly a big, blue bus drove by, and the driver hit the horn when he saw their van.

"That's Tom and Sasha!" shouted Louis.

Pookey Bear waved, a sad expression on her face.

"I'm gonna miss that little piggy," she said.

By the time they got the kids in their pajamas the woods along the shore had turned shadowy.

"Wow, it's getting dark so early," said Dee as she looked at the dash clock.

They got the Vinniman ready, but just as Dee put it in reverse she noticed the lights in the sky above.

"Look!" she shouted, and they all stared out the windshield.

Far above the lake, the sky was alive with vibrant ribbons of light. A few moments before there had been nothing, but now, suddenly, the ribbons of green and blue spanned the entire sky.

The lake before them offered up a dim reflection.

Dee turned off the car and Louis pulled down a few camp chairs that he had strapped to the roof, next to the Thule.

The girls were getting sleepy. Louis had Pookey Bear on his lap, her body stretched out while she stared straight up, and Say Say snuggled with Dee.

"Is that magic?" asked Pookey Bear.

"Well, not really," said Louis. "There is a scientific explanation."

She looked into his eyes, a bit disappointed.

Louis smiled and added, "But it is magical, huh?"

She stared up and all of them followed her gaze.

At the Bartender's Bash, Louis had seen the northern lights, but what they saw on this night was much more dazzling, with an assortment of green, blue and red, like someone had taken a rainbow and stretched it across the sky.

"No," said Pookey Bear after a moment, "it is magic."

Many years later Louis would tell me that he thought this was the moment Pookey Bear began thinking for herself. It drove him half mad because he had all these theories and beliefs that he just expected his daughters to follow, and he couldn't accept it when she just said, "No." I can only imagine the fights he would have gotten into if he had had sons.

The lights above them shifted and moved like neon paint floating on a river. A few times a ribbon broke away, and seemed to sink toward them before rippling off.

Louis thought of the adventures he'd had with his family since leaving their home back east, but none of them compared to these lights. They seemed bigger than anything he'd ever witnessed. Bigger than the Tormented Valley or the many thousands of miles they'd driven. Bigger than the Inside Passage or the Rocky Mountains. Bigger than the Yukon, even.

With relief he realized this was even bigger than the hole in his stomach he'd sensed on their desperate drive across the country.

He looked down at his girls and knew that they could feel it also.

Even little Say Say watched the lights with sparkling eyes.

He knew they should get driving, but instead they just stayed, watching the sky ripple with magic.

Bison along the highway, the Yukon

Chapter Nine

Liard River Hot Springs, B.C.
(September 2002)

Two days later, they all woke up when the birds began twittering outside their tent. It was still early, but Pookey Bear was too excited to stay in the zipped-together sleeping bags.

"Let's go," she pleaded, tugging on Louis's arm.

Yesterday they'd driven three hundred miles from their campsite a few miles outside Whitehorse to the Liard River Hot Springs. They'd arrived after dark and had told an impatient Pookey Bear she would have to wait until morning to go to the hot springs.

Slowly, Dee and Say Say sat up and then reluctantly wriggled out of the warm sleeping bag, their breath jumping before them in white puffs. Dee slipped into her swim suit, shivering, and then helped the baby into hers. They had left the snow behind, but it was still chilly out.

Pookey Bear already had her bathing suit on, and stood by the tent door, impatiently tapping her pink slippers.

Soon they were wrapped in their towels, following a boardwalk through a lush, boreal spruce forest. On either side of the walkway, clouds of mist floated over a warm-water swamp, and the temperature around them had risen by at least ten degrees before they took a dozen steps. Dee held the baby close to her chest, and the infant seemed content to drift back to sleep; she was like a little heater under Dee's towel.

In the trees around them hundreds of birds chatted noisily.

"I thought they all migrated south already," said Dee.

Louis stopped and listened. There were several different bird calls echoing through the pre-dawn, but the mist obscured the trees and he couldn't see the birds themselves. A cloud of fog rolled over the boardwalk, and for a minute they waited because they couldn't even see the wooden slats under their feet.

"I doubt many winter over here," said Louis, "even if this water never freezes. Winter hasn't tightened its grip here like it has on the coast—these birds are still moving south."

Pookey Bear peered into the fog and said, "I'd stop here for a little swim if I was a birdy."

She reached down and felt the water and then shouted, "It's hot!"

Several minutes later they reached the pools. These were the second largest hot springs in Canada, and Louis had expected to see more people, but between the late season and the early hour they had the place to themselves.

Several natural pools sat steaming between the trees, each around twenty feet wide, and it appeared that they flowed into each other. Dee stepped into the closest one, and her eyes lit up when the warm water engulfed her feet.

She grinned at Pookey Bear. "This is just like a tubby—you're gonna love it."

Louis piled their clothes on a bench by the first pool, and then they lowered themselves into the water.

Dee held the baby over it and carefully dipped her toes in. Suddenly her eyes opened wide as she stared down at the water.

"This really is warm," she said. "I'd guess it's gotta be at least a hundred degrees."

Louis pointed at a plaque near the bench. "It says there the temps range from 107 to 125 degrees."

"Yikes!" exclaimed Dee. "Let's keep the kids away from the hot spots."

The water in this pool was just two feet deep, and Pookey Bear slowly explored the spring, crossing to the vegetation on the other side, then following the perimeter. Wherever she went she called out the temperature.

"It's warmer over here... now it's cooler... now it's real hot."

Say Say remained silent, but her eyes took in everything.

Dee continued to lower her until her feet barely touched the sandy bottom. If she stood on her tippy-toes, her mouth was an inch above the water.

She stared back at them, her chest rising and falling, her eyes still brimming with uncertainty as small clouds of mist floated by her head.

Dee moved her to a section where it was shallower and cooler, and the baby began to relax.

They sat in the springs, breathing in the warm vapor while the chirping and twittering rose in crescendo with the coming sunrise.

Now that they were all immersed in the warm water, they could feel the chill in the air even more sharply. Nobody was anxious to leave.

Louis soaked the bruises on his chest and arms from the outings with Timber. They were still black and blue and the hot water helped soothe the sore muscles.

They stayed until their skin began to wrinkle, and then climbed out and dried off.

The sky had begun to lighten, but the sun was still beneath the horizon. The mist had gathered into dense fog banks that repeatedly overtook them.

While they waited for one cloud of vapor to move on, Pookey Bear peered off to the side of the boardwalk.

"There's something out there," she said.

The others crept next to her and tried to see through the mist.

Then the cloud dissipated, and revealed the biggest bull moose that Louis had ever seen, not ten feet from them. He sucked in his breath, not sure what to do.

The moose just stood there in the water, eyeing them. He was chewing on aquatic plants, and water dripped from his mouth and the dewlap dangling beneath it. He continued to stare, curious, but not alarmed.

A slight breeze blew through and brought in another cloud that obscured the moose. Pookey Bear looked up at Louis, her face calm but serious, and said, "We should go."

They still had well over three thousand miles to drive to get to New Hampshire, so after getting dressed and taking down the tent, they were on the road.

Although they had left the tropical warmth of the hot springs behind, it was warmer now that they were away from the coast and the weather had lost its bite. Their intended route slanted southeast through Canada, aiming for Edmonton, over eight hundred miles away. After that it was a straight shot east, until they hit Montréal.

At this early stage of the journey Louis avoided dwelling on the thousands of miles ahead of them. Instead he focused on Fort Nelson, British Columbia, roughly one hundred and eighty miles away.

They cruised along with the windows half-down, enjoying the morning. Dee opened the plastic cage with Lotion, the guinea pig, and handed her to Pookey Bear, who soon had the little critter wearing a dolly dress.

An hour into their drive Louis was squinting into the rising sun, when suddenly Pookey Bear shouted, "What's that?"

Ahead of them a large bison stepped into the road.

Louis slowed, then stopped.

The bull paused, and stared at them.

"He's big," said Pookey Bear.

Louis nodded. "I'd guess over two thousand pounds."

Pookey Bear whispered into the guinea pig's ear, "Don't worry, Lotion, I'll protect you."

The bull lowered his massive head and shook his horns at them; they were two feet long and surely deadly. Its hump and muscular shoulders were intimidating, and Louis blanched at the prospect of the bison charging or ramming the Vinniman.

Then the bull glanced over his shoulder, back the way he had come.

Pookey Bear looked in that direction and shouted, "Holy shit!"

Dee had a reprimand on the tip of her tongue, but as she followed the girl's gaze also blurted out, "Holy shit!"

Emerging from the woods on their right were at least sixty bison, mostly cows and calves. The females also had horns, but were less bulky.

They moved casually, grazing as they walked. The young ones bounced around energetically; they'd been born that spring and now, after almost six months, were confident in their movements.

One young male flopped into a grassy mud puddle near the road and rubbed his back into the mud.

"Tubby time!" shouted Dee. She unbuckled Pookey Bear, and then took Say Say out of her car seat and held her on her lap so she could look out the window.

Pookey Bear held Lotion above her while she scrambled down, and then tucked the guinea pig by her side and peered at the bison.

The big bull had moved on, but the rest of the herd seemed content to graze and relax by the side of the road. They watched the bison for the next half hour, alone. There was no traffic on the road.

Louis couldn't take his eyes off his oldest as she in turn stared at the bison. Her gaze went from one thing to the next, and Louis tried to guess what observations she was making.

As a guide he'd seen a lot of animals and was in the habit of noting details. Did they have antlers? How many points? Were they traveling alone or in a group? Had the animal's coat thickened for winter? He wondered what his daughter would note.

"What do you think?" he finally asked.

She smiled. "They look happy. I think it's one big family."

Ten minutes later the herd was gone and Louis put the Vinniman in gear and drove on. He smiled inside, feeling an observer might call his family a happy one, too.

At noon they rolled through Fort Nelson. They had sandwiches planned for lunch, their little cooler still filled with supplies which they'd picked up at the Whitehorse Walmart, so they only stopped to gas up.

After filling the tank Louis looked at the map.

"Two hundred and eighty-three miles to Dawson Creek," he said to Dee who had just returned with a few coffees.

"Want to stop there for the night?" she asked. They had planned on driving five hundred miles a day, but didn't mind figuring in a rest day — or two — before they reached New Hampshire.

I'll bet Louis had made that plan figuring they would spend the rest day camping in a national park, and Dee imagined relaxing in a soft hotel bed. Luckily, the season had been lucrative enough that all options were open.

"We'll see," he grinned. "That's only four hundred and seventy-one miles — that's twenty-nine short."

Dee made sure Pookey Bear wasn't watching her, then smirked and flipped him off.

Dee drove the next few hours. She found a good country station, and the girls drifted into a movie. Louis watched the forest pass by, and was soon lost in his own thoughts.

He was returning to New Hampshire with mixed feelings. It was where his family and most of his oldest friends lived, but his beloved travel office job in Walpole was gone, and he didn't think he was ready to settle down in Hollis where he'd grown up.

While he scanned the woods for deer, or more bison, in his mind he envisioned the old New Hampshire home that they had lived in before moving into the Chase house by the lake.

That home had been built in 1796, and sat in the rolling hills between Walpole and Keene.

It was known as the Crehore House and was named after its builder, Ebenezer Crehore, who had arrived in Walpole in 1780 when he was fifteen.

The house did indeed feel like it was over two hundred years old. Half the interior doors wouldn't close, most of the floors sagged in the middle, and there was always a corner of the bed that needed to be propped up on a piece of wood, or a book.

Dee told me that if she used a novel Louis often replaced it with a Bible. He claimed this was the only reason he took one from the "thumpers" that came around every few months. "You don't need a book to tell you what God is," he would say. In Louis's world, God was an experience, not a conscious entity, and I think bashing religions was his way of re-enforcing that.

The house's stone foundation needed repair, and from the basement you could see through it to the outdoors from a dozen places; and the heater conduit that fanned out from the basement often creaked and groaned as if complaining about the weather.

The yard and the surrounding grounds had a spooky feel about them, as if the past wasn't ready to let go and fade away. Directly across the street a plaque was mounted to a rock, and an inscription told the story of a group of soldiers who had marched by here in 1758, on their way to the Battle of Ticonderoga. And a few hundred feet up the road was an old cemetery with graves dating to before the civil war.

Behind the house, a network of trails wound through the woods with little man-made bridges across several streams that trickled by with either snow melt or rainwater.

Dee loved these trails and especially the bridges, but Louis worried about several heavy, dead branches that dangled in the tired old oaks above. Some had so many leaves and twigs piled up on them that they looked like they'd been there for decades, just waiting for the right moment to come crashing down.

"They call these Widow Makers," he told Dee as he pointed at one. The branch looked like it weighed at least a hundred pounds and seemed to be held in place by only twigs.

Pookey Bear was only one and a half, but she craned her neck up to see from the back of a pack Dee wore.

Many graves in the cemetery were inscribed with the name Crehore. According to Louis's research, Ebenezer had died in 1819, at the age of fifty-four, and left the house to his son, Charles.

·I don't recall ever hearing anything about Charles, but I certainly heard about his wife, Lucy. Dee had read the facts of her life etched into her tombstone, and — typical — Louis had become a bit obsessed with Lucy and learned everything about her he could.

She had married Charles at age twenty-nine, Louis discovered, and over the next four years bore four children, of which she lost one. Shortly after the delivery of the fourth child her husband also died.

Seems to me the house and grounds still echoed her passing, even after more than two hundred years.

If you turned left out of the driveway, a dirt road faded off into the forest. A locked gate guarded it, and no cars ever went down it as far as I know, but the town maintained it for historic reasons. Apparently this was the original road through the region and among others, the soldiers in 1758 had used it.

As Louis looked up a sign for Edmonton flashed past and he realized he had daydreamed right through Dawson Creek.

"I thought you wanted to stop back there," he said.

Dee smiled. "Everyone seemed to be chillin' so I just kept driving."

An hour later they stopped at a campground and set up the tent. Louis cooked up two pork chops on the propane stove, and when it got dark they crawled inside and went to sleep.

Over the next few days they continued their southeast trajectory and the miles ticked away... Edmonton to Saskatoon, three hundred and twenty-six miles... Saskatoon to Winnipeg, four hundred and ninety-one miles... Winnipeg to Thunder Bay, four hundred and thirty-five miles.

The Vinniman chugged along.

The wildlife became scarcer and the highway wider, but yet the trans-Canada seemed more personal than I-70.

After a few days Louis had them start later in the day so they wouldn't have the rising sun right in their eyes.

Louis continued to dwell on the Crehore house in his thoughts. He remembered long walks he'd taken down the old road, and when his stomach filled with butterflies at the prospect of the road ahead, he returned to an experience he'd had on the cellar steps on a dark night in October.

Dee had flown south to Florida, to visit her mom, and had taken little Pookey Bear with her. Say Say wasn't born yet; it was still a few months before Dee would be pregnant again.

Louis had remained behind, working at the travel office by day, and pacing through the old house by night. His thoughts kept returning to Lucy Crehore.

One night a strong wind blew through the woods, making the old house creek and groan. The leafless branch of an ancient oak kept scratching against the bedroom window and kept him awake.

He walked through the house, checked on the dog, Missy, and made sure the wood stove was damped down properly.

While he was passing through the kitchen he heard a muffled sound coming from the basement. He stopped, then walked to the cellar door and opened it.

Darkness greeted him. The only light in the old basement was controlled by a pull-string down in the dark, fifteen feet from the bottom of the stairs. You always had to grope around for it before you found it and could turn it on.

But something prevented him from descending.

There were so many holes in the stone foundation that the cellar was always colder than the house, even though that's where the furnace was.

He sat on the top step and listened, wondering if a raccoon, or maybe a bear, might have found its way inside. A cold breeze rushed up at him, and as he shivered he thought he heard someone crying in the darkness below. He pricked his ears up to hear more clearly, and the crying became more distinct.

He could tell it was a woman.

He sat, riveted. Listening. The hair on his arms and the back of his neck was standing up.

He knew without a doubt it was Lucy Crehore. She had good reason to cry, having lost a husband and a baby in this house.

You might remember me mentioning earlier that Louis believed in spirits, not ghosts. I guess you could say he thought it was all internal, and this situation frustrated him, because the crying woman felt pretty real.

He shook his head to clear his mind. If he just walked down into the basement and turned on the light, of course he would discover that the sound had been caused by wind racing thought the air ducts, or a creaky vent in the furnace. But try as he might, he couldn't summon the courage to descend.

Throughout his life, Louis claimed that one of his strengths was his ability to face fears. If you told him there was a monster in a cave he would feel compelled to explore the cave, and if you claimed a house was haunted, he would have to go into it at night, armed with flashlights.

According to him, he'd never encountered anything that made him question his convictions about the world.

But now, sitting on the top of the stairs and staring into the dark, he just couldn't walk the ten steps it would take to prove that this ghostly crying really had its source in something natural.

Instead he sat there for twenty more minutes, listening to the woman crying.

Finally, he stood to leave, stiffly, aware of the step creaking beneath him, and whispered, "I'm sorry for your loss."

Near Thunder Bay, they stopped at Uppsala to visit some of Dee's relatives for a few days. Her grandparents, Bunny and Melissa, lived here, as did her Aunt and Uncle, Paul and Gay, as well as their kids: Heather, Sharon and Christopher.

Louis was apprehensive because they lived on a Christian compound. He was afraid they would be trying to cram religion down his throat. But it quickly became evident that the compound revolved around community more than dogma and nobody seemed to mind when he didn't go to church with them their first full day there, which turned out to be on a Sunday.

Bunny couldn't bend his right leg at all, it stuck out straight. He showed it off by placing Pookey Bear on it and bouncing her in the air.

"Again!" she begged. And after a few more turns Dee took her away before her boundless energy exhausted him.

Dee's uncle, Paul, was an artist. His cabin was decorated with photographs of the wilderness, and he had beautiful recordings of birds and trickling water that they listened to late one night after dinner.

"I like the birdie songs," said Pookey Bear with a yawn.

It was good to see family, but Montréal was still over a thousand miles away, and it seemed even the girls were restless, hankering to get to New Hampshire where they might stop long enough to keep the world from spinning under them. So after only two nights with the relatives they were on the move again.

Being with the family had relaxed them all, and they played games on the road, counting animals, or red cars, or Walmart trucks. Say Say usually got placed on the team of whichever adult was in the passenger seat because the driver was busy enough and therefore needed Pookey Bear's help. Dee offered up single M&Ms as prizes and Pookey Bear tried her hardest to win every game.

That afternoon, while the others floated in and out of naps, Louis let his mind drift back to a walk in the woods which he'd taken when he was living in the Crehore House.

He had left the house with Pookey Bear wiggling around in a backpack carrier, and turned down the historic old road, hoping to find a quiet place for them to have a picnic.

I've heard him say that each step he took down that forgotten country lane felt like it went further back in time. Thick tree trunks lined the way, and the large boulders between them were covered with dense moss and ferns. Several small streams trickled by, gurgling under the road, and then sneaking away.

Past the gate, all traces of modernity disappeared, and only the quiet forest accompanied them.

It was a week past peak foliage, and many of the maples and oaks were shedding their leaves which lay piled on the road, crispy and brown. Nobody had seemed to have walked down the road in a long time, and Louis plowed through the dead leaves, kicking them in the air while Pookey Bear cheered him on. "Go dada!"

After a mile Louis stopped, took off the carrier, and set his daughter down. He was wearing a jacket, and the hike had warmed him up, so he set it on top of a pile of the leaves and the two lay on it.

Sunlight filtered through the trees, and they lay on their backs staring up, soaking up the warmth. Pookey Bear sighed and snuggled into the crevice between Louis's right arm and his ribs.

She only had a few words, but her eyes were alert as she watched the leaves slowly tumbling out of the trees towards them.

They shared a peanut butter and jelly sandwich, and shortly after the toddler fell asleep. Louis felt a warm glow flow over him, loving the uncomplicated moment.

He listened to two old trees creaking, one on each side of them, and smiled at the thought that they were talking to each other. Their language was like an ancient lullaby and soon it lulled him to sleep as well.

I asked him once how long they slept like that, and he gave me a strange look and said, "A little over two hundred years."

I didn't understand what he was talking about until he told me about his dream.

Sleeping there with his young daughter cradled in his arms, Louis dreamt that an army of men marched by. Their uniforms identified them as the 16th New Hampshire Militia Regiment, on their way to reinforce the Continental Army during the Saratoga Campaign. These were the very men honored by the plaque across the street from their house.

He remembered the plaque stated that they had had a big feast the night before, eating plenty and drinking their fair share of the beer provided by an old tavern.

Now they were marching to New York, five thousand strong. They were stepping confidently to the beat of drums while the fifes carried the melody. The men joked with each other and gave off an air of confidence; with full bellies and a good night´s sleep, they seemed to be ready for anything. Several officers rode alongside the men on horseback.

Louis sat up, and Pookey Bear waved to the men as they passed—not very differently from the way she would eventually wave to her "people" on Skagway's *White Pass Railroad*.

And then he woke on the side of the forgotten road, the toddler sleeping quietly by his side. But in his mind he could still hear the music, and the steps of the passing soldiers.

It seemed so real that he glanced down the road to see if they might still be in sight. Pookey Bear wasn't ready to wake up, so he allowed himself to fall back asleep as well and it was another hour — or maybe another hundred years — before he woke again, shouldered his daughter, and walked away, returning to civilization.

He thought of those soldiers, marching to battle, while they were approaching Montréal in the Vinniman. He knew their campaign had been successful, but also that many had not returned home.

The thought of his own returning home was weighing heavily on Louis's mind. But then he had to concentrate hard to navigate through a city whose road signs were French. They soon turned south and left Canada, entering Vermont from its narrow top. Louis realized he was only two hundred and fifty miles from Hollis.

He tried to feel positive about their homecoming, but again and again was overwhelmed by echoes of the past. There, in the lonely corners of his mind, Lucy Crehore cried for her losses, and there also the brave militia weren't marching to war, but limping home months later.

Their numbers were diminished. They trudged along without fife or drum, or mounted officers. He imagined the vacant look in their eyes as they mourned comrades who had fallen by their sides. He wondered if they had been feeling proud. He guessed it had been like most modern wars — complicated.

Rather than picturing the weary soldiers, he tried to remember napping with his oldest on that peaceful old road in the woods.

That was where he drew his strength. Or at least that's what he told me years later. He always claimed that a part of him was still there, napping under the ancient oaks with Pookey Bear by his side, while the soldiers marched by.

When they entered New Hampshire Dee and Pookey Bear became excited, and he found it contagious and chuckled at one of Pookey Bear's jokes. "Finally, he cracks a smile!" shouted Dee. She had uncorked a bottle of red wine and was sipping it.

"Loosen up, luv," she said, "we just completed a great journey! How many miles did we drive?"

Louis scratched his head. "Well, I'd guess the drive there and back was seven or eight thousand miles. At least."

"And now we're almost home," she said. A moment later she fell into a silence, lost in her own thoughts on home. Honestly, I don't think at that point either of them knew where home was.

"At least we're heading to family," said Louis.

Pookey Bear cheered and added, "And no more car seats!"

And then Say Say blurted out some word that none of them understood, but they all cheered her on like it was brilliant.

Robert Louis DeMayo

Driving the Grasshopper

Chapter Ten

Hollis, New Hampshire
(October 2002)

In the middle of a hard October downpour, they turned the Vinniman into Louis' parent's driveway in New Hampshire. Nobody was home, so Dee hopped out and opened the garage door, and Louis pulled their vehicle into the empty stall—forgetting he had a Thule on top.

After scraping its way in, the storage box popped up and they couldn't back out until they took it off.

This was their first mishap on the long trip from Skagway all the way across North America.

"Just a few scratches on the garage door," said Louis, after. "The Thule seems unfazed."

Dee laughed. "Not bad considering how far we traveled—better than hitting one of those bison, or blowing the transmission on the way."

Over the next weeks they enjoyed the brisk fall weather while they were catching up with family and friends. The orchards were ripe with fruit, the trees vibrant with color, and often the honk of geese drew their eyes overhead where their v-formations pointed south.

Two weeks later, Louis's father, Pip, had a lamb cooking on a spit; and a dozen people, mostly guys, were sitting around the coals passing around a bottle of Black Velvet. Louis's best friend Bone was there, with Pookey Bear on his lap, and Dinty had just finished telling the story of how he'd disappeared at the Haines fair and returned ten days later with buckets full of salmon fillets.

Most of the other guys were also friends from Louis's past. Pistol Pete, Reilly and Stubby had gone to high school with him. Pearl Fish, Seano, Gator and Big Wes used to be part of his painting crew. John E. Rotten had been one of his best friends since high school, and he'd gone on to marry Louis's sister, Kathleen, who stood away from the fire pit — out of the smoke — holding her one-year-old boy, Dean.

A motorcycle rumbled down the driveway, driven by another friend, Satchmo. As he parked and took off his helmet, Dinty yelled out, "There goes the neighborhood!"

Pip's house had been built on a hill overlooking the Nashua River, and down by the dock Louis could see his brother, David — nicknamed the Gouch — pulling a canoe on shore while his daughter, Bella, carried the lifejackets. The Gouch owed his nickname to a bully on an 80s TV show called *Different Strokes*.

When it was just the two of them Louis always called him Diggy.

Louis glanced at the scratched garage door and chuckled.

His father followed his stare and said, "You better paint that door before you go traipsing off again."

Louis grinned and nodded, actually enjoying being nagged by his dad. "I will."

This is what I've been missing, he thought, while he looked over his friends sitting around him. For all his life, this place, and this circle of friends, had been what he called home.

But he knew he couldn't stay.

Dave from Southeast Tours had called him about the upcoming season, and Louis had committed to returning to his Alaskan guiding job in the spring.

They had ample time until then, but as much as he loved the people that surrounded him, Louis had no intention of waiting through the New Hampshire winter which was about to set in.

It saddened him to think they'd be moving on again and he tried to soak up as much of the gathering as he could.

His father knew all the guys sitting in the circle as long as Louis had known them, and he teased them by bringing up embarrassing stories from their past. Pip had a memory like an elephant, and it was a bad day when he got the goods on you.

"How's Erin doing?" he asked Bone, referring to a girlfriend he had years ago.

"You should just forget all that stuff," said Bone, shaking his head.

Pip poured himself a shot and toasted Bone before he downed it, saying, "Don't you wish."

A pretty blonde exited the house and approached the group. She was carrying Say Say, who snuggled against her neck, almost asleep. This was Lucinda, and for years she'd run the local coffee shop.

"Pat Pat wants to know when the meat will be done," said Lucinda.

Pat Pat was Louis's mother—even she had a nickname. She'd operated a day care for ten years, and this was what the little ones called her.

Pip gave Lucinda a death stare, and then grinned. "It'll be ready when it's ready—tell Pat Pat to chill out."

"Shouldn't be mean to Pat Pat," said Legga, Louis's cousin. He was sitting next to his sister, Joanne, who added, "Unless you want to take over in the kitchen."

"Who's that?" asked Dinty, nodding at the driveway, and everyone looked that way. A hundred feet away a tall man with curly black hair was walking up with a woman and two young girls.

"That's Brian!" exclaimed Louis. Brian had worked with him on a dairy farm all through high school. "Who told him about this?"

Pip squeezed Louis's shoulder and said, "Your old dad takes care of you, doesn't he?"

Before Louis could respond, his attention was drawn to a large RV that was slowly cruising up behind Brian. It was a Class C, a behemoth almost as wide as the driveway.

"And who the hell is that?" he asked.

Nobody answered, but then they saw that Dee was driving it. She wore a huge smile. "Oh shit!" exclaimed Louis.

Dee put the vehicle in park, and then opened the side door. Pookey Bear slid off Bone's knee and ran to the RV.

"What is this thing?" she asked.

Dee looked at her for a moment, and then at Louis, before she finally said, "It's our new home."

Soon everyone was standing around the RV checking it out. Their new home was a 1998 *Sea Breeze*. It was shaped like a giant box: thirty-three feet long, nine wide, and ten high, and it took a while to figure out where to park it until they eventually backed it up next to the barn.

The RV's body was white with two thick blue and green stripes running down the sides. The roof sported two small skylights, and a roll-down canopy was mounted to the side, but what interested Pookey Bear the most were the large black mirrors that were attached on the sides just behind the front window.

"They look like big mouse ears," she said and stared up at them.

"Maybe we should call her Mousey," said Dee. "She needs a name."

Before Pookey Bear could reply, Louis asked, "Her? How did it suddenly become a female?"

Pookey Bear grinned. "Don't even start, Dad. You're outnumbered by the girls in this family."

Dee asked, "Aren't all vehicles female?"

Louis shrugged. "I don't know. I knew a few old trucks on the farm that had male names."

Dee and Pookey Bear stared him down until he mumbled, "Well, it needs a name anyway."

They went inside the vehicle and the girls scrambled around exploring. Say Say was eighteen months by now and could clamber around, and she followed Pookey Bear who acted like a tour guide as she pointed out the small bathroom and dining table.

The two front seats swiveled, and Dee sat in the passenger seat and spun it around until she faced away from the front window.

She smiled at Louis. "No more wet Skagway tents for this girl."

Pat Pat stepped up into the RV and looked around. Louis sat behind the wheel, looking over the dash. Dee and the girls had gone down to the river, and everyone else was back at the fire where the bottle of Black Velvet was making its way around the circle again.

"You sure know how to live," she said.

Louis smiled proudly, but then a shadow of doubt crossed his face.

He said, "Sometimes I feel guilty that I'm not creating a more financially stable world around my girls—most times we seem to be barreling along on a wing and a prayer."

He looked at her and grinned. "Well, maybe not a prayer."

She smiled back. They understood each other well enough that they never fought about religion. Pat Pat's maternal grandmother came from Cork, Ireland, and she had passed on to her many descendants a strong emotional core—or at least that's what they all told me. All I know is those of us with that core went through life with a deep well of emotion just beneath the surface.

None of us knew this ancient Irish ancestor personally, but we knew Pat Pat, and if one of us wept while watching a movie, or sobbed when telling a story, we would say they had the Pat Pat gene.

Louis had it for sure. He choked up all the time. And now, sitting in the RV with his mother, he felt overcome with emotion.

He thought of when they'd lost their jobs after 9/11, and of the desperate drive up to Alaska. He thought of discovering halfway there that his friends were no longer in Denali, and the jobs they'd been counting on were no longer waiting for them. And he thought of sitting in front of Dave at the Southeast Tours office, ready to beg for work.

He wanted to say something, but his throat was tight and his tongue lay heavy in his mouth. He wanted his mother to know just how scared he had been. How desperate.

But when he looked into her eyes, those deep pools of green that had watched over him as he grew up, he knew she understood. Staring into these emerald circles, he melted away, held only by the thin tangent of a smile that hinted she knew already how this adventure had changed him. As if she could see Timber bucking in the rain on that steep slope, Louis gripping the saddle horn with one white-knuckled hand. As if she could see him quietly stepping through a herd of elk in a snow-covered campground, Pookey Bear on his shoulders.

"You'll do fine—and so will they," she said, touching his forearm. "You just keep chasing your dreams."

She went to say more, but now she got choked up. Louis hugged her, and sobbed, and felt all of the worry from the last year slowly dissolve. She wiped a tear of her own and managed to say, "But you should run up to the cabin with your father before you leave town."

Louis nodded. He couldn't go anywhere before he returned to the woods of Maine. In many ways, the cabin up there had shaped who he was, and after any big trip he always made it a point to go there and recharge.

It took Pip and Louis almost six hours to drive there from Hollis a few days later. They had planned on leaving early, but didn't actually get on the highway until noon, when they had finally loaded the truck and gassed up. Soon after they crossed into Maine, Louis noticed the ground lay covered with a dusting of snow.

They stopped in Portland for lunch, and by the time they reached Millinocket—an hour south of the cabin—the sun was setting. The snow-covered flanks of Mt. Katahdin briefly reflected a cold pink glow as they cruised north up I-95, but it was soon extinguished by nightfall. They slowed down after they sighted white-tailed deer standing close to the edge of the highway.

"I don't mind driving," said Pip, nervously, "you just keep an eye out for any critters."

Pip had good reason to be a bit anxious. Ten years earlier he'd nearly been killed when a deer ran out in front of his station wagon on the highway, and many of his Maine friends had lost loved ones in collisions with moose or deer crossing the road in the dark.

"Last year it was real bad up here," he said. "Nobody drove at night. The deer flies were so thick that they chased the moose right out of the woods."

They arrived at the cabin with three feet of snow on the ground, but the neighbor had recently plowed the driveway and they could drive right up to the porch.

Louis hopped out and climbed the steps. It was much colder here than in Hollis and his breath jumped ahead of him in puffs of white. He smiled inside, and took in every detail: the empty porch, the silent woods, the swaying poplars, the snow-covered pines, the bright stars above, the crisp air.

He didn't know how soon he would be able to come back here, and the thought scared him. If they did indeed spend another summer in Skagway, the entire North American continent would separate him from this refuge.

But he knew he'd eventually be standing here again.

The family might someday leave the place in Hollis behind, but never the cabin.

Pip unlocked the front door. It was chilly inside. He grabbed a hand full of kindling from a box by the wall, and walked to the wood stove to get a fire going.

The cabin had been built almost thirty years ago. The walls were made from hundred-year-old cedar trees, and the main supports were large spruce logs. Numerous antlers and a few pelts from white-tailed deer decorated the walls. The two racks over the front door were from a moose and a caribou.

The cabin had been built by friends of the family as a favor — the story I heard was he'd saved one of their lives once — and Louis used to tell me tales about the cabin-raising days when several families would show up and all work together. The first year they'd put in the foundation, cut the logs and stripped the bark; the next year the walls went up and eventually the roof; and the final year all the doors and windows as well as the plumbing and electrical were completed.

During the first summer — when Louis and the Diggy weren't even teenagers — they'd slept in the open, looking up at the stars. During those long summer nights, Pat Pat would entertain her boys with stories about Africa and Alaska; places she'd always wanted to visit, but had never been able to.

Louis walked around the cabin, looking at all the mementos from his past. The walls were decorated with images: photos of the family over the last three decades, arts and craft projects he'd created with his siblings, oil paintings and pen and ink drawings made by Pat Pat, who'd been an artist in her thirties.

Since he'd been a young man, he had known the cabin was where he wanted to be when he was old. He imagined himself in his seventies, sitting on the porch and listening to the birds.

But not now. He didn't want to settle here with young daughters that would need to be driven to school through long, cold winters full of big snow storms. He wasn't ready yet.

He stared at a photograph of himself, sitting astride a pony when he was twelve. That summer they had boarded two ponies and had ridden them everywhere. He remembered the time he'd been on one named Sheba and came upon a black bear in the back field. The bear was more than five hundred feet away, but still close enough to scare Sheba half to death; she tore off for home, blazing a trail straight through the woods.

He was knocked off by a branch halfway. It wasn't until a half-hour later that his family found him, his pride hurt, but uninjured other than a scrape over his eye. He thought of riding Timber in the Yukon, and how much more dangerous those rides had been: just remembering them sent a surge of adrenaline though his arteries.

On the fridge, a polaroid showed Louis kneeling next to a six-point buck he'd shot when he was seventeen. Pip still claimed it was "the ugliest deer I ever saw."

"That truck isn't gonna unload itself," said Pip, still crouching by the wood stove. "Think you can haul in our gear while I turn on the water heater?"

Louis laughed and said, "Believe you can, and you're halfway there."

Pip stood and brushed his hands off, wiping them on his jeans.

"So we're on to Roosevelt?" he asked, recognizing the quote. The former owner of this property was a man named William Sewell, whose grandfather had been a young Theodore Roosevelt's guide. When Louis visited the cabin with Pip they tended to talk history — not religion—and eventually their conversations always turned to Roosevelt, or TR for short.

The fire began to crackle and Pip shut the stove door and damped down the flu a little; Louis stepped outside and began grabbing items from the truck.

TR had come to Maine as a weak, asthmatic twenty-year-old. He was grieving for his father who had passed away six months before. Under Sewall's guidance, he explored the Maine woods, and it was here—in these very woods—that Roosevelt had learned to be an outdoorsman.

Pip thought a minute and when Louis returned he offered his own Roosevelt quote, "If you could kick the person responsible for most of your trouble in the pants, you wouldn't sit for a month."

Louis stopped and grinned. "Why do I feel like you're saying I've been responsible for most of your trouble? You do know the quote suggests we each create most of our own problems, right?"

Pip paused by the cellar stairs. "You never caused me trouble as much as worry with all your crazy travels. It's good to have you here, at the cabin—I was just kidding."

Louis stepped outside again and felt the cold air filling his lungs once more. Every time he breathed it in he thought of Sewall and Roosevelt, because the first thing those two men discovered on their jaunts—one-hundred-and-twenty-five-years-ago—was that the extremely cold weather didn't aggravate TR's asthma.

It was here, in northern Maine, that he overcame the weaknesses of his body that he'd always feared would prevent him from accomplishing his goals. After that he was unstoppable.

During the coming year Roosevelt put his body to the test. He worked out with weights and a routine of vigorous exercises, he boxed, he ran, he swam, he didn't stop, until by the end of the year he had transformed himself from a frail weakling to a fit young man. Louis liked to claim that the spruce-scented air that wafted through the Maine woods was to blame.

This was also the year Roosevelt met, and romanced, his first wife, Alice Hathaway Lee, and soon he was head-over-heels in love. Maybe the scented air was to blame for that too—Louis thought so, after all, he'd gone on to marry a Maine girl himself.

As a boy, Louis had roamed these woods, pretending he was young Roosevelt sneaking up on a bear, or trying to find his way to Crystal Lake, which was located about a mile behind the cabin on the edge of a cedar swamp.

By the time Louis was in his twenties, William Sewell—the grandson of TR's guide—had passed away, but his wife, Cleo, still lived in nearby Island Falls. In between trips to Africa and Asia, Louis would retreat to the cabin to regroup. Once a week he would visit Cleo and talk about the old days, when young TR visited. Before Cleo passed away, Louis also got to know her son, David, who'd been a game warden most of his life and knew the Maine woods well.

TR was Louis's favorite president, and he liked the fact that they shared time in the same Maine woods. He always missed the cabin when he was away, and his happiest holidays were those when all of his family drove to the cabin to be together.

Later that night Louis and Pip sat on the porch smoking cigars and sipping whiskey. The temperature had plummeted once darkness had fully set in, settling at well below freezing, and they sat on rockers, each with a warm blanket spread over them.

To their left, a row of poplars creaked as an icy wind swayed their upper branches, and somewhere in the woods behind the cabin a pack of coyotes howled at a sharp-horned moon that had just risen over the trees. "Boy I've missed this place," said Louis.

Pip silently leaned over and clinked his glass against Louis's and they sipped the whiskey in silence.

When Pip went to bed, Louis stayed a little longer on the porch, watching the stars twinkling overhead. Louis often told me he'd lived his life backwards because he always knew where he wanted to be when he was old—on the porch—but he'd spent most of his life trying to figure out where to go until then.

"I'll be back," he said out loud, then stepped inside the cabin and retired for the night.

*

Louis and Dee had hoped to leave New Hampshire the day after Christmas, but the weather forecast was warning of a big nor'easter heading into New England, so they reluctantly left on the twenty-third.

"I don't want to drive in the snow if I can help it," Louis mumbled while stuffing some extra camping gear into one of the holds underneath the RV.

The RV was huge in comparison with the Vinniman, but after they had loaded the storage compartments underneath, and then filled every spare storage space inside, there was little extra room. The fridge and cupboards were overflowing with groceries and snacks, and even the compartment under the bed in the back was stuffed with jackets, scarves and hats.

It seemed the more space they had, the more stuff they brought.

They had not only supplies that they would need on the road, but also items for when they got to Alaska. After completing one season up there they had a better feel for what they would need — and what was tough to obtain in Skagway or at the Whitehorse Walmart.

On the RV's back hitch, Louis had mounted a rack for several bikes and a carrier that could be towed by one of them. He'd also given up one of the storage compartments so the girls could bring some toys, and now it was bursting with dolls and stuffed animals.

"I'm bringing baby Pip," said Pookey Bear as she defiantly placed the doll on the driver's seat. She stepped outside and returned with the guinea pig cage and set it down boldly. "And Lotion."

When Louis went to protest, Pookey Bear put her hands on her hips defiantly. Dee giggled and said, "I think we have to take the pig."

Pat Pat knocked on the door and entered with a bag full of Christmas presents.

"These are from all of us," she said. "They're mostly for the girls."

Pookey Bear's eyes lit up, and it was clear she wanted to tear into them right away.

"We'll stick them in the shower for now," said Dee. "And I'll let you open one every day — how's that?"

Pookey Bear frowned. "Can I open one today?"

Dee nodded, and the young girl spent the next ten minutes trying to decide which one.

The front of the RV seemed to be all window. There were two captain chairs, and behind the driver was a couch where the two child seats were buckled in.

Between them was the VHS player that Bone had bought the girls the year before. It was still functioning, although it had once fallen down a flight of stairs, and several glasses of milk had been spilled on it.

They had celebrated their last night in Hollis with a family dinner, and after the girls said goodbye to their cousins and aunts and uncles. Now, all that was left was a final kiss for their grandparents.

Dee fired up the engine. As they pulled out of the driveway they were all crying.

Pat Pat and Pip waved from the house steps.

In a few minutes they were out of Hollis, heading down the highway towards Boston where they would turn onto I-95. A light flurry had started and Louis couldn't get south fast enough for his liking.

Dee tried to cheer up the girls by shaking a bag of M & M's.

Instantly, Pookey Bear snapped out of her wet-eyed funk.

"Can I have some?" she asked.

"Well," said Dee with a mischievous smile, "I told you we need a name for the RV—we can't just keep calling it the RV. I'll give you ten if you can come up with one."

Pookey Bear scrunched her eye brows together and concentrated.

Then her blue eyes lit up and she smiled, saying, "We'll be jumping all over the place, so let's call it *The Grasshopper.*"

They didn't shake the snow until they reached New Jersey. It hadn't accumulated on the highway, but flashbacks to being stuck on the side of the road outside of Chicago kept Louis pushing forward.

"We should stop for the night," said Dee. The girls were asleep in their car seats, but the dark, cold highway looked uninviting and she knew they weren't planning on driving all night.

This was the first time Louis had driven the rig, and he wasn't looking forward to searching the suburbs for a place to park.

"Hey!" shouted Dee. "There's a Walmart."

People had repeatedly told them they could always park at a Walmart if they needed a place.

"That place is gonna be crazy there," said Louis. "It's Christmas eve."

Dee shrugged. "You got another suggestion?"

Louis took the next exit and tried to make his way toward the blue sign. Somehow he got funneled into a construction zone, and when they were finally stopped at a light, Dee sighted the Walmart behind them on the left. Three lanes of traffic were bumper to bumper, trying to get in.

"I'm gonna make a U-turn," said Louis.

"Here?" asked Dee, incredulously.

Louis nodded ahead and they could now see large mud puddles in the road. Flashing dividers were funneling all the vehicles into one narrow lane ahead. "I'm not going into that."

When the light turned green he began to turn, but couldn't make it all the way. He put the Grasshopper in reverse.

Horns honked all around them. Traffic was so dense that after backing up a mere five feet he had to pull forward again, then back up some more.

"This is gonna be a twenty-point turn," said Dee as she sank lower into her seat. She stared out the window at the stopped cars all around them.

"Some of those people look pretty mad," she said.

"I don't care," he said. "I'm not driving into that construction – they can all just chill out."

It took several minutes for him to pull it off, and during that time the light ran through all of its colors twice.

Soon honking around them had become a shrill concert and Dee started to laugh at the absurdity of it.

"This is crazy," said Pookey Bear as she stared out the front window.

They pulled into the Walmart parking lot a few minutes later and settled down to sleep.

The next day they drove over four hundred miles, and parked the Grasshopper at a Walmart south of Richmond, Virginia. Pookey Bear opened another present: crayons and a few coloring books. They were preparing dinner, when suddenly someone knocked on the side door.

"Hi there—Merry Christmas!" said a man of about sixty wearing a light jacket. "I own an RV as well, and I understand why you park at Walmart, but this is no way to spend Christmas Eve."

Louis and Dee stared back, not certain what he wanted. The guy looked friendly enough, but for a moment they feared he wanted them to move their vehicle somewhere else.

"Any other suggestions?" asked Louis.

"Yes," he said with a smile. "My name is Richard, and my wife and I live about ten miles away. We've got a cement pad on our property where you can park for the night—it's even got electrical and sewer hookups."

A half-hour later they pulled into Richard's property. A large sign by the street read: "The Stantons."

Shortly after they parked, Mrs. Stanton appeared, inviting them to dinner, and five minutes later they followed her up to the house.

The Stantons lived in a beautiful two-story house on a grass hill. The place was lovingly decorated for Christmas with candles, wreaths, and other ornaments. Many of the decorations seemed like they'd been handed down for generations. A sparkling Christmas tree stood in the corner, surrounded by presents.

Pookey Bear slowly circled the room, inspecting everything.

On the fireplace mantle stood numerous photos of children and grandchildren, but it was clear the Stantons were celebrating their Christmas dinner without them.

Mr. Stanton left the room, and his wife whispered to Dee, "We've got two grown children: one lives in Seattle with his family, and the other is currently not getting along well with my husband, so until you came along we thought we'd be spending Christmas alone."

Dee looked over the lovely home and smiled. "Well, I'm glad you invited us."

They ate a large, delicious smoked shoulder, with lots of side dishes: mashed potatoes, stuffing, sweat yams and carrots. Pookey Bear capped each of her fingers with a black olive, and then tried to see how long she could leave them there and keep eating.

Say Say devoured three helpings of cranberry sauce.

After, they moved to the living room and sat by a fire while eating dessert. While Mr. Stanton entertained Louis and Dee with a story about the property's history, Mrs. Stanton walked Pookey Bear through her house, showing her knickknacks and decorations. At one ceramic bowl she grabbed a handful of sweats and stuck them in the young girl's pocket.

She said, "Here are some treats for you on your journey."

The woman held up a finger to her lips indicating it was a secret, and Pookey Bear winked back in response.

The next morning, they had coffee with the Stantons before returning to the highway.

"I'm gonna miss that nice lady," said Pookey Bear as she quickly stole a glance at her parents, and then plopped a sweet in her mouth.

In the years to come, they would often think of the Stantons on Christmas Eve, and recollect how their hospitality had brought warmth into their lives.

They made good time on I-40 heading west, skirting underneath the bad weather which was hitting the northern half of the country, and began each day with the sun on their backs. They found Walmarts in Memphis, Oklahoma City and Albuquerque and didn't spend any money at RV parks or campgrounds.

From Albuquerque to Flagstaff they were buffeted by a strong wind and they drove slowly so they wouldn't overheat the engine.

By the time they approached Sedona it was nearing sunset. Louis remembered a guest on one of his tours in Skagway mentioning guiding jobs in Sedona and he crossed his fingers.

He was in the back, cooking mac and cheese on the stove, while Dee drove. The cassette player was blasting Johnny Cash, and Louis was having a whiskey-coke.

"Love is a burning thing,
And it makes a fiery ring.
Bound by wild desire,
I fell into a ring of fire."

"Shouldn't be much further," he shouted over the music. "Less than thirty miles."

Dee turned off I-40 onto 89a, heading south. Soon they passed a sign and she said, "Looks like we're about to drop down into some kind of canyon."

"Hold on a minute," said Louis and turned off the stove and put the pan in the sink.

Suddenly the front end of the vehicle slanted down as they descended into Oak Creek Canyon.

"What the hell?" shouted Louis. He scrambled to put the plates away and grab his drink.

Dee shrieked, and suddenly the entire front end of the vehicle swung to the left as she entered a switchback.

"What's going on up there?" screamed Louis as a butter dish tumbled off the counter. He bent to pick it up, but the road was now bending right and he fell over on his side.

"Help!" shouted Dee.

He half-crawled, half-climbed into the passenger's seat while the Man in Black continued to belt out his tune.

"I fell into a burning ring of fire,
I went down, down, down, and the flames went higher
And it burns, burns, burns,
The ring of fire, the ring of fire."

They were approaching another switchback, and this one looked tight. "Do you think we can make it?" she asked in a trembling voice.

Pookey Bear and Say Say watched silently from their car seats.

"I sure hope so," said Louis. "I don't know how we'd turn around."
They slowed to a crawl and made it around the turn, narrowly missing a vehicle coming from the other direction.

"Alright!" shouted Dee. "Here comes another one."

"Go momma!" shouted Pookey Bear.

"Seems like we're just twenty miles from Hawkeye RV Park in Uptown Sedona," said Louis as he was looking at a map of the southwest. "Let's keep going and see."

By the time they had backed the Grasshopper into a lot, leveled it, and hooked up the septic and electrical, it was almost dark. Pookey Bear pleaded to be unbuckled the entire time, but it was easier when the girls were confined.

"Why am I a prisoner?" she asked each time Louis walked past.

Soon they were ready to relax, and Dee unbuckled the girls. This was the first time since leaving New Hampshire that they would be in one place for more than one night, and they had no plans yet on when they would leave.

Say Say slid out of her car seat and with her sleepy legs, staggered across the Grasshopper. Pookey Bear quickly swooped in and checked her car seat for fallen M & M's.

Dee uncorked a bottle of wine and gawked at their surroundings. In the last traces of daylight they could see it was a great location, with red rocks rising up beyond the cottonwoods and sycamores that lined a gurgling creek. The bedroom back window looked down towards the creek, a hundred yards away, and the front faced a little road that circled the RV park.

They had neighbors on either side, in total maybe forty other vehicles. Some looked like they belonged to tourists passing through, but other sites had a more permanent air. There were three renovated school buses in the mix, one with a second floor, and the back row of lots—closer to the road—was lined with dilapidated RVs and mobile homes that looked like they'd never drive again.

To the right of the permanent camps a large fire blazed. Standing around it were a dozen people.

"What do you think's going on there?" asked Dee.

The twilight had faded into darkness and Louis and Dee observed the group by the flickering light of the fire.

Louis noted they wore an assortment of ethnic clothing, much of it pretty ragged, and most of the men had long hair and beards. Lots of bandanas and necklaces, too. They were all drinking beer, and as he watched, one skinny, blond kid fired up a joint and passed it around.

An older man was tending the fire in a sarong and a black leather vest. His bare chest was covered with tattoos.

"That looks interesting," said Louis. "Can you put down the girls?"

Dee smiled and pulled Pookey Bear against her. She said, "Oh, we are so glad not to go anywhere. You go have fun."

With a Heineken in his hand, Louis exited the RV and walked up to the fire.

"Hey! Coyote! No more wood," said the vested man as Louis walked up. The scrawny blond kid put his hand up defensively.

"Just trying to help," Coyote said and dropped a log he had been ready to place on the fire.

The vested man grinned. "The fire is too strong already. If you want to help, then step over here."

Coyote walked around the fire to a large table made from a sanded half-tree. On it sat the hindquarter of what Louis assumed was a deer. It had been just recently skinned, and the hoof was still attached.

Louis stepped closer and listened.

"Take these," said the vested man, and handed over a handful of peeled garlic cloves. He then took one, stuck his finger into the meat, and poked the garlic into the hole he'd created.

"Do that with all the garlic," he said. "Spread it out."

The vested man turned and noticed Louis.

He smiled. "Company!" he shouted and extended his hand, saying, "My name is Foolish Thunder!"

Louis shook his hand and introduced himself, then asked, "What are you guys up to?"

Foolish Thunder rubbed his chin. He was badly in need of a shave.

He said, "Well, a trucker hit a deer this morning—right over there by the edge of town. And before the Forest Service got here we claimed the hind quarter that hadn't gotten all banged up."

"They should have just given it to us," said Coyote without looking up from his task.

"Well, they should have," admitted Foolish Thunder, "but they don't always do things in our favor." He looked up at the stars and shouted, "EVEN THOUGH IT'S OUR FOREST!"

Coyote finished inserting the garlic, and then Foolish Thunder rubbed a sage-smelling mix into the meat.

"Smell that," he said and held his hand up to Louis's nose.

"What else is in there besides sage?" asked Louis.

Foolish Thunder grabbed a long metal rod and began impaling the deer leg on it. He paused, and then with a crooked smile said, "Secret."

"Help me with this, Chewy," said Foolish Thunder, and a guy with dreadlocks stepped forward and held the deer leg while they forced the rod clean through it.

Louis had heard of Sedona's vortexes—or energy spots—and the psychics and new agers that operated all over town, and he hoped he hadn't fallen in with a group of them. They did look like hippies in a grungy kind of way.

"You guys aren't all new-agers are you?" he asked.

Coyote turned and spat on the ground. Foolish Thunder laughed and said, "Heck no. We worship the earth. We're the Rock People."

Foolish Thunder placed the metal rod on two forked sticks that bracketed the fire, and soon the meat was sizzling. When the delicious smell began to float through the campground other residents showed up, some with plates and cutlery in hand.

"Funny how everyone becomes more sociable when there's free meat cookin'," said Foolish Thunder.

Coyote sat on a log next to Louis. "How long do you have in Sedona?" he asked.

"I guess that depends on if I find work," he said. "I'm supposed to be back in Alaska in April—but that's months away."

"What do you do?" asked Foolish Thunder from across the fire. He now held a smoldering bundle of sage, and he blew the smoke over the meat.

"Well, up in Alaska I was a tour guide."

"Then you should drive jeep tours."

The next morning Louis took Pookey Bear on a walk through Uptown Sedona. He located several different jeep tour offices, but it was too early and they were all closed.

One store called the Cowboy Corral had a mechanical, waving cowboy in front of it and the young girl stood next to it giggling.

"Shouldn't laugh at him," boomed a loud voice next to her. "You might hurt his feelings."

She looked up to see a tall, silver-haired Indian staring down at her. The man wore chaps, spurs, and a big white cowboy hat.

"Are you a real Indian?" she asked.

He nodded. "Sure am. I'm a Sioux Indian."

He also wore a six-shooter on his side. The young girl stared at it for a minute, but held her tongue.

Instead, she asked, "How old are you?"

The man's eyes sparkled. "How old do you think I am?"

She held his gaze, then looked over his attire again before saying, "Three hundred."

He laughed hard, slapping his chaps.

"Well, sometimes I feel that old."

Pookey Bear's attention drifted to a storefront window with chocolate in it and Louis turned to the Indian.

"You work for one of the tour companies?"

The man smiled. "I do."

"Well, I'm looking for a job. They hiring?"

The man smirked and extended his hand. "Name's Jimmy, and yes, we're always looking for drivers. Let me get my coffee and I'll swing you by the office."

Robert Louis DeMayo

Sea of Conception, Baja

Chapter Eleven

Baja, Mexico
(January 2003)

The Grasshopper barreled its way north, up I-17, heading towards Flagstaff; this time they avoided Oak Creek Canyon and its switchbacks. As they ascended the Colorado Plateau, the red rocks disappeared, and the trees changed from piñon pines and junipers to towering ponderosa pines.

In no time they were on I-40, heading west.

Louis had applied for a guiding job at a tour company called A Day in the West, and although the manager had sounded encouraging, he also said there wouldn't be any openings until mid-February when the tourist season began. So now they had time to kill.

Sedona had been chilly so they decided to drop down into Mexico's Baja Peninsula.

"Come on, girls," said Dee. "Let's go find the perfect beach!"

Louis rode shotgun, and the girls were buckled in their car seats, watching *The Jungle Book*. Dee hummed a tune as she drove, a steaming mug of coffee in one hand; she liked being behind the wheel of the big rig and didn't often give Louis a chance to drive.

He didn't mind. The swivel chairs up front were the perfect place to sit and watch the countryside pass by, and Louis stared at the white-capped San Francisco Peaks hoovering above Flagstaff, then slowly fading away in the side mirror, while the west opened before him. The panoramic vistas seemed to expand forever, or at least until they eventually blended into the soft horizon.

Oddly, all this reminded him of riding in an overland truck in Africa.

Overland trucks crisscross Africa to nearly every corner of the continent, on journeys that last from two weeks to ten months. If you were lucky enough to find a driver on his way back to a starting point like Nairobi or Harare, you could usually give them fifty bucks and catch a ride. Both Louis and Dee had traveled that way, and as the plateaus, mountains and pine forests passed, Louis replayed a few of those journeys in his mind.

With his bare feet up on the dash, he eventually picked up a novel: Jon Krakauer's *Into the Wild*. The book recounted the adventures of Christopher McCandless, a young vagabond who eventually died in Alaska on the Stampede Trail—the very trail Louis and Dee were camped on when Pookey Bear was conceived.

They turned south at Kingman, and when Louis looked up next he saw a sign for Needles and said, "That's funny."

Dee looked over at him. "What's up?"

He lifted the paperback he was reading. "This book about McCandless has a chapter on a young guy named Everett Ruess. Apparently he disappeared in 1934 after four years of roaming the southwest."

"That's random," said Dee. "Why did he get included?"

Louis read the next few paragraphs. "It seems when Krakauer was researching *Into the Wild* people repeatedly said to him, 'Heck, McCandless barely made it one hundred days in the wild—you should be writing about Everett Ruess, he did it for four years.'"

Another sign for Needles appeared and Dee nodded at it.

"So what's Needles have to do with that?"

Louis smiled. "He hitched a lot, and he got stuck in Needles several times—for days at a time—waiting for someone to pick him up."

"I have to go to the bathroom!" shouted Pookey Bear.

Dee smirked. Throughout their journey from New Hampshire the young girl tried repeatedly to find excuses to get out of her car seat.

"Okay," said Louis and unbuckled her.

He tried to hold her hand and walk her to the bathroom, but she shrugged him off. "I got it," she said and stumbled to the back of the Grasshopper.

Say Say held up her arms, as if she was next. Louis snuggled with her, and then checked her diaper. "You're fine."

Five minutes later Louis knocked on the door and was greeted by a shout, "I need my privacy!"

He left her alone for another ten minutes.

"What do you think she's doing in there?" asked Dee.

Louis grinned. "I have no idea."

She eventually returned and staggered to her seat.

Four hours later they reached Joshua Tree National Park, where they intended to stay for the night. They got a site at the Jumbo Rocks campground, connected the electrical hookup, and closed all the shades while they cooked dinner.

There was a bedroom in the back where Louis and Dee slept, and the side couch turned into another bed where the girls snoozed, side by side. Louis did the dishes while Dee read a bedtime story, and before long they were all in bed with the lights out.

But even after crawling between clean, crisp sheets Louis couldn't fall asleep. He still felt like the road was moving underneath him.

Again he thought of his travels in Africa.

*

The sun was peaking over the horizon of Botswana's Okavango Delta and winked at Louis and Dee through a tangle of dense reeds. Riding low in a dugout canoe, Dee sat in the front, Louis behind her; they couldn't see more than ten feet ahead of them, and put their trust in their guide, Thaba, who stood in the back.

The three of them had set out early, before the crocs could muster, but now the flared, bobbing tops of the papyrus were crackling with light as they swayed in the wind. The sun had risen.

From a soft pink to a burning orange, it rose in the sky and the wilderness came to life. Birds darted before them, others twittered and chirped out of sight, and now and then they heard the light swish of something sneaking away, off to their side in the high reeds. Now the animals were moving again and they would have to be more careful.

For the last week they'd been exploring the Delta, and they had the injuries to prove it: Louis's right eye was covered with gauze; he'd sliced it on a reed and even after three days it still hurt like hell. Both of them were covered with insect bites and bruises, and their forearms were crisscrossed with scratches and cuts.

Dee reached down to touch the water and let her finger trail along for a few seconds, but then thought better and lifted it away.

The source of the Okavango River was far off to the west, in Angola; and it covered hundreds of miles, forcing its way straight through the Kalahari Desert to get here. Depending on the time of the year, the delta was either a flooded plain or bone dry.

They hadn't picked the best time to visit; Dee and Louis had arrived just a few months after the floods, and now the water had receded into narrow channels connecting the remaining lagoons, limiting where they could go.

Thaba stood perfectly balanced in the back. He wore threadbare green army fatigues and a floppy green hat, sun-bleached to faded khaki, which also looked military. His name meant 'Mountain' in Sesotho, his language, and Louis thought he'd been aptly named. He looked solid, like he was made of oak, and in the same way as an ancient oak tree, timeless, having existed since the plants and trees around them had first sprouted up, but from stories he'd told of his earlier life Louis guessed he had to be at least sixty.

He carried himself like a younger man, but his deep, dark eyes glowed with experience. His stern countenance was a result of maintaining a constant alert. He had worked in the South African gold mines for twenty-five years, but considered guiding in the delta to be far more dangerous.

He kept his guests at a safe distance from elephants and carnivores, showing respect while offering up observations, but tended to steer clear of the hippos whenever he could.

"They are the enemy," Thaba said. "The mines were dangerous, but they weren't a thinking creature that wanted to hurt me."

In his hand he held a long pole called a *ngashi*, and with it he pushed the dugout canoe, or *mokoro*, deeper into the channel. Louis and Dee had been on safaris in East Africa, but this was different. The Okavango was a vast wilderness area where you hardly saw any other tourists; and it wasn't nearly as tightly controlled as the national parks where rangers strictly limited your activities. In the delta, you were pretty much on your own, and you could get into real trouble here. The dangers were tangible—and they felt close at hand when you were sitting only inches above the water.

"This must be what the early African explorers felt like," said Louis as he pushed a handful of reeds away from his face.

Suddenly Thaba glanced ahead and stiffened, but then he smiled and whispered, "Sitatunga."

A few seconds later they emerged into a small clearing where six antelopes stood in a few inches of water.

The sitatungas froze for an eternal second, and Dee held her breath while she watched. Their shaggy coat had a deep chestnut color, and faded white spots and stripes decorated their necks, backs and snouts.

"All females," said Thaba, and they noticed that none of them had horns.

In slightly deeper water, one majestic doe timidly drank, trying to see beyond her own trembling reflection, in case a croc was lurking there, underneath.

She suddenly lifted her head and sniffed, and a second later they all shot off, appearing to dance over the water.

Thaba liked to joke about the antelopes, because they had a unique ability to hide underwater with only their snout sticking up. It was an effective subterfuge against lions and leopards, but Thaba knew the crocodiles just loved it when they stumbled upon one.

"Dinner time for the crocodile I think," he said with a grin.

They were now making their way east, trying to find a channel that would lead back to their camp.

These channels through the reeds were made by hippos, and because of their narrowness they weren't the best places to come upon them, but the lagoons which the channels connected were even more dangerous.

"When the water is low," Thaba had told them, "the hippos become very territorial and the big ones claim the lagoons."

Five minutes later Thaba stopped, a concerned expression on his face. "Put your hands inside," he said while nodding ahead.

The passage before them was only ten feet wide, and ahead a large crocodile lay along one side, his left flank submerged in the water.

Thaba made a grunting sound and banged his *ngashi* against the side of the *mokoro*. The croc failed to acknowledge him.

The bush lining the canal was disturbingly quiet.

The *mokoro* was fifteen feet long, carved out of a single log, and sat deep in the water with the sides only extending a few inches above the surface. As they approached Louis realized the croc was bigger than the *mokoro*.

"That thing has to be eighteen feet long," whispered Louis.

Thaba shushed him and slowly poled past the croc.

Dee watched the massive crocodile and as they passed it she sank deeper into her seat, leaning away from it. As they slowly cruised by, the croc eyed them and Louis felt his blood run cold — if it pulled down even slightly on the closer side of the *mokoro* they would spill sideways right on it.

An hour later they were still trying to travel east through land that resembled the Florida Everglades. They reached an open section where the reeds were flooded by a foot of water and they plodded ahead for about a mile. Leaving the channel gave them more freedom of direction, but you never knew where the water might become shallower and leave you stranded.

Ahead a large lagoon appeared, maybe eighty feet long and forty across. The great dawn had unfolded, and now the morning rays stained the water orange; the surface lay so flat and still it seemed made of marble.

Beyond the far shore of the lagoon a herd of impala grazed.

Thaba paused and listened. A single bird repeatedly called out, as if warning them.

Finally, he inched the craft forward.

They reached the edge of the lagoon and listened again. Nothing moved. The water was dead still.

Thaba shook his head and whispered. "This lagoon is too nice not to have a large bull. I think he is down there, waiting."

He banged his *ngashi* against the wooden hull and the three listened, not moving, for two long minutes. Even the squawking bird had gone silent.

Thaba's eyebrows sank low while he watched.

"We will try," he said, his dark eyes simmering.

With one strong push they left the reeds and began to cross the lagoon. A third of the way across Louis noticed a swirl in the water by the far shore.

"There!" he shouted and pointed.

Suddenly the water appeared to boil and bubble upward. A hippo was coming at them, underwater. From the *mokoro* it looked like someone had fired a torpedo at them.

Thaba cursed under his breath and began pushing backwards.

The flooded reeds lay just a few feet behind them, and they reached the shallower water just as the hippo was upon them.

Thaba put all his weight on his staff and shoved them back further.

The hippo reached the end of the lagoon and rose out of the water until his front feet were on land. He was huge—at least three thousand pounds—and water poured off his barrel-shaped body while he trembled and shook his massive head.

In the front of the *mokoro*, Dee felt helpless.

They were barely ten feet away when he opened his maw, unbelievably wide, and roared. Dee stared at the beast's foot-long canines and incisors and thought she was about to die.

The water around them was barely a foot deep and for a split second she considered hopping out and running, but before she could react Thaba gave another great shove of the *ngashi* and they moved a few paces deeper into the reeds.

The hippo appeared content to stand his ground, but he roared again to make sure it was clear that they'd entered the wrong lagoon.

His lagoon.

Two days later they were celebrating at a bar in Maun, just south of the delta. Dee felt drunk already on all the wildlife they'd seen, and couldn't stop talking about it to a young couple from England who were preparing to fly into the Okavango for a week-long safari.

"When that hippo came charging out of the water, I thought we were done," she said and emptied the last few drops of her fourth gin and tonic. "I thought he was gonna run right over us."

The English woman turned pale as she listened, and her boyfriend tried to calm her. "I'm sure it's not all that dangerous."

"Nope," Dee giggled. "We did have about five minutes when I thought we were safe — but then we cruised by a humongous croc."

The guy quickly led his girlfriend away.

Dee hiccupped and said, "I'm gonna need another drink."

Louis grinned. "Well, you're out of luck, because I've run out of *pula* — I'll change some dollars in the morning.

Dee searched her pants, and in a back pocket she pulled out a fifty. "Not me!" she said before she disappeared to purchase another round.

She returned to find Louis standing outside by a large pool. There were no lights, and the dark water reminded him of the delta.

"You want to take a swim?" asked Louis, half in jest.

"I jussst might," slurred Dee as she set the drinks on a low table by a few reclining chairs, but then she looked down at her jeans and boots. As a precaution against malaria, Louis and Dee had made it a habit to change out of their shorts and Tevas into jeans and boots an hour before dark when the mosquitos came out.

"I'm way too buzzed to take all this stuff off," she said.

She stopped when she heard a male voice coming from one of the reclining chairs beside them. "I wouldn't do it anyway if I were you."

She turned with a surprised smile and snapped. "And why-the-fuck not?"

A man in his early thirties sat up. He was five foot, with a shaved head and stubbly chin.

"Well, you never know what might be in there," he said with an Australian accent and flipped on a flashlight. "Sometimes hippos drop in at night when the delta water is low."

The three stepped to the edge of the pool. The guy aimed the flashlight and they stared into the depths, looking for a hippo, but their attention was diverted to the surface when a four-foot snake slithered through the beam of light.

"Holy fuck!" screamed Dee and jumped back.

The man turned off the light and the snake slithered into the shadows. The two men moved away from the pool.

The guy extended his hand. "Name's Geoff," he said.

Louis shook his hand, and from behind them Dee said, "Very pleased to meet you—and your little snake. Please keep him in the pool."

They moved to the chairs and sat down. Dee sipped her drink.

"You guys look like you've been in Africa a while," commented Geoff.

Louis nodded. "We have. About three months. We started in Malawi and then dropped down into Zimbabwe."

Geoff gestured at Louis's wounded eye, which still looked red and angry. Today was the first day he'd gone without the bandage.

"You get that in the delta?" he asked. At last minute Louis resisted the urge to touch his eye. "Yes," he said, "on a reed."

"I did that once," said Geoff. "Hurt like hell."

Geoff rubbed his chin. "Where'd you stay in the delta?"

"Oddballs," said Dee.

Oddballs was a safari camp located deep in the delta. For thirty American dollars a day you got a tent site, three meals, and you could take out a *mokoro* whenever you wanted. Louis was going to say more, but then he saw Geoff nod and figured he'd already been into the delta and knew his way around.

Instead, he asked, "How about you? What are you doing here?"

Geoff gestured toward the parking lot. "I drive a truck for Encounter Overland. I've got a group that's in the delta right now, and when they get back we're heading west."

Louis picked up his drink, a little fearful that otherwise Dee would consume it after she had finished hers. He took a sip and said, "We're trying to get to Namibia. Any chance we could catch a lift?"

"I'll ask my people in the morning," he said. "You'll like Polly.

"Who the hell is *Polly?*" asked Dee who now was fully reclined in the chair.

Geoff laughed. "Actually, that's the name of my truck. But I'll ask the passengers if they mind me taking on a few extras."

"What are our chances?" asked Louis.

Geoff shrugged. "We've got a pretty loose itinerary. There's a general direction—right now we're on our way to Namibia's Etosha Pan—but the group decides on where to stop and for how long."

He must have noticed their expressions because he quickly added, "I only have six passengers, so there's plenty of room. I'd suggest you meet me on the highway heading west no later than nine tomorrow morning. I'll pull over and we can talk then."

The sun was glaring down on them as they stood on the side of highway A3, heading southwest out of Maun, and looked around for Geoff's truck. They'd walked at least a quarter mile and now stood on the city limits.

Dee was quiet, and clearly hungover. "Christ," she mumbled, "my sweat smells like alcohol—I'm never drinking gin again."

"I knew you were gonna be a mess."

She held up her hand. "I don't wanna talk about it."

They crouched on the side of the road, their backpacks behind them.

Not a single vehicle had passed since they'd arrived thirty minutes ago. The trees lining the road were full of birdsong.

"Do you think he'll show?" she asked.

Louis shrugged. "I don't know if he'll even remember us—he was pretty drunk by the end of the night, too."

A motor rumbled from down the road.

They both looked up, and soon a large, blue overland truck appeared. "*Polly*" was painted on the driver's door. Behind a rugged cab sat a square, canvas-covered structure. It had roll-down plastic flaps for windows, a large one up front that looked over the cab, and a small door near the driver door that led to a metal ladder.

The big truck screeched to a halt and the driver rolled down his window. "There you are, my Yankee friends!" shouted Geoff.

"Morning!" yelled Louis over the rumble of the engine. "What did your people say?"

Geoff gestured to the metal ladder behind his door.

"Climb in the back," he said, "you can ask them yourself. I've got an hour's drive to Sehithwa, to gas up. It's on the way to Namibia. If you guys can't work out something by then I'll leave you there."

"Thanks!" shouted Dee and climbed the ladder. Louis handed up the backpacks and followed her.

Geoff grabbed the stick shift and worked his way through *Molly's* lower gears as he again crept up to speed.

They stepped into the truck through the small side doorway. Three rows of padded benches slowly came into focus, with an alley down the middle—much like a school bus. Closer to the front a table was bolted down with two wooden benches on either side. There were numerous cupboards and book shelves attached to the walls near the front and back, each with latches or netting to prevent items from tumbling out.

A half-dozen passengers were sprawled out in the back, although it took a while to make them all out. Several were hunched down low, trying to read, and the two benches furthest back were occupied by two people who were sleeping.

The side flaps in the back were down, and the morning sunshine filtered through as light blue. Louis and Dee stood awkwardly just inside the doorway, holding the metal ribs of the inner canopy for support as their eyes adjusted.

At the table near the front of the truck a man and a woman were playing cards. The guy looked to be around sixty, with short, brown hair and metal-rimmed glasses; the woman was in her early twenties, and had her blond hair held in place by a light green scarf.

She jumped up right away when Dee stepped aboard.

"Hi," she said. "My name is Meg. What are you guys doing here?"

Dee shrugged. "Trying to get a lift to Namibia. I guess it depends on whether you guys are willing to take on stragglers or not."

Meg grinned. "Heck yeah!" and then leaned closer to Dee and whispered, "I'm the only one on board under forty—please stay."

The other card player extended his hand to Louis.

"I'm Martin," he said, "and I don't care if you ride along, but you should know that we plan on taking a detour to a bushman site called Tsodilo Hills."

"But you'll continue on to Namibia, right?" asked Louis.

Martin smiled and nodded. Now that the truck was moving along it was easier to use gestures than shout. He put the cards away.

Louis was fine with the detour. Ever since their arrival in Malawi they'd utilized numerous buses, taxis and private vehicles to get around, and he was happy not worry where the next lift might come from.

At Sehithwa, Meg told Geoff while he was pumping gas that they didn't mind if Dee and Louis stayed on. Martin leaned out the small door and said, "We all voted on it, Geoff, and we want to go to that bushman site I mentioned.

Geoff frowned. "Tsodilo Hills? I looked at it on the map—it's not gonna be easy."

Martin nodded. "I've heard that. We're all willing to help in any way we can."

Geoff turned and spat. "Oh, if we do it I'm gonna need some help for sure. You might regret that offer before we're done."

They left Sehithwa and turned north up A35, skirting to the west of the delta. Geoff informed them that they had a hundred miles ahead of them before the Tsodilo turn-off so everyone settled down to enjoy the ride. "Might not be a big deal to you," said Meg, "but this is one of the only smooth sections of road we've been on for weeks."

Louis sat on one of the benches by the side flap and watched the street while Dee slept with her head on his lap, using a daypack as a pillow.

There were pedestrians on the outskirts of Sehithwa, and as Polly sped past Louis watched them through a break between two plastic panels.

These were the first San he'd seen—the first Bushmen. They were golden-skinned and slender, and he could see why they were referred to as Earth's oldest folk. There was something childlike in their lovely elfin features: a hint of innocence that made you yearn for the past. They seemed more like a part of the wild desert they now skirted, a part that had only recently been blown into town.

Beyond the town only thorn bushes lined the road, and Louis drifted off, his head against the plastic flap while he dreamt of a time when only the Bushman walked through the hot, flat desert.

*

Back in the States, the Grasshopper was slowly cruising through southern California. They didn't rush. The RV had begun to feel like home, and that yearning for a destination slowly faded. They *were* home.

There were lots of campgrounds along the way, but they preferred to camp in natural settings, and searched out state parks. A friend in Temecula offered to put them up for a few days, but after only a night there they moved on.

I think Dee was yearning for her 'perfect beach' and that's where she wanted to park. Until then, nothing really mattered.

They finally checked into a campground in Chula Vista, less than nine miles from the Mexican border. Louis wanted to make sure the Grasshopper was in tip top shape before leaving the country, and he repacked all the storage compartments under the rig, and tied down the bikes securely on the back.

The next morning they drove to the border.

They were still a few miles away from the crossing when they were swept into huge lines of traffic. They crawled along doing a few miles an hour.

The U.S. Customs Agent didn't even ask for their passports. He just knocked on the side door and then entered, saw that they were all white, and waved them through.

"That was a little too easy," said Dee.

"I do hope they're tighter on the return journey," said Louis. "That was the easiest border crossing I've ever gone through—a little security isn't a bad thing—that was a joke."

The traffic didn't move much faster on the other side. Along the highway men peddled hammocks, ceramics and other goods. Some walked alongside the vehicles holding up enchiladas or shrimp tacos. One guy shadowed Dee in the driver's seat, and kept calling to her as he held up a small statue of the Virgin Mary.

"*Hola!*" he shouted. "How much you pay for this?"

She waved him off, but he persisted.

In front of them, a large sign read: Zona Central.

"Did you see Mexican Customs?" asked Louis. Most people didn't get a visa, but they needed one or the RV insurance wouldn't cover them.

"I didn't see anything," said Dee, nodding at the vendor outside her window. "I'm just trying not to run over this knucklehead."

Suddenly the traffic surged forward and picked up speed.

The vendor faded away.

A sign read: Route 1.

"I think we missed customs," said Dee.

"Shit!" shouted Louis. "Pull a U-turn. Take that exit."

"I have to go to the bathroom!" shouted Pookey Bear, and both Dee and Louis yelled back, "Not now!"

Dee managed to make the exit, but then the road spilled onto a monstrous roundabout with four or five lanes of traffic all somehow circling together. Cars were cutting each other off, horns were blaring. There were hundreds of vehicles, and none seemed happy about the fact that the Grasshopper was just too big to stay in any one lane.

"Oh my God!" shouted Dee.

"We gotta do it. Just slowly follow your way around. I can see the north exit on the other side."

Not only were they in the heart of the city, but it was now noon and they were caught in the lunch rush. The smaller vehicles swarmed around the Grasshopper.

Louis looked out the side window and saw a young guy running alongside them. He reached down and tried the latch on one of the storage bins under the vehicle. When he felt that it was locked he moved on to the next one.

Louis opened the side door and yelled at him.

248

"Get away from there!"

Dee made it halfway around the circle and located the exit. She headed directly towards it, ignoring the crescendo of honking around her.

Another guy tried to take Pookey Bear's bicycle off the back of the RV but it was strapped down too tightly.

Somehow they got back on the highway.

A mile up the road, they saw the customs office on the other side.

"How do we get there?" asked Dee.

Louis sighed. "Forget about it. Let's just go back to Chula Vista and we'll try it again tomorrow."

Within thirty minutes they were parked again at Chula Vista.

Louis would later often tell the story of circling that crazy roundabout, and he always said it seemed like a thousand ants attacking a caterpillar.

*

The overland truck continued north. After an hour the road got bumpier and Louis and Dee sat up. The six overlanders were stirring too, and soon everyone moved to the front table to get to know the newcomers.

The two who had been reading were an American couple from the Midwest. They looked to be in their late forties, were a bit overweight, and dressed in matching khaki pants and shirts. Their names were Nora and Jonathan.

"Hope you guys have plenty of sunblock," said Nora. "We're 'bout to cross the Kalahari. Don't bother using the African stuff—it's worthless."

Louis and Dee found it strange to hear an American accent after traveling with mostly Australians and Europeans for months.

The two sleepers had both woken. One was a Canadian named Adam. He was forty-two, and when he joined them at the table it was obvious he had eyes for Meg.

"Do you want some coffee, Meg?" he asked. "I filled a thermos before we left this morning."

Meg smiled. "As long as you have a cup for my new friend, Dee."

Adam nodded and happily made his way to the kitchen area in the back of the truck, holding onto the backs of the benches as he went.

Meg blushed and whispered to Dee. "He's really sweet—but he's like twenty years older than me and I'm not interested."

The other guy was an Englishman named Richard, an avid birder. He looked to be in his fifties, and mostly kept to himself, except when the others were talking about birds or natural history.

On Polly's right, they could make out a band of green where the delta began. Above it low clouds hovered, as if drawn by the flooded plains. To their left the land lay parched, with a fine red sand covering the base of the small acacia trees and scrub brush that somehow took root here.

Soon Adam returned, precariously balancing two coffees.

"Hope you don't mind it black," he said. "I put in some sugar, but we're out of cream."

"Thank you!" said Dee, "I so desperately need a coffee."

The mugs had lids, but the women still held them at arm's length in case they hit a bump. There were plenty of surprise potholes.

Louis hit it off with Martin, and the two sat at the table up front and watched the countryside pass. It turned out this was Martin's first visit to southern Africa, but he had traveled all over the world and been to many of the same places as Louis. He was an expert on sacred sites, and had selected Encounter Overland because their loose itinerary allowed them to visit several places he was interested in.

"I've never been to the Kalahari," said Martin, "but I do know it's not a true desert like the Sahara, more of a sandy savanna with more plants and animals."

From guide books Louis knew that the Kalahari Desert stretched across seven countries, and covered 350,000 square miles. They were about to cross one of the largest continuous stretch of sand on the planet.

"It reminds me of the Australian outback," said Louis.

Martin nodded, and then smiled and slid sideways to make room when Richard joined them.

"Have you talked with Geoff about the rock art site yet?" asked Richard. "I believe Tsodilo Hills would be a good place to see some of the migratory birds that pass through—I would at least hope to see a few eagles nesting in the rocks."

Martin shook his head. "I told him we decided on going, but I've got a feeling he's going to try to talk us out of it before we turn off the main road."

Martin, it turned out, was right. Later that day Geoff pulled over and climbed in the back with the others. He opened a well-worn map, laid it out on the table, and then pointed at a patch of green in the middle of southern Africa.

To the left of the green area ran a thin line of a road.

"This is where we are," said Geoff, and touched the map on the left of the road. "And those are the Tsodilo Hills."

Meg said, "It really doesn't look that far away."

Geoff nodded. "It's not. Maybe thirty-two kilometers. But the road is as bad as it gets around here—and if we break down the chance of help coming along is pretty slim. I doubt we'll make it without sand mats, either."

Martin exchanged glances with Richard and both nodded.

"Let's give it a try."

Louis didn't have a vote but listened attentively. A primitive rock art site did sound interesting and he wanted to see it. He did a quick calculation and thought, twenty miles—how bad could that be?

Geoff sighed. "Okay, the first twenty-two kilometers are bad enough, but then the road surmounts a dune, and it'll be nothing but low-gear four-wheel drive for the last ten kilometers."

"Let's do it!" shouted Nora. The look in her eyes said clearly that she was in the midst of a once-in-a-lifetime experience.

"Okay," said Geoff, grudgingly, and gave Nora an annoyed glare. "We leave in ten minutes."

Everyone climbed out of Polly and relieved themselves. Dee, Meg and Nora stepped behind the truck.

After they scrambled back inside Nora scurried around excitedly.

"Cover the bags so they don't get dust on them!" she said to Jonathan and Richard, "Put all those dishes in the plastic tubs!" Then she set about clearing all the backpacks and food bags out of the alleyway between the back benches. It appeared that organizing relaxed her. But the way the others helped her made it obvious that these were chores they all did when they went off road.

Louis worked with Meg and Adam to roll up the side flaps. Martin climbed down the ladder with a detailed map and compared it with Geoff's.

They left the highway, and the truck began to bounce all over the place. The road was so rough that the eight of them rode standing for a full hour, holding onto the back of the benches, using their legs as shock absorbers.

"What the fu...!" shouted Dee right before Polly's left back tire hit a rock and sent her flying. If she hadn't been holding onto the bench in front of her she would have punched a hole into the truck's canopy.

The sun crept higher in the sky; it got hotter by the minute. The coolness of the delta was long forgotten. The low, desiccated scrub outside here offered no shade.

Eventually the road grew so bad that Geoff had to slow to a crawl.

Louis's legs felt like rubber. He had drunk the last of his water, and anxiously waited for a chance to refill his canteen.

At this slow speed, the clouds of dust Polly was kicking up engulfed the truck. The air was stifling. Dee's mouth and nose were covered with a fine red dust. She splashed the last of her water on her face, then tied a bandana around it and put on her sunglasses.

Reluctantly, they rolled down the side flaps. This kept the dust down, but turned the back of the truck into an oven.

With a running start, Geoff managed to propel Polly over a large dune, and then the road turned into a narrow, sandy track. Polly's wheel base was very wide, which forced Geoff to drive on the soft sand on either side of the primitive, narrow road. The ruts were too deep for him to put two wheels in one rut and two on the side because the narrowness of the road would have forced one side into the brush.

They went so slow that when a piece of trash blew out through the gap by the ladder, Adam hopped out, walked back to pick it up, then casually caught up and jumped back onto the ladder.

The land around them seemed to be succumbing to sand. Acacia trees dotted the low dunes, but their bases were buried, just the trunks were sticking out of the sand. All other ground cover had disappeared.

Eventually the dunes levelled out and the land lay perfectly flat. It was a letdown not to see the Tsodilo Hills in the distance.

Then they got stuck. The back left tire was spinning, kicking sand into the air. Geoff turned off the engine and everyone piled out.

Louis guessed they had at least six miles left to go.

The sun beat down on them oppressively while they stared at the half-submerged truck tires.

"Time for the sand mats," said Geoff.

Bolted to the side of the truck were a dozen metal mats, each a foot wide by four feet long. They were a half-inch thick and weighed about twenty-five pounds each.

Geoff took them off with a big wrench, then cleared away the sand in front of each tire and lay down four mats.

"Stand back!" shouted Geoff, engine revving. He glanced in the mirrors to make sure nobody was too close, and then drove up onto the mats and gained enough momentum to stay on top of the sand when he dropped off the other end.

His arm shot out the window and motioned them all forward.

It was clear Geoff didn't want to stop for fear of getting stuck again. The passengers trudged behind the truck, carrying the mats.

Geoff continued in low gear, but soon Polly was got stuck again. When the travelers caught up with her, they trudged around and placed the sand mats in front of the tires.

The fine, hot sand was burning Louis's feet in his Tevas. For a moment he considered changing into his boots, then didn't because he feared they would fill with sand and weigh him down.

They bogged down over and over again, and soon resorted to simply placing one mat in front of the next. Only every so often a section of hard ground appeared where the sand had blown away, and they caught a small break.

The sand was so deep that every step took effort. On a few occasions they sank in up to their knees.

Earlier they had each carried a sand matt, but soon this proved too tiring and they started to work in teams, each carrying an end of a mat. Dee and Meg were working together.

"I'm never gonna drink again," said Dee. She was pale, but kept working, weakly holding up her end of the sand mat.

They had to walk around the truck in order to lay down the mats, ducking under barbed branches and trudging through deep sand full of small thorny twigs.

Sometimes they had to dig sand out from around the tires so Geoff could drive onto them. A spade that had also been bolted to the truck passed from hand to hand.

After one serious digging session, Louis squatted on Polly's shaded side, catching his breath. By this point they were all scratched and sunburned. Martin was filling his water bottle from a nozzle on the side of the truck.

"Help yourselves," said Geoff to Louis and Dee. "There's a hundred gallons of water in there."

Louis's sliced eye had been healing fine, but now looked irritated after being battered by the sun and dust. "Remind me to put some ointment on that later," said Dee.

Martin capped his bottle, looked over the scrub and said, "Kalahari is actually a Tswana word, derived from *Kgala*. It means *the Great Thirst*."

Geoff tilted his head back and poured some water onto his forehead.

"Thanks for that, Martin," he said and grabbed his shovel. He trudged heavily back to the front end of the truck.

"Put on some more sunscreen," said Louis to Dee while he filled his canteen. He handed it to her, and she drank from it in long, slow swallows, wincing when her lips cracked.

After an eternity the Tsodilo Hills finally rose up in the distance like stone giants. The closest was now a mere half-mile away, and Louis guessed it might be a thousand feet tall.

They walked behind the truck, almost as tired of climbing the metal ladder as trudging through sand. The sun still beat them with long, slanted rays, but it had lost some of its fury.

Around the hills, only the never-ending desert extended, fanning out majestically. Thankfully the sand petered out ahead of them, and dried yellow grass covered their final approach. The acacia trees grew thicker, and looked taller now that their trucks weren't covered with several feet of sand.

Termite mounds bulged suddenly from the red earth, and Louis kept catching glimpses of them off to the side, thinking they were people. Richard shouted, "Look!" and they turned to see a secretary bird ducking behind a cluster of low bushes, its black spatula-shaped feathers still visible for a second as it sped past.

Ring-necked doves fluttered before them, hopscotching from tree to tree as the truck advanced. The travelers were walking slowly, tired but in awe, as the sacred place in front of them came to life. Richard was having a great time spotting birds and plants. He nodded at a vine with spikey, orange fruit and said, "Horned melons."

Martin took a closer look. "This is an ancient site, I would think we'll see lots of the trees and plants used by the San here—some grew here naturally, but they cultivated others."

The trees became denser, and in between the acacia there now appeared reddish-brown-barked camelthorn trees, some fifty feet high. Ahead at the base of the cliff Louis could make out several enormous baobabs.

Geoff shifted up a gear and drove the last quarter mile, leaving the six of them to approach on foot without being enveloped by his dust.

They watched him park Polly in the shade of a large stone hill, which looked like a pile of giant boulders. It was late afternoon now and the shadows were finally lengthening.

Eventually, the travelers reached the shade of a large boulder and sank down. All afternoon they had walked due west, directly towards the sun. Louis told me once that by the time he finally sat down he felt like he'd been dragged there, and I do believe it was many years before Dee ever drank gin again.

They downed what was left in their canteens. They were thirsty, but too tired to get more water from the truck, so they just sat and rested for a long while.

Finally, Martin broke the silence. He'd never been here, but he had a good guidebook with a detailed map of the hills and various rock art panels. "The San were the original inhabitants of the Kalahari," he said. "To them these hills are filled with significance and legend."

They silently looked around. They could make out several rock art panels by the base of the rocks. They had yet to see another person, but still sensed there were people all around them.

They knew they were in a place of ancient beginnings.

Martin pointed at the hills around them, "These hills are comprised of four large chunks of rock: the Male, the Female, the Child and North Hill. We're parked at the base of the Female which has more paintings and is a bit easier to climb than the others."

"I'm so excited to see some of the rock art?" said Meg, and Martin frowned.

He said, "I'm very hesitant to call these rock 'art' panels for the reason that they were not originally created as pieces of art, but rather for ceremonial and shamanic purposes."

Meg nodded awkwardly, and Adam said, "I'm not climbing anything today."

The others grunted agreement.

Adam shuffled over to Polly, climbed in the back, and returned with a small cooler full of beer. He handed one to Meg and then distributed the rest.

Geoff soon came over from the truck and joined them. He looked a bit crazy: his face was smeared with dust and sweat, and his eyes bulged and darted around. Wiping his forehead, he looked at his passengers and said, "Now that we've come all the way here, I'll kill anyone who doesn't walk around and look at the bloody paintings."

Adam tossed him a cold beer and Geoff glared a rough thank you at him.

"We're gonna need two days here," said Martin and Geoff shot him an angry glance, too, but then took a swig of the beer and softened, realizing a day of rest wasn't such a bad thing.

"Take your time," he said. "I might look around as well—because I promise you I'm never coming back here again."

*

At the Chula Vista campground in California, Dee was up early making coffee.

"Okay," she said when she had a cup ready, "let's try that again."

They drove to US customs, were waved through this time without the guard even stepping inside, and continued toward Mexican customs. This time they stayed in the right lane until they saw it, and exited early.

After parking their vehicle, they discovered they were the only tourists in the office. A man stamped their passports and charged them fifty dollars.

They got back on the highway, glanced at the crazy round-a-bout from above, and followed Route 1 for sixty miles until they hit Ensenada.

"We should fill up," said Louis. "I don't know how many gas stations we'll see when the highway turns inland, away from the coast."

Dee pulled into a gas station.

Louis walked around to the pump, where an attendant was already placing the nozzle in their gas tank. The man stood there awkwardly for a minute, then pulled out the nozzle and hung it up.

He then pointed at the gas dispenser where the counter read 50.00. The man said, "Fifty dollar, *por favor.*"

Louis figured the meter counted pesos, not dollars, and the guy couldn't have put more than an ounce of gas into the tank.

He leaned forward and stared at the man. "Don't even start with me. I know you didn't put anything in the tank yet."

The man shrugged, indicating he didn't speak English, then pointed at the meter. "Fifty dollars, *por favor.*"

Louis looked into the guy's eyes.

He said, "Stop screwing around. Reset the meter and start pumping." Louis had once driven all the way through Central America to Panama, and knew these sleazy tricks.

The man eyed Louis for a moment, then smiled like he'd just been playing a practical joke, and reset the meter.

Louis took the nozzle and filled the tank himself.

"You just back off," he said. "I'll pay when I'm done."

He pointed at the meter. "And don't even think of telling me that meter is in dollars."

They followed the coast south for the next few hours. Dee scanned the coastline for a nice beach, but it all looked too developed.

Just before the town of El Rosario she spotted a small campground by the water and they registered there for the night. The sun was setting, and after parking the Grasshopper they all walked to the beach. The tide was out, and the sand reflected a golden sunset. But there was a chill in the air and Louis ran back for a blanket.

A vendor passed and sold them five pounds of crab claws for five dollars. Dee uncorked a bottle of red wine from a case which she had bought at Trader Joe's before leaving Arizona.

Pookey Bear helped cook the crab claws on the propane stove, outside because Dee didn't want to stink up the RV. They sat at the table inside eating the crab, dunking it in butter, as the sunset faded from the wide front windows.

"If only it was a little warmer," said Dee. "This might have been our beach. We gotta keep moving south."

*

It took a while for the overlanders and Louis and Dee to muster enough energy to unload the camping gear from the back of the truck. But sunset was only an hour off and they didn't want to have to set up camp in the dark.

When the tents were up and the matts and sleeping bags rolled out, Louis and Dee washed their legs and feet with the water of one canteen, then put on their jeans and boots.

258

"What are you doing?" asked Nora.

Louis said, "Mosquitos are attracted to the smell of sweat and the feet and ankles are their first target."

Geoff was already snoring in a hammock he'd strung between a tree and Polly. He was planning on sleeping in the cab and had no intention of showing his face until dinner.

Louis was moving in slow motion, still foggy from the heat. He sat down for a minute to gather his strength when Nora called over to him.

"You should camp under the stars," she said, "like we do."

Louis shook his head. He liked his own tent—and some privacy.

One time in Kenya his guide had wanted him to use the camp tents, instead of his own. He had declined when he noticed numerous holes in the canvas, and around two in the morning his friends in the other tent were screaming, because army ants were attacking them. The ants had crawled into the camp tents—there were three of them with two in each—and at the same time bitten all six people.

A sturdy little man, mostly naked, came around just before dark. His skin had a yellowish color, and his gentle features seemed more Asian than African.

He wore two pieces of hide; one had been trimmed into shorts, the other was draped over his shoulders like a cape. Maybe impala, or some other antelope, Louis had thought.

Martin tried a Khoisan phrase from his guidebook and said, "Wueyho." The man smiled at the greeting, and then replied with a series of clicks that left Martin baffled.

They both laughed, and then the man said, "Maybe English is better. I am the site caretaker—do you need anything?"

Martin looked at the others who were relaxing in the cool night air. "I think we're okay," he said.

Nora was laying on her cot, and the little man said to her, "Be careful—there are leopards here."

She smiled. "We've been camping all over Africa—I'm not afraid of animals."

He smiled and moved on.

Louis knew that the modern San were irregularly settled with some cattle and crops, but many still lived a nomadic life, hunting game with bows and poison arrows, and gathering edible plants, like berries, melons and nuts. They even ate insects.

Watching the little man walk away, he was impressed by his toughness. Louis didn't know if he could survive on getting his water from plant roots and desert melons, even if one of the San showed him how. Many still lived in huts built from branches and thatched with long grass.

That night they all lay out in the open, staring up at the star-studded heavens, hundreds of miles from any city lights. Meg and Martin had each set up small one-man tents; the others lay on four cots side by side.

Louis and Dee stretched out on a reed mat in front of their tent, and Martin sat a few feet away on a roll mat.

"So Martin," asked Dee, "what's so special about the rock art here?"

Martin sighed, and Meg said, "Here we go again."

Martin shrugged. "This matter has bedeviled me for many years and recently I have begun simply denoting the places as sites with rock paintings and/or rock etchings. Personally, I believe that calling the paintings and etchings 'rock art' preconditions the viewer to pigeon hole them as such, which disallows a fuller, and probably more accurate, understanding of them."

Meg stared at Dee. "See what you did."

Martin chuckled. "All that aside, I can easily tell you why this place is so special: It's been inhabited for almost thirty-five thousand years, and the thousands of rock paintings here record this long history."

"Well, I can see why modern humans should preserve and study it," said Dee, "but why was it special to the San?"

He nodded. "According to the San, the gods lowered themselves and their cattle down a rope onto the Female Hill and that's how it all started—in their eyes, this is the place where life began."

Meg sat down on a corner of the mat next to Dee. "I read that North Hill was an argumentative wife of Male Hill who was sent away, "she said.

"You can do that here?" asked Louis with a smirk.

Dee stared him down. "How many other women would follow their guy to a crazy place like this?"

Louis thought for a moment and said, "Not many." He'd traveled for ten years before he met Dee, and not one of his old girlfriends in America had been willing to follow him abroad.

They were up early the next morning, sharing a breakfast of scrambled eggs and toast with the overlanders. A flock of helmeted guinea fowl foraged in the brush around them, and they were making such a racket that it sounded like something much larger.

Nora yawned. "Those birds were at it all night — and I kept thinking it was that leopard the caretaker mentioned. Didn't really sleep well."

Richard was in a great mood. He pointed to the base of the hill and said, "There's a much higher diversity of vegetation here than along that horrible drive we made yesterday: over there are horned cucumbers, and closer to the rocks the acacias have given way to shepherd's tree and blackthorn."

Meg teased him. "But have you found your eagle yet?"

He laughed and held up a finger. "Actually I sighted an eagle nesting up on Male Rock, and I think it might be a Tawny eagle."

After breakfast most of the crew followed Richard to Male Rock to take another look at the eagle. Nora had a headache and decided to lay down. Martin set off by himself to North Hill to see a particular cave. Geoff glanced at a few rock art panels then went back to his hammock.

Louis and Dee ventured off on their own, following a steep path that led right over the top of Mother Hill and down its backside. They were walking stiffly from sore muscles and thorn punctures in their feet, and both had sunburns on their arms, neck and face.

They passed dozens of murals with Bushman paintings. Martin had told them that the oldest paintings were in red, and the white ones were done latter by the Bantu people.

Many of the white paintings depicted men standing with their hands on their hips, and several showed men astride horses. All of the panels had images of rhinos, giraffe, antelope and other animals.

The bush was quiet around them, with only the occasional bird call.

At the pass over Mother Hill a giant grass nest hung suspended from a tree. Weaver birds darted all around them as they passed under it.

"Let's stop here," said Dee, enchanted with the birdsong.

They sat down and tended to their feet, rubbing antiseptic into the sores. "This is about the last place I want to get an infection," Dee said. They let the ointment soak in for a few minutes before they put their shoes back on.

They eventually reached the other side of the hill, and began to follow its base clockwise. When they rounded a corner on the meandering trail they heard the startled snort of an animal, but it was out of sight, and only the clop of hooves on loose stones came back to them.

The rocks and caves that lined the hill looked like they hadn't changed in tens of thousands of years, and it seemed by spiraling around the Mother Hill they'd gone back in time, back far before there were cars, or planes, or computers.

At one cave, they stared at a panel of dancing men, painted in red, with large, erect penises. "Well that's something you don't see every day," said Dee.

By the entrance to the cave a massive baobab tree, at least twenty-five feet wide, reached up toward the sky, which lay cloudless and perfectly blue. Years later they would see that same soothing color in the eyes of their first-born, Pookey Bear.

Dee leaned back against the tree, and motioned for Louis to come closer. They embraced, and she gave him a mischievous grin. Soon they were making love, listening half-heartedly in case someone came along.

"What kind of child do you think we would conceive here?" she asked, after, when they sat in the shade.

He shook his head. "No babies yet or you won't fit into your wedding dress."

In two months they would return home to get married at Pat Pat and Pip's house along the river. Almost three hundred people would attend, and they would celebrate the union until three in the morning.

In his tent that night, Louis dreamt of embracing his wife against the baobab, while painted animals roamed around them.

They broke camp early the next day. Louis had washed his shorts and hung them overnight on a make-shift clothesline. In the cool morning air he retrieved them, and only at last minute saw a scorpion in its folds. "Dodged a bullet there," he said and shook it off outside the tent.

They had all been dreading the long drive out, but as it turned out Polly cruised back easily on top of her own tracks. They didn't get stuck once, and were all cheerful until they reached the bumpy stretch back to the highway.

Nora looked pale as she held the seat in front of her and Louis figured she had spent another sleepless night. When they reached the sun-scorched crossroads where the track met the highway she collapsed on the floor of the truck.

"I'll be okay," she whispered to her husband, Jonathan, but the others were skeptical when they realized she was feverish.

*

From El Rosario they turned the Grasshopper inland, into the *El Vizcaíno Biosphere Reserve*; the largest wildlife refuge in Mexico, covering almost ten thousand square miles.

Their destination was the small town of San Ignacio, still three hundred miles away, but when the highway turned into a slim and winding road after they entered the reserve, they knew they wouldn't get there in one day.

The road became narrower still as they drove on. The RV was nine feet wide, eleven if you counted the mirrors, and the road was barely twenty feet wide with sharp drop-offs of up to two feet in place of a shoulder.

When an eighteen-wheeler approached from the other direction, they gasped: there couldn't possibly be enough room for both of them in the road. Louis pulled the Grasshopper as far to the right as he dared, Dee screamed that they were going to hit the truck charging at them and Louis screamed right back that there was no more space to move over.

In seconds it was over. They could hardly believe they'd made it through this confrontation unscathed. A few minutes later, another truck came into sight, and again louis pulled as far over as he could, white-knuckled, Dee shrieking. Then another one. And another. After only two hours that seemed like an eternity they pulled over and parked for the night.

Dee was rattled and opened a bottle of wine to calm her nerves.

In the morning the desert plants drank up a thick fog that had rolled in before sunrise. It was a magical world out there, and Louis took Pookey Bear for a hike while Dee and Say Say snuggled in bed.

They got back on the road by nine. Dee found some mellow Mexican music on the radio, and Louis had just handed her a coffee when suddenly the road dropped into a deep gully ahead of them.

As they started descending a large truck at the bottom of the hill came into view. It seemed to be broken down. The Grasshopper gained momentum on the steeply dropping road, and Dee turned into the other lane to go around the stranded truck.

Just then another truck appeared at the top of the hill ahead of them, now charging down at them.

"There's not enough time to break!" shouted Dee.

"Keep going! That other truck is coming right at us!"

Dee floored the gas pedal desperately and clenched her teeth.

As they raced past the stranded truck, a large BANG sounded, and Louis half expected the front window to shatter. Dee cut hard to the right and for a moment, the Grasshopper swerved crazily as the truck coming at them blared its horn and shot past.

"Oh my God!" shouted Dee.

At the top of the hill Dee pulled into a bay by the roadside and sat there, trembling, for a few moments. Then they got out to inspect the damage.

They had torn the passenger mirror right off.

Louis looked back down the road and could see it laying in the ditch. He ran back and got it. The glass was cracked, but otherwise it looked fine. Its four attachment bolts were somehow still there. Louis finagled with it for a while and eventually got it mounted on the Grasshopper again.

They continued down the highway in a state of shock, afraid of what might come at them.

Later that day they reached the town of San Ignacio and parked next to a freshwater lagoon. This wasn't the beach they'd been looking for, but it was beautiful and peaceful and relaxing, and they needed just this after the tense drive. They stayed for five days, and at least for a while the clock seemed to stop ticking.

The rest of the world faded from view without television or news. The guiding job in Sedona would wait. The sketchy highway would wait.

Instead they put a good dent in their wine supply and took lots of naps.

On the day they left the lagoon they stopped at a gas station so Louis could check the tire pressure and top off the tank. At the register he picked up a USA Today and read that NASA had lost the Columbia space shuttle. It had disintegrated upon reentering earth's atmosphere, killing all seven astronauts.

*

At first all of Polly's passengers were euphoric about getting on the highway. They enjoyed the breeze as they moved along. Adam, Meg and Dee put up the side flaps and a cool wind blew away the dust that had accumulated over the last few days.

Nora was clearly sick, but she put on a brave face and claimed she'd caught some flu-like bug.

But she still burned with fever, and they decided to stop at the next town, Rundu, and maybe finding a hospital or pharmacy.

Three hours later, however, her fever broke, and the color returned to her face. When they passed through Rundu she seemed fine and joked about how badly she had soaked her clothes with sweat. From Rundu, Geoff was going to drive one hundred and sixty miles to Grootfontein where he would turn off for the Etosha Pan.

Louis and Dee decided to get off Polly there—at Grootfontein—and head directly to Windhoek where Louis had a friend they wanted to look up.

Two hours later—and halfway to Grootfontein—Nora suddenly groaned and spit up a gush of yellow vomit. She then collapsed and began to convulse.

Jonathan dropped beside her, panic-stricken, and Louis and Richard helped him hold her down as she thrashed about. The side flaps were still open, and the wind whipped through, splattering the three men with vomit.

"What's happening to me?" Nora cried out, her eyes wide.

Jonathan soothed her, although his own eyes were filled with terror.

Adam banged on the cab until Geoff pulled over in the shade of an old acacia.

"What the hell is going on back here?" he shouted as he ascended the ladder, but he shut up instantly when he saw her.

"My guess is *Plasmodium Falciparum*," said Martin.

"Cerebral malaria?" asked Geoff. "Fuck!"

Geoff ran a hand through his hair and took a deep breath.

"We're two hours from Grootfontein," he said, turning for the ladder, "but that's the closest town. Try to keep her hydrated—I'm gonna drive like hell."

Suddenly Richard looked out the side of the truck, at the tree they were parked next to, and saw a large black and white bird with an enormous orange beak.

"That's a southern yellow-billed hornbill," he said, smiling.

He realized his comment was out of place when he saw the others staring at him, not the bird.

Nora was momentarily calm. Her hair was matted to her face which was flecked with yellow vomit. She met Richard's eye and gave a weak smile and said, "It really is quite beautiful."

Over the next few hours Nora's fever spiked two more times, each time it seemed to go higher. They rolled down the side flap to keep the wind down, and covered her with a blanket when she got the chills.

They pulled into Grootfontein and Geoff parked the truck across the street from the hospital.

Jonathan, Adam and Richard helped her walk, very weakly, to the entrance.

Geoff approached Louis. "We passed a bus station about two blocks back," he said. "You could walk there, or when we're done here I could drive you to the edge of town—your call."

They were almost three hundred miles from Windhoek, and Louis didn't feel up to hitching.

"We're gonna bus it," he said. "Thanks for the lift."

They said goodbye to Martin and Meg and walked to the bus station. A bus was leaving in forty minutes, and they decided to wash up in the bathroom.

"Think she'll be okay?" asked Dee.

"Should be now that she's at a hospital," said Louis. "But that cerebral malaria is bad stuff."

"Think she caught it at Tsodilo Hills—sleeping in the open?"

Louis shrugged. "Not sure, but I would think she picked it up somewhere in the last few weeks with all that open camping."

Dee shook her head. "I love our tent."

*

The drive from San Ignacio to the town Mulegé was easier. The road was wider, less winding, and they only had eighty miles to cover. They found a nice RV park that seemed filled with expats. The campground host was friendly and offered tips on where to find the best beaches, and what roads to avoid.

They took the double stroller down from the roof to put the girls in and walked through the pleasant, sleepy town. A grocery store offered lots of fresh produce at low prices, and Dee and Louis stocked up.

On the walk back the girls sat between shopping bags. Say Say was almost invisible between the big bags, but both girls soon fell asleep and Dee and Louis walked along slowly, enjoying the quiet moment.

They passed people sitting on shaded benches along the sidewalk, and a few leaned forward to see the girls.

"Que bonita!" said one elderly woman.

Others just smiled and nodded. The town appeared to accept them and slowly the nightmare experience on the highway faded.

*

The bus ride through southern Africa passed like a lazy dream; it was a modern bus with air-conditioning, and after the hot, bumpy passage in the overland truck this felt like they were gliding. They were now in Namibia, which had once been a German colony, and the road system and some of the houses they passed seemed to resemble Germany more than Africa.

After five hours on the bus, they arrived in Windhoek, and then took a taxi to Louis's friend's house. With a fiery red sky behind them, they knocked on his door. Louis had only an address, no telephone number, and hoped desperately the guy still lived there.

A tall, muscular man with short blond hair opened the door and gawked at them for a moment until recognition swept over his face.

"I would have been less surprised if the devil was standing here," he said and embraced Louis.

Louis had met Fritz five years before, in Kenya. At the time Louis had been trying to get a ticket on the overnight train from Mombasa to Nairobi, but all that was available was third class. Fritz had been in line behind him when Louis reluctantly purchased a ticket and walked away.

On the street, Fritz had approached him. "You cannot spend the night in third class—you will have everything stolen. Come with me, you can spend the night on the floor of my first class cabin."

Months later Louis had flown down to South Africa and stayed with Fritz for a few weeks in Pretoria, and their friendship grew.

Now, Fritz led them through his house to a guest house by a garden. He seemed to have done well since they'd last seen each other.

"Why don't you rest," he said, "we can have drinks and a bite to eat in a few hours."

He handed Louis a stack of clean, white towels and said, "And you should wash up—you're as stinky as ever."

Louis grinned. He honestly couldn't remember his last shower.

Dee shut the door to the guest house. Their clothes were so dirty that they stripped down to their underwear to not soil the covers. Their upper thighs, bellies and chests were white and contrasted with the dark red of their forearms and face.

They both sat on the edge of the bed, not sure what to do next. They still felt like they were moving, and since they'd seldom stayed in a room over the last few months, it felt strange to be enclosed.

They had covered over two thousand miles since leaving Malawi, most of it on pothole-ridden dirt roads, and they needed a break. Neither wanted to think about the nine hundred remaining miles they would still have to travel to get to Cape Town, where their flight back to America departed from.

The numerous game parks they had camped in over the last five months would provide fabulous memories down the line, but for now the journey was taking its toll on them.

The lights in the bathroom were very bright, so Dee turned them off and lit a candle instead. They stood awkwardly, looking at each other, noticing the sand clinging to corners and crevices of their skin, cemented in place by sunscreen.

They took a long shower together. Clean water pouring from a shower head, shampoo and conditioner—it all felt like such luxury; they took their time, for once unconcerned that the water might run out. The shampoo truly smelled like a bouquet of flowers.

Louis leaned against the cool, tiled wall with a towel wrapped around his waist. He watched Dee combing her hair, noting the sunburned skin, the pealed patches, and the scratches on her arms and legs. She looked like someone had dragged her through the Kalahari, but she didn't appear defeated; instead she had a glow about her, a radiance that comes from accomplishment.

She'd crossed southern Africa, from Malawi to Namibia, and her eyes said she could do much more. Louis was proud of her, and in love, and while he watched her run the comb through her hair he couldn't help thinking he'd found the perfect match.

He couldn't wait to get home and marry her.

The image of them in that candlelit room is one they often recalled over the years. As if the flickering candle glow captured something the daylight hid. Years later Louis would look at Dee, and still see the young woman that looked back at him that day, neither of them saying anything, just watching each other while they took pride in what they'd accomplished together.

*

Only twenty-five miles south of Mulegé, Dee finally found her perfect beach on the Sea of Conception. I have a photo of her laying in the water with a floppy hat and sunglasses. In her hand is a glass of wine.

They stayed there six days, soaking up the sun and swimming a lot. During the low tide you could walk across a narrow stretch to a couple of islands and Louis and Pookey Bear explored them all.

Dee bought a small inflatable ring that fit snuggly around Say Say and the infant appeared to enjoy herself most of all.

Eventually they had a talk concerning whether they should continue south, or begin heading back to Sedona. Louis—always obsessed with achieving geographical goals—wanted to reach the bottom of the Baja Peninsula, but Dee thought it might be better to head north and slowly make their way back.

They still had a few weeks before they were due back in Sedona for the guiding job, so they made a compromise and pushed on to see what might be around the next bend.

Forty miles south of their perfect beach they saw a sign for the town of Imposible.

"We gotta stop there," said Louis. "I love the idea of getting to a place that's impossible."

But then they came upon another section where the road narrowed with no shoulder. There were no curves or hills, but each vehicle they passed seemed too close.

Suddenly Dee spotted a large eighteen-wheeler coming at them. It was painted flat black and belched exhaust as it approached. There was a dip in the road ahead of them, and when the truck passed through it leaned over the middle of the road and both Dee and Louis thought for sure that they would collide.

At last minute it straightened up and shot past them, but not before knocking off the driver's side mirror.

"Okay, I'm done," said Dee to Louis when he got back from retrieving the mirror. This one was a bit more smashed up, and couldn't be reattached.

When they got back on the highway they were heading north, and Louis was driving. The town of Imposible had truly been impossible to reach.

Scout in dad's hat, Rimrock, Arizona

Chapter Twelve

Rimrock, Arizona
(February 2003)

I could go on all day with stories I've heard about Louis and Dee and the girls crisscrossing North America in the Grasshopper once more, or about their second season in Alaska and the Yukon, but I'm gonna jump ahead.

So rumble down the road with me, if you will, from Skagway to New Hampshire. Cousin Sal and a cat named Gracie, whom they had picked up in Sedona, had joined them for this journey, but now the journey was done and it was time to sell the RV. Unfortunately, this wasn't an opportune time to sell recreational vehicles—over the past year gas prices had risen from a dollar twenty to two dollars forty a gallon, and nobody knew how high they might still climb. So they sold the Grasshopper at a loss, but felt lucky to unload it at all.

Pookey Bear, becoming smarter every day, had taken to quoting her favorite kindergarten teacher, Ms. Beedle: "You get what you get and you don't throw a fit." Louis and Dee tried to heed that advice and accept the loss.

Cousin Sal helped clean up the Vinniman and get it running again.

For the last year it had sat quietly at Pip's house, in the back field by the river, under a tarp — hibernating, Louis said, like the vehicle was a big bear.

Pookey Bear had peeked under the blue plastic and whispered, "I hope you had a good nappy."

Their plan was to drive back to Arizona and pick up in Sedona where they'd left off. They rented a U-Haul trailer and put most of their gear in it, but it was tight quarters in the Vinniman for four people, their belongings, a guinea pig and a cat.

They drove the Vinniman to Arizona, crossing North America for the sixth time in two years.

In the RV, Gracie the cat had lounged like a queen wherever she pleased, but now she rode in a cardboard box, and meowed unhappily from time to time.

They rented a house in Rimrock, about thirty minutes from Sedona; the rent there was far cheaper, and the place had enough bedrooms that Sal could have her own. Within a week they were all working: Louis driving jeeps at A Day in the West and Dee waitressing at a restaurant called Savannah's. Sal also got a job at the jeep company, as a receptionist at the departure desk.

And I can see them there in their little rental home. Pookey Bear was four, and Say Say two. The house had a covered porch with a cement floor and Pookey Bear circled it for hours on a tricycle that had also made the journey in the trailer. In the shade of the porch Say Say played dolls with Lotion, dressing the little guinea pig like a princess in pink fabric.

They were happy when they arrived, even if they were broke again; the season in Alaska had been profitable, but after selling the RV they were left with a ten-thousand-dollar debt on a vehicle they no longer owned.

They managed to pull off Christmas that year with a total budget of seventy dollars, which bought some lights, stocking stuffers, and even a few presents. For a Christmas tree, they used a tumbleweed that had got stuck underneath the Vinniman on I-17. They decorated it with one string of lights and a few homemade ornaments, and hung it from the ceiling by a tack and some string.

274

The house in Rimrock occupied a very unique location on a small mesa that overlooked a field. Beaver Creek flowed by the far end of the field, about a quarter mile away; a line of massive cottonwoods marked the water's edge and after a rainstorm you could hear the water gurgling past.

One morning Louis sat on the mesa's edge. The sun was peeking over the distant rim of the Verde Valley, and it majestically washed the tops of the other mesas around them in light. Birds sang everywhere, chirping so loudly that he could hear them by the creek.

Golden rays lit up the uppermost branches of an ancient sycamore near the water. Large herons perched in its branches, one stretched and flapped its wings in the early sunlight.

For the first time in his life, Louis felt ancient.

He told me that when he sat on that limestone rim he was overcome by a sensation that he'd been sitting there all his life. It was like a buried memory that suddenly surfaced, he said, and the longer he sat there, the clearer it became.

I'm not exactly sure what he was talking about, but I think he sensed the lives of the ones who had lived there before, thousands of years ago.

Along Beaver Creek, about a mile upstream, was an Indian ruin called Montezuma's Well, and it was evident that this settlement had extended to the mesa he now sat on, and the field below. The limestone around him was marked by numerous depressions where these ancient people had ground their corn, and the modern owner of the property had framed collections of arrowheads and pottery shards which she had found here.

Just like when he'd learned about Heman Chase, or Lucy Crehore, Louis now read whatever he could about the pre-Columbian inhabitants of the Verde Valley, mainly the Sinagua whose lifestyle captivated him. He read that they traded with the Anasazi to the north, and the Hohokam to the south. They grew corn, beans, and squash, and bartered cotton and pottery with people as far away as Mexico and the Pacific Coast.

Everywhere he hiked he discovered evidence of past cultures: half-buried foundations, pottery fragments, etchings and paintings on cliffsides and in hidden canyons—even corn cob husks on the dirt floors near the ruins of these dwellings. He searched the grounds around their house and once found half of a metate, a rock bowl that had been used to grind corn, as well as some reddish-brown pottery shards with a black polish on the concave side.

The land here fascinated him as much as the ancient Sinaguans. The rock layer that he sat on was hundreds of millions of years old—not twelve thousand like the granite in New Hampshire that had been left behind by glaciers—and whenever he hiked he felt transported back in time.

His young hippie friend Coyote was also interested in the long-ago inhabitants of the area. Louis and Coyote had met at the Hawkeye RV Park in Sedona when Louis and Dee had stopped there with the Grasshopper before their Mexico trip. Now, Louis had again bumped into him in Sedona, and when he explained where he lived Coyote had said he wanted to "show him something special".

The twinkle in Coyote's eyes hinted that what he planned wasn't the kind of thing one did every day. "You just wait and see," he said.

Pookey Bear came out and handed Louis a coffee. She took some marbles from her pocked and placed them in one of the old depressions created by the Sinagua, rolling them from one to another in a game only she knew.

Dee's waitressing job came with hours that extended late into the night, and Louis worked days, so they barely saw each other. She was up now—making coffee—because she knew he would leave for work soon. Sal babysat the girls when she was around, but on this day she was catching a ride into town with Louis because she had a shift, too.

Louis loved the jeep guiding job as much as he had loved the tours in Alaska. Not only was there the fun of driving a jeep full of people across some very rugged trails, but he was also tasked with offering his passengers insights into the geology, the plants, the animals, and the history of Sedona's high desert; and he could talk about it all day long.

Tours departed throughout the day, and most guides enjoyed the ones at sunset most. But Louis preferred the early tours because there was more game to see. When he was out there before the sun was too high, he often encountered coyotes and bobcats, mule deer and javalinas, black bears, and a few times even a mountain lion.

The company had a fleet of ten modified CJ-7 and Rubicon Jeeps to explore the canyons and rock formations surrounding Sedona. Some trails were technically challenging, climbing up and over the rocks, and Louis loved the thrill of this and he was happy that he wasn't using his own vehicle.

Other tours offered fantastic photographic opportunities, ascending 2500 feet above Sedona to the rim of the Colorado Plateau, or exploring the western canyons during sunset when the desert was awash in reds and oranges.

The guides dressed as cowboys—or Indians if they were Native, which some were. Louis's New Hampshire accent might have sounded odd coming from under his cowboy hat, but his enthusiasm made up for it.

Dee came out of the house with Say Say on her hip and joined him. The little girl was wearing Louis's cowboy hat, and it wobbled on her head as she looked up at him and beamed.

"I guess I should be going," said Louis, reluctantly.

He took the hat from his youngest and stuck it on his head.

From inside the house Sal yelled, "I'll be right out!"

Louis kissed Dee and the girls goodbye, and then hopped in the Vinniman and turned the ignition.

Twelve hours later he was back at the same spot, sitting next to Coyote and sipping a couple of Heinekens with him. To the east, a pale full moon was rising over the cottonwoods. Coyote had been adamant about bringing flashlights, which Louis found strange because the night was awash in moonlight.

"You been to the Well yet?" asked Coyote, his stringy blond hair shining under the moon's glow. He wore a rawhide vest over his bare chest, and around his neck hung several leather necklaces, each with a pendant or charm.

Louis shook his head. He'd read about the Montezuma Well National Monument, a flooded sinkhole that had formed long ago when a limestone cavern had collapsed. There were ruins there, too. Over one million gallons of water rose up into the sinkhole from below each day, creating a unique oasis for both humans and wildlife.

"It seems like a neat place," said Louis. "I just haven't had time to get there—by the time I get back from work the gates are locked."

Coyote's smile had a mischievous edge to it as he pointed to the huge cottonwood at the end of the field. "See that big tree down there?" he asked. "Ever notice all the water by its base?"

Louis nodded. "There's a small canal that empties out there."

Coyote stood. "That water comes from Montezuma's Well, and the Sinagua dug that canal almost a thousand years ago."

He caught Louis's eye and shook his head. "A thousand fuckin' years ago, I still can't wrap my head around that—and it still flows."

He gestured at the field again with his forehead. "See how the ancients shaped the land? The canal empties on the high end of the field, right near that tree, and then the water fans out over the field before draining into Beaver Creek."

Louis stood also and looked down at the field. After a moment he asked, "Why is it named after Montezuma?"

Coyote scoffed. "The Forest Service says it was mistakenly attributed to the Aztecs, but they're just tryin' to mislead us. People in the know say that Montezuma II, the ninth Aztec emperor, sent a treasure north, right before he was captured by Cortez, and many think it's hidden around here—maybe in the Well, or in the caves underneath it."

Coyote grabbed his daypack and shouldered it. Louis snatched up his own which contained a canteen of water, a flashlight, a bandana and a power bar.

"Come on," said Coyote, "we're burnin' moonlight."

Louis followed him off the small mesa, down to the old cottonwood. Coyote walked right past the tree, and began following the canal of water upstream.

It flowed strongly, and the gurgle was reassuring as they crept alongside it, ducking under low branches. The moonlight lit their way; no need for flashlights, just as Louis had thought.

At first they passed a few houses, but eventually the land grew wilder and traces of modern civilization faded away.

Coyote's eyes appeared to glow in the dark. He was loping ahead excitedly. You could tell he loved prowling around in places where he wasn't supposed to be.

"People have lived in the Verde Valley for thousands of years," he said over his shoulder, "but those early guys were just scavengers. Sure, they harvested agave, manzanita, and scrub oak—but they didn't build anything."

Louis said, "And then came the Sinagua, right?"

Coyote nodded. "Yeah, the Sinaguans were cool—and they lived by the Well for over four hundred years. They kept dogs and parrots as pets, and wild turkeys as a food source."

Coyote told Louis how the Sinagua used Yucca roots to make soap, how they wove strands of bear grass together so tightly that their baskets could hold water. He gestured at a cluster of snakeweed and told Louis how this was used to make a poultice against rattlesnake bites.

Then he pointed at a prickly pear cactus and said, "They harvested the fruit from those for flavoring, and you can eat the whole pad if you burn off the needles."

"How's it taste?" asked Louis.

He shrugged. "Kind of like a soggy French fry—but it'll keep you alive."

They had to climb a low fence to enter the National Monument. Here Coyote veered to the left, away from the canal and across a field of mesquite, creosote and catclaw acacia. They stepped carefully, trying not to cut their legs on the catclaw, an aptly named thorny bush.

"How much trouble will we be in if we get caught?" asked Louis.

Coyote grinned. "We're not gonna get caught, so don't sweat it—I come here all the time."

Several other canals appeared, each angling down, away from the Well. These canals were wider, and their walls were encrusted with lime that had built up over the years.

Soon they came upon a paved pathway, and they followed the slanted trail up, to the rim of the Well where they were buffeted by an erratic wind.   Along the trail and near the rim stood ancient foundations of cliff dwellings. They stopped on the top and stared down at a pond of black water, about a hundred feet below them.

The perfectly round sinkhole was about four hundred feet in diameter. Down below they could see the dark, still water that seemed to resist reflecting the bloated moon which now rose high above them.

Along the upper walls of the Well other dwellings were tucked into caves behind manmade walls. The walls had small rectangular doors.

"Ever been inside one of those?" asked Louis.

Coyote nodded seriously. "I've been in all of them."

"Ever find anything interesting?"

The young man glared at Louis. "I would never take anything, or even search for stuff in there. I just sit there and commune with the elders."

"Really?" asked Louis.

"Look," said Coyote and raised his hands up defensively, "when I go into one of those ruins I don't touch anything. I even bring a small branch with me so I can erase my footprints."

Coyote lifted a small leather pouch by his side. "And this is full of pollen. When I leave I sprinkle some where I was crouched."

"And what does that do?"

Coyote scratched his head. "I don't know—but it seems like something an Indian would do. They use pollen in a lot of their ceremonies."

Louis read from a plaque which stated that the water had a high concentration of arsenic and carbon monoxide, and because of that there were no fish in the Well, only water scorpions and leeches.

"Doesn't sound like there's a lot of life in the water," said Louis.

"I wouldn't think so," mumbled Coyote, his expression suddenly downcast.

He picked up a rock and threw it deep into the pond. The distant splash echoed off the walls, and the moonlight rolled with the ripples as they expanded outward.

He looked at Louis. "The Yavapai and Apache lived in this area after the Sinagua left, and they have a creation myth that begins in that black water down there."

He took a breath and Louis waited, sensing there was something gloomy coming up.

"According to the legend, their ancestors used to live in the bottom of the Well—it was very deep then, and dry. And one day, one of them did something that offended the gods and one of the gods decided to drown them all."

"All of them? The entire tribe?" asked Louis. "That's definitely an old-school god."

"Yup," said Coyote while he pulled out a joint and put a flame to it. He had a big hit, then offered it to Louis.

"I'm all set," Louis said, already nervous about sneaking into the place.

Coyote exhaled and continued. "Anyway, while everyone was treading water, tryin' not to drown, they decided that at least one of 'em should survive—so they took a young girl, sealed her in a hollow log with pitch, and she eventually floated to safety."

"That's pretty ominous," said Louis.

Coyote hit his joint one more time before putting it out and stowing it in his backpack. "It might be beautiful here, but this is a dark place."

He stood and shouldered his backpack. "Come on," he said, "we're not done yet."

A cement stairway led down into the well, skirting the right wall. Large boulders sat along the trail and Louis wondered if they'd tumbled down recently, or in antiquity. Various plaques indicated trees and bushes like black walnut, hackberry and one-seed Juniper, whose seeds the various tribes had harvested.

It was quieter down in the well, all traces of wind had died.

On the far wall a cluster of ruins glowed by the base of the cliff.

Signs along the path said to stay on the trail and keep out of the ruins. Moonlight passing through the trees above left skeletal shadows.

The ruin that sat furthest back had a mortared, stone doorway in its front wall, and beyond that lay only darkness.

They paused there and Coyote took out his flashlight.

Louis followed suit, not sure where his friend was about to lead him. The night was still, but somewhere in the darkness Louis thought he could make out whispering.

He peered into the foreboding doorway and asked, "What do you think eventually happened to the Sinagua?" Louis had read theories that they had migrated north to the Hopi Mesas to join other ancestral Puebloan cultures. That made sense, the Hopi name for their legendary home was *Palatkwapi* "Red House". But sitting in the shadow of a ruin by the black water, he sensed the reason for their exodus was a sinister one.

Coyote crouched next to him and said, "Archaeologists call it the Great Abandonment, and it's one huge friggin' mystery. At the peak of their civilization there were, like, five thousand Sinagua living in the area. And they were happy, man. This place had everything — so why leave?"

Coyote took a few steps forward, into the ruin, and turned on his flashlight.

Louis flipped his on too and followed.

"What do you think?" he asked.

Coyote stopped and twisted around. He said, "I think the Sinagua holy men saw the coming of the white man and knew it was time to go — they could see the future, you know. Heck, not long after the Sinaguans left, the Spanish came through the area."

Louis thought about the Yavapai and Apache, who he'd been told had showed up before then. But he didn't say anything.

Beyond the mud-brick doorway, a cave extended into the darkness. The ceiling was low, less than four feet, and ahead of them in the dark a sign appeared in the beam of Coyote's flashlight. It read:

"Do not enter. Poisonous gas."

"Whoa," said Louis. "What's up with that?"

"Oh," answered Coyote, "the Forest Service put that there to scare people away — it's nothin'. There's probably some carbon monoxide in here, but I've been all through these caves and it never killed me."

"Where's the gas come from?" asked Louis.

Coyote began moving forward again, crouching low.

"It's Montezuma's treasure, man, I think it's here—and over the years it's given off fumes—like those Egyptian tombs."

He looked back toward the entrance and said, "If I could ever get into the water with some scuba gear I know I could find it. I'm pretty sure it's at the bottom of the Well."

He stopped and grinned. "That is, if it's not hidden in this cave."

"I thought you didn't disturb the ruins," said Louis.

Coyote shrugged. "Oh, I wouldn't dig in the dwellings, but in the cave itself, or under the water in the Well—that's fair game."

Trailing a few feet behind, Louis followed Coyote deeper into the cave, feeling he shouldn't be there for multiple reasons. Within a minute they were beyond the ruin and in the cave, bent forward to avoid the low ceiling.

Louis pulled his t-shirt up over his mouth and nose, not confident of Coyote's disclaimers. He could feel his heart pounding, and he feared this might be an effect of the gas or fumes or whatever might be present here.

They paused in a low chamber where water pooled on the floor in several puddles. It dripped from dark patches in the ceiling into the puddles with a "plop" that echoed through the confined quarters.

They squatted low to collect their breath, and Louis asked, "So what happened to the young girl that was sealed in the log?"

"Her name was Kamalapukwia," said Coyote," and according to the creation myth, she floated for days before the log settled just west of Sedona. There, she stumbled upon a hidden canyon with a cave in the back—the cave where the water always drips—and made it her home."

Louis glanced around them at the cave they were in, thinking how aptly it fit the description of the hidden cave. The ceiling was barely three feet high here. The place seemed peaceful and scary at the same time.

Coyote nodded ahead. "It gets lower, but we can keep goin'."

Louis shook his head. "I'm gonna stay here and wait," he said.

"I won't be long," said Coyote.

Louis put a hand on his elbow and asked, "And what happened to Kamalapukwia? Did she live alone in the cave in Sedona?"

Coyote's eyes glimmered in the low light.

"For a while," he said. "Eventually she got lonely and made her way to Mingus Mountain. She saw the sun for the first time there, and it scared her, and she ran all the way back to the cave. When she got there, she lay down and a drop of water fell on her. That's how she became pregnant with the first Apache—a daughter—and after that she wasn't alone. Isn't that awesome?"

With that Coyote scurried off, on all fours like a crab. Louis could see the ceiling dropping even more and was surprised when his friend disappeared around a corner and Coyote's flashlight was suddenly extinguished.

Still nervous about the gas, Louis reached into his pack, took out his bandana, soaked it with water and held it in front of his mouth. He didn't know if this would do any good, but it made him feel calmer.

He could still hear him scrambling around for a little while, but soon the only sound was that of the water dripping.

Louis sat by himself in the chamber. It was suddenly painfully quiet. He held up his flashlight to look around, but the light began to flicker. He knew he'd put in fresh batteries.

He pointed the light above his head. The beam caught a red handprint on the ceiling. Again the light flickered. Then, a dark shadow seemed to appear in front of him, but as he lowered the flashlight the beam died.

Louis sat in the dark, breathing heavily. Was there someone in here with him? His heart raced. Again he had to think of the warning of poison gas.

He thought of the red handprint he'd seen.

He banged the light against his side and tried the switch again.

Nothing. He peered into the darkness.

He couldn't see a thing. But then his eyes began to play tricks on him, and again he thought he could make out a shape moving toward him.

He desperately banged his flashlight again.

There was no sound other than dripping water, but suddenly he felt clearly that he was not alone. Part of him wanted to just start scrambling toward the exit, feeling his way out, but he knew he'd just hurt himself.

Instead he just closed his eyes and tried to control his breathing.

Had he really seen something—or someone—moving towards him? And if he concentrated on it long enough, didn't the dark shape begin to resemble a young woman?

He wet the bandana again and tied it in place in front of his mouth and nose.

The darkness closed in on him. Just when he felt he could take it no more he heard Coyote scrambling toward him, and a moment later his light came into view.

The young man grinned after crab-crawling up to Louis, and then Louis followed him out of the cave.

On the rim of the well they stopped and once again stared down at the dark water. Louis wanted to ask more questions, but he knew Coyote didn't have any more answers than he did. There might be some clue hidden in that dark cave, but he was too scared to return.

Under the soft glow of the moon they made their way back to Louis' house.

Sedona, Arizona

Chapter Thirteen

Sedona, Arizona
(July 2004)

Under the harsh glow of a spotlight, a guide was spraying down his dust-covered jeep while another stood nearby, waiting for the hose. Louis approached and noticed both men were quiet while they listened to shouting coming from the guide shack — an old fifth-wheel that was permanently parked about twenty feet away.

Moths and a few large beetles buzzed around the light.

It must have been on a timer because suddenly it turned off.

The overhead night sky glittered with stars, and in the sudden, comforting darkness the heavens appeared to expand.

A few miles away, Thunder Mountain lay silhouetted by a reddish-purple sky. The night was hot and dry and Louis wished the late afternoon clouds had brought rain.

One of the guides took two steps to the edge of the wash bay, reached up, and turned a knob on the pole on which the light was mounted.

Instantly the wash bay was flooded with a bright pool of light.

The side door of the trailer burst open and Jimmy stepped out, shaking his head. Louis had first met him looking for a job in Sedona a little over a year ago. Jimmy was a tall, silver-haired Lakota Sioux; in his younger days he'd been a rodeo bull rider, and he still wore the chaps and belt buckle to prove it.

Jimmy called over his shoulder. "You get caught taking another jeep out at night and you're done — tighten that shit up, Perky."

A guy in his forties with a handlebar moustache was now following him out the door. In his hand he held a dirty cowboy hat, and he raised it up while he gestured defensively with his other hand.

"Nobody saw us, Jimmy" said Perky.

Right on Perky's heels was a tall blonde in skin-tight jeans and a western button-up shirt. This was Miss Lynn, who was sharing the guide manager position with Jimmy.

In a stern voice she whispered, "For Christ's sake, you should know better. If you had got caught, we would have lost our permit."

A few more jeeps pulled into the lot and lined up behind the two jeeps already in the wash bay. Jimmy walked up behind a driver named Custer who was wiping down his vehicle with a towel. Custer claimed to be descended from General George Custer's brother, who — according to Custer — died right next to him, but was more respected.

"You missed a spot," said Jimmy and bumped against the man.

Custer grinned. "You wanna to fight about it?"

Louis loved it when Jimmy and Custer teased each other. He always thought this was the closest he would get to a real cowboy–and-Indian-scuffle; here were two men whose ancestors had fought at the infamous Battle of Little Big Horn.

A hundred years ago they would have tried to kill each other, but today, instead, they were driving jeep tours in Sedona.

Jimmy grabbed a beer from a fridge and handed it to Custer. "Not today, Yellow Hair. The guide meeting's gonna start in ten minutes so get that jeep outta-here so somebody else can wash theirs."

A lot of the guides had a connection to famous people in the past — or at least claimed to. You never knew where the facts ended and the story began. Louis had met one driver whose ancestry supposedly included Pat Garrett, the guy who shot Billy the Kid; and another driver, nicknamed "D Square" because of his initials, asserted to be related to Jefferson Davis, the President of the Confederate States during the Civil War.

D Square was sitting in a plastic chair on the edge of the wash bay, drinking beer, waiting for the meeting to start. He'd been living at Hawkeye RV Park when Louis had first showed up in Sedona, and now he nodded a hello.

Custer maneuvered his jeep out of the way, and Brad pulled his in. Brad had moved down here from Minnesota to drive jeep tours and was having a blast. Unlike the other dusty jeeps, his was covered in dried mud. It was everywhere: the tires were thick with it, the back end was caked over, and the windshield lay smeared where Brad had tried to use the wipers.

When Brad hit the jeep with the hose, mud dropped off it in large clumps.

Five of the senior guides—Daniel, George, Rusty, Mario and Harold—had arrived, and now sat in plastic chairs, watching Brad clean his jeep. The older guides were wary of enthusiastic new drivers because sometimes the greenhorns broke the jeeps, or didn't clean them up right after they got them all dirty.

"Looks like Brad found a mud puddle," mumbled Harold.

Harold was in his seventies. He'd been a mechanic and could often diagnose a problem by just listening to—or glancing at—a jeep. He caught Jimmy's eye and nodded at the front end of Brad's jeep.

"You better make sure he didn't break that left shock. The jeep seems to be leaning."

Jimmy gave it a quick look. "It's fine. Get this thing out of here—dry it off over there. Make room for Jerry and Terry."

Brad's jeep still had some dirt on it, as Mario noticed. Mario was Apache with a wicked sense of humor and seemed to only show up at guide meetings to give the managers a hard time.

"Oh, sure," he shouted, "give the white guy a break. If that had been my jeep you'd have me spend half the night cleaning it."

Miss Lynn passed him and in a raspy voice, said, "Give it a rest," and he saluted her and said, "Yes, ma'am." Custer had parked his jeep, and now returned to grab a plastic chair. When he passed Mario, the Apache stuck out his tongue and hissed, "Indian killer."

Custer grinned, took a swig off his beer and sat down.

George eyed the still-dirty jeep as it pulled away. He was half-Cherokee and half-Sicilian and you didn't want to get him mad.

He yelled, "I better not get stuck with a dirty jeep in the morning!" From the darkness Brad shouted back, "It'll be fine when I'm done!"

George had served in Vietnam. They called him Buzzard for his nearly bald head, and he was as tough as a buzzard, too. The year before he'd had some shrapnel removed from his back and he often rubbed the spot saying, "That damn thing bothered me for almost forty years."

Daniel, sitting next to George, rolled his eyes.

He said, "We'll see how well Brad can clean a jeep in the dark."

Daniel had also been to Vietnam, but where Buzzard was fiery, Daniel was mellow, and Louis just couldn't picture him as a soldier.

A half-dozen more guides showed up. In the front were Cush and Matt, the two wildlife experts. They left every fall to guide hunting trips, and returned in time for the spring rush, which always started a big kerfuffle over seniority. The senior guides got to pick their schedule first, and some of them thought the part-time guides should start fresh each year. Louis had gone through a similar battle when he'd returned from Alaska.

Cush was descended from some of Sedona's first settlers. His mother's family were Purtymans, and through marriage they could claim Bear Howard—one of the first Anglos to homestead in Oak Creek Canyon—as an ancestor.

There were also three Germans: Nina, Chris and Christian. Shortly after graduating high school, Christian had moved to Arizona from Berlin. He'd been friends with Chris and Nina since kindergarten, and eventually he talked them into joining him. They now called the Southwest home.

Nina smiled at Louis and said, "Great sunset, eh?"

Nina was a journalist and drove tours a few days a week for fun. She was a great guide, and people raved about her tours. She was also an editor, and had helped a local author develop several novels.

And then there was Doc. Doc looked like he had stepped straight out of the 1880s. He wore a black vest over a white, billowy shirt, and a top hat. In between tours, he entertained tourist by cracking his whip. He'd once been a big deal down in Tucson at a well-known western show called *Rawhide*.

Jimmy stepped into the middle of the wash bay and tried to get everyone's attention, but there were now close to twenty people standing around, all talking at once, and nobody paid him any mind.

Doc stepped into the middle of the crowd and began circling his whip. He wasn't as accurate as he'd once been, and everyone quickly stepped out of range just as he cracked it.

"Let's get this show moving!" he hollered hoarsely.

Miss Lynn stepped into the middle of the circle.

"Okay everyone! I need you all to do a better job at filling out your time sheets—I can barely read them. Really, one of you used a crayon."

A few guides grumbled, and Jimmy stepped forward.

"Listen up!" he shouted, "the reason we called this meeting is because the monsoon is about to hit us, and we need everyone to be alert out there. It's been baking hot, there's been no rain for months, and when the first rains do come they'll bring flash floods."

"Or spark fires where lightning strikes," added Miss Lynn.

"So be smart out there," continued Jimmy. "Keep your radios on, and watch the weather."

"Also, drink plenty of water and use those vitamin C packets!" said Miss Lynn. "Stay hydrated."

Suddenly the lights went out again.

Before the timer was reset a crazy cacophony of coyote howls came at them from the flanks of Airport Mesa, a quarter mile behind them.

The lights came back on, but everyone paused for a moment longer, listening until the coyotes quieted down.

Later, when the group was dispersing, Rusty noticed all the empty beer cans lying around. Rusty was in his late sixties and had come down from Alaska; he had a well-trimmed white beard, a spotless cowboy hat, and a deep, baritone voice that seemed to rumble right through you.

He shouted, "Hey, clean up your goddam beer cans so management don't see 'em—were you guys raised in a barn?" and a few of the newer guides scurried around to pick them up.

Louis and Dee no longer lived in Rimrock by Montezuma Well. They had moved to West Sedona, to a small, three-bedroom house on View Drive. Its owner was a builder and just about everything in the place had been salvaged from one of his jobs. The garage was the owner's storage room and was off limits; he was in and out of it every few days, but the rent was cheap, so they signed a year lease. The house had a little front lawn which Dee loved, and it was centrally located; not too far from the schools or work.

Cousin Sal had returned to Alaska so it was just the four of them again, plus Gracie the cat and Lotion the guinea pig.

Dee still waitressed at Savannah's but she was in the process of re-activating her national massage license and getting the Arizona state certification. The girls were checked into a daycare and their lives had taken on a stable routine.

They had moved into the house on Pookey Bear's fifth birthday and before they had even finished unloading the Vinniman she'd climbed every tree in the yard and met all the neighbors.

Next door lived a small girl named Annabelle, and Pookey Bear and her became instant friends. There was a break in the fence between the two houses where two slats had fallen away, and the girls could just barely squeeze through it to see each other.

The house across the street was the home of a screenwriter named Mark; Pookey Bear nicknamed him Question Mark and he in turn called her Tavy-Two-Tone, playing on a shortened version of her first name.

Mark was a colorful character, but a little dark sometimes. He had graduated from Grinnell College with BA in English, had taught English in Korea, and had been a radio personality on a popular station in Kansas.

He'd also spent time in Alaska some years back and right away Louis and Mark hit it off. They traded stories about the great north while playing video games: Mark was addicted to HALO—and pretty lethal at it.

Louis pulled in the driveway, parked the Vinniman, and walked into his house. He wore cowboy boots, jeans, and a heavy duster and was moving stiffly. He'd driven six tours that day, logging about eight hours in a jeep on dirt roads and four-by-four trails.

When he entered the living room, Pookey Bear ran up and gently pushed him onto the couch so she could take off his boots. She did this every night, wrestling with the boots until she fell backwards with them.

"Thanks Tavy," said Louis and piled his boots, hat and a duster by the door. At five, the young girl was now embarrassed by her old nickname.

"It looks like I'll be busy tomorrow so I'll be off pretty early in the morning," he said.

"Can you bring the jeep home and take us for a ride?" asked Tavy. Louis smiled. "I will as soon as we have a slow day."

The next morning Louis pulled into the Uptown departures office with his jeep. Jimmy was standing in the parking lot talking to two guides: Rhoda and Dave.

Dave was also from back East, from Cape Cod, but he looked like he'd been born in the west. He wore a thick mustache and a leather vest, and spoke with a relaxed air.

Rhoda had once worked as a cook at the old Bradshaw Ranch, but now drove tours. She had lived in Hawaii for much of her life and talked of returning there from time to time.

Louis parked his jeep and waved to the guides as he stepped inside the office to see what tours he had lined up. A rotation system dictated the order in which the tours were assigned, but it all could change if a new tour was booked, or if one of the guides passed a tour on to the next guide on the board.

July was a busy month and behind the counter three women scurried around answering calls, printing out receipts, and entering information into the computer system. The first to notice him was Gina.

"Hey Louis," she said and picked up a ringing phone. "Give me a minute."

The other two women, Jamie and Amber, didn't even look up. But Jamie said, "Hope you're rested — looks like you'll be busy today."

From the back room Lauren called out, "Louis! Get back here and drink a couple vitamin C packets! It's gonna be over a hundred and you'll get at least six tours."

Lauren was the office manager and she ran a tight ship, oftentimes playing the middle man between the drivers and guide managers.

Five minutes later he was in his jeep, racing across town to pick up four passengers at the Hyatt hotel.

Five tours later Louis was back at the front desk, standing on shaky legs. He'd done the Broken Arrow trail three times, followed by a tour on the Pioneer Trail up Schnebly Hill Road, then another tour that visited the Van Deren Cabin on the Red Rock West trail. So far, he had logged six and a half hours of talking and driving.

It was indeed now over one hundred degrees out, and he tried to pull himself together for one last tour. His skin was dry, his throat parched, and his eyes felt crinkly. The air was so dry that the sweat evaporated right off him, and even though he drank water constantly, his thirst seemed unquenchable.

On the horizon the clouds were stacking up, but the rain seemed no closer.

In the parking lot Jimmy was staring at Accuweather radar on a small flip phone, talking to Rhoda. She peered at it while he shook his head.

A minute later he walked to the front desk and began talking with Jamie. Rhoda intercepted Louis on his way to the desk.

"Hey, you better watch out," she said. "Jimmy just saw a big storm heading our way and he's gonna pass his next tour to you."

They both looked to the southwest where dark clouds were accumulating.

"That's fine," said Louis and reached behind the driver's seat of his jeep to retrieve his waterproof duster. "I'm sick of this heat."

She shook her head. "Well you better be ready. On the radar it looked like a lot of rain, and most of the other tours are dropping off the board."

Louis entered the office where sure enough Gina told him he had the next tour.

"I told them there was a big storm brewing, but I couldn't talk them into cancelling," she said. "They're leaving town right after and really wanted to do the Broken Arrow."

"It's fine," said Louis and grabbed the paperwork.

The Broken Arrow trail had been created in the late Forties as a horseback trail by Bob Bradshaw, the founder of A Day in the West jeep tours—now run by Bob's son John. Back in the Forties and Fifties, Bob had been recruited by film production companies who were coming to Sedona to contribute to the Golden age of westerns. Bradshaw worked as an actor, wrangler and location scout. He was also Jimmy Stewart's stuntman and double on *Broken Arrow*.

Bradshaw senior eventually purchased a 90-acre ranch near Loy Butte and opened it up to the movie industry. Five movies, two TV series, and numerous commercials were filmed there. It also saw the likes of Elvis Presley, Kenny Rogers, Beau Bridges and Paul Hogan.

The Broken Arrow trail had been monopolized by another jeep tour company, Pink Jeep, over the past years, but recent litigation had changed that, and considering Bradshaw's role in the construction of the trail, all the ADW drivers were happy about this.

On the way to the trail, Louis noticed heavy, dark clouds gathering in the sky. The air suddenly had a crisp intensity to it, but the rain held back. To the south he could see long, dangling tentacles of virga rain that evaporated before they hit the ground.

He didn't mind driving in the rain, but he didn't want to get caught on the trail in a lightning storm—and the clouds above him had just that look. This trail had a few difficult technical sections, and there was a deep wash to cross—no place to be when you had passengers on board.

He glanced up again and desperately hoped he could outrun the clouds on the trail and be outta there before the rain hit.

The jeep's front doors had plastic windows, and the canopy offered some protection, but the sides were open.

Louis stopped at the trailhead and handed back some disposable rain ponchos. He had four passengers: a mother, father, and two teenage boys who looked a bit bored.

He watched them awkwardly put on the ponchos and tried to remember their names; the boys' he'd already forgotten, but he was pretty sure their parents were Bill and Melissa.

He put the jeep in four-wheel drive and crawled over a large speed bump. His passengers shrieked excitedly and Louis quickly looked back to make sure they were all buckled. The trail ahead wound through some junipers and then opened to slick rock.

There were three benches in the back of the jeep. The two boys sat in the 'trampoline seat' in the far back where the ride was bounciest. Bill sat directly behind Louis, and Melissa across from her husband.

They emerged from the trees and were greeted by towering red cliffs that rose before them. The sky overhead was clear blue and Louis wondered where the storm clouds had disappeared to.

They reached a small rocky ledge and crawled up a slab of slick rock, the back tires spinning for a second before they finally gripped the rock.

On the right, a short spur road led to a sinkhole called the Devil's Dining Room. Normally, Louis would have pulled into it, but he decided to keep moving; if the weather held, they could always stop there on their way back.

The track entered the forest again, wending its way through a grove of smooth-bark cypress, then skirting a dry creek bed; Louis was beginning to relax into his tour. He slowed down, pausing to point at a grove of manzanita bush and explain how the Sinagua would harvest the little berries, and then again by a soap-root yucca.

"You can make soap from the roots of that yucca," he said, nodding at the plant.

He put the jeep in gear, and Bill said, "We love tall tales—you got any?"

Louis grinned. "Funny you should say that right now."

"You see these trees?" said Louis and indicated with his chin a stand of cypress they were passing. "The Native Americans call these the 'Keepers of the Forest' because of a legend revolving around forest fires."

Everyone peered at the trees while they slowly passed, and Louis continued. "The trees soak up a lot of water, and the water has a lot of iron oxide in it—just like the soil. As the trees get older they turn into natural lightning rods."

They passed a tree whose trunk was black and looked burnt.

"That's so cool," said one of the boys.

"It's when the tree gets struck that it earns its nickname. As it burns the water inside vaporizes and turns to steam, and the steam then shoots out the limb that's on fire and puts it out," said Louis. "Despite the fact that we have had a ten-year drought here, there hasn't been a major fire mostly due to these trees—every lightning bolt goes straight to a cypress and the fire is quickly extinguished."

Bill caught Louis' eye in the mirror. He raised an eyebrow as he asked, "So how much truth is in that story?"

Louis shrugged. "According to the Forest Service, none. But I think that just makes it irresistible."

They passed a very steep trail on the right; this was the infamous Hill of Death and they would have to crawl down this hill later on.

"We got a couple Barbies on our tail," said one of the boys in the back, and Louis glanced in his side mirror to see two Pink Jeeps. It was tempting to take the next left to Submarine Rock, but he didn't want to get swept into the parade of Pink Jeeps that went there every hour. Even though the permit system was no longer in effect, they still acted like only they were allowed there, blocking trails and glaring at the non-Pink drivers.

"We'll lose them in two minutes," said Louis.

Up ahead he turned right, up onto some slick rock again.

This was his favorite section of the ride. Here the trail rose above the trees and led across some pancaked red rocks, winding up and down and following exposed ledges up to a spectacular overlook called Roundabout Rock.

But when Louis reached Roundabout Rock and circled it, the open view of the sky made his heart sink. What ten minutes before had appeared as a cloudless blue pool was now a brooding, threatening black mass.

He'd never seen a more ominous sight looming over him.

Right then a bolt of lightning struck a tree about five hundred feet away.

They all saw it. The crack of thunder was instantaneous, and seconds later the skies opened to an enormous downpour.

"Shit," he mumbled.

He told his passengers to hunker down and slowly drove forward. The wind swooped down mightily and buffeted the canopy. The rain was pelting down with a vengeance. He warily glanced ahead. The most difficult section of the trail still lay ahead, and the slick rocks were now shimmering with wetness and covered with little rivulets.

Slowly and carefully he maneuvered the jeep across the rocks to the top of the Hill of Death. As they paused to look down at the steep trail Melissa gasped and whispered, "We're not going down that."

"Yes, we are," said Louis with a nervous grin.

Thousands of jeeps had skidded their way down this hill, and over the years they'd worn rough steps into the rock.

He put the jeep in low gear and slowly inched ahead. The jeep leaned forward into a 45-degree angle and his passengers sharply drew in their breath. Mud and small rock pebbles were rushing down the steep trail, threatening to undo the tire traction. Soon they were sliding more than driving. Louis put the brake down heavily but still slid and bounced down, step by six-inch step. With a great gush it began to pour even harder.

Melissa screamed at each drop, and the boys perked up. They whooped and shouted, but as the storm intensified, Louis could see their knuckles turn white as they gripped the roll bars.

Lightning continued to crash down around them, echoing off the surrounding cliffs. Streams of water were cascading down the steps.

"Get out of there!" boomed Lauren's voice over the radio.

They thumped down the last step and everyone cheered.

At the bottom of the hill he turned left, pulled ahead about twenty feet and stopped. He grabbed the radio and tried to call in, but the thunder and pounding rain made communication impossible.

"What? I can't hear you!" Lauren´s voice squawked from the radio.

Louis looked around; again, he had to skirt the dry wash, which was now swirling with a river of mud, at least a foot deep. In the back of his mind he could hear Jimmy's warning about flash floods.

They inched past it as quick as he dared, and Louis could see the water rising in the time it took him to put it in his rear view mirror.

Lauren continued to holler garbled warnings, and Louis turned off the radio.

Finally, they reached the easy section of the trail. The cypress canopy softened the force of the downpour.

"Everyone okay?" asked Louis.

Melissa responded, but her words were lost when another lightning bolt struck to their right—this time only a hundred feet away. It seemed to be pulsing for several seconds, like a hand gripping and shaking the tree.

"Time to go!" shouted Louis and sped the jeep up as much as he dared.

By the time they reached the pavement the lightning seemed to have jumped ahead of them, flashing to the north, and the rain still came down in buckets.

Louis picked up the radio. "We're on pavement, heading in," he said, but all that came back was static.

But even the road was flooded with water so deeply that several people had pulled their vehicles over to the side. Louis kept the jeep in four-wheel drive and slowly crept down the middle of the road, spaying up gushing fountains of water.

And then it began to hail. His passengers started laughing, and he grinned, too. "I'm glad you guys got to experience some of our lovely Arizona weather," he said.

A strong wind blew through, making the clouds overhead race by.

"That was some tour," said Bill when they reached the parking lot. The hail had stopped, but it was still sprinkling. They shook hands, and Bill palmed him a note when he said goodbye. Louis pocketed it without looking.

Later, at the bar with Jimmy, Louis pulled out Bill's tip hoping it might be enough to buy a couple Heinekens.

He unfolded the note and with a huge grin, he held up a hundred-dollar bill. He remembered how he'd last gotten a tip like this for guiding the Star Trek writers around Skagway.

"Drinks are on me, Jimmy," he said with a smile.

If it wasn't for a few remaining stories, I'd end my narrative here. But hold on, the best is yet to come, so we're gonna keep rolling. Louis, Dee and the girls stayed in the house on View Drive for another five years, which by all accounts seemed to fly by.

Tavy, formerly Pookey Bear, made friends with some more girls in the neighborhood, Taylor and Elise, and when Annabelle joined the gang they became the View Street Girls, or the Fab Four. They all took dance lessons from Miss Danielle, who had a studio up the street, and more often than not the house was filled with the music of Taylor Swift and Justin Bieber.

Say Say, formerly The Shrimp, progressed from daycare to preschool to kindergarten. She began using her middle name, Scout, which had been inspired out of Pat Pat's love for the main character in Harper Lee's novel *To Kill a Mockingbird*. Whenever Scout was in the presence of the View Street Girls she stood on her tippy-toes, trying to look taller, and perhaps because of that she began to sprout up.

Dee quit her waitressing job and began offering massages at a one-room office on Jordan Road. After hours she often sat on the front porch of the home watching the sprinklers pepper their little lawn, with Gracie on her lap.

Lotion, the travelling guinea pig, passed away during those years.

They had a funeral in the back yard where they recited her accomplishments: born in Alaska; crossed North America five times; best friends with a cat.

"She took good naps, too," said Scout.

Louis continued driving jeep tours until his back couldn't handle the rugged driving anymore. He moved into marketing, and before the five years were up he was general manager of A Day in the West.

But he also grew restless, despite taking his girls to India and Thailand for month-long trips. He often told me that the further he got from actual tour guiding, the less he enjoyed working in tourism. These were also the years of the recession and making a buck in the vacation industry became more difficult.

One afternoon, Dee came home announcing she'd found a house for rent and they were moving. Louis was ready to move; the skylight over their bed dripped from condensation, and no matter where you placed the bed in the small room, someone got wet.

Over the years they'd mentioned it to the landlords, who were sympathetic, but not willing to replace the skylight.

Dee had already put money down on the new place, and all that was left was to give the old landlord notice.

The new house was vacant, and the new landlord said they could move in anytime. They chose April 12th, which was the same date they'd moved in five years before — Tavy's tenth birthday.

Their rent was paid until the end of April, so there was no rush.

Their current landlord's wife, Beverly, asked if they could vacate the property early, so she could have some time to paint and still get it back on the market for the first of the month.

"I can get our stuff out no problem," said Louis, "but I'll need the last week of the month to clean it properly."

Beverly smiled. "Don't worry about that. We've got a whole crew — we're gonna paint all the walls and replace all the carpets. If you can get your stuff out a week early, we'll take it from there."

Louis had seen the landlord's Hispanic crew in action and figured it would take them less than a week to renovate the house.

Two weeks later, Louis stood in the driveway, fuming mad. He had met with Dee to load up the last of their things, but found the landlord's crew had started two days early, and now Louis' computer, photos and all of his clothes were all covered with a fine white dust.

To make things worse, while they loaded their dust-covered belongings in the Vinniman, Beverly ran around photographing the building.

"I'm keeping your entire deposit," she said. "This place is a mess."

Louis was still angry about the condition of his belongings and fired back, "You're here two days early."

Dee looked at her and said, "And you said to not bother deep cleaning."

Beverly gave Dee a strange look and proceeded to show them digital photos of the clutter they'd left behind. "Why would I say that?"

Louis said, "Well, I'm paid until the end of the month. I'll clean up after we unload the minivan."

Beverly shook her head. "We already cleaned everything—you would have just been in our way. I'm keeping the deposit." With that she turned and walked away, leaving Louis and Dee feeling like they'd just been conned.

Louis now waited with Tavy for Dee to return from the Kindergarten. She stood next to him, fidgeting in the shade of a telephone pole. By their feet were the remaining toys they'd collected in the yard.

Across the street they could hear Question Mark yelling inside the house. It was nine in the morning and Louis figured Mark had been up all night.

"What's up with Question Mark?" asked Louis.

"He's been shouting since we got here," said Tavy. "You didn't hear him?"

Louis really needed someone to vent upon. Normally he wouldn't have hesitated to cross the street, but Mark seemed angry himself today.

Question Mark was having a big year. He'd written a half-dozen screenplays over the last few years, and several producers were interested in them. He was always brimming with energy. Sometimes he worked off some steam on hikes; he'd checked off just about every hiking trail in Sedona. But other times — like now — he went on multi-day benders of caffeine, alcohol and weed. This could make him incredibly productive: once he wrote multiple screenplays in a three-day stretch. But it also took its toll on him.

He seemed to be on a good binge now. Louis could hear Mark shout: "*Humanity? You never had it to begin with!*"

He recognized the quote from Charles Bukowski, the drunk poet. Not a good sign, he thought. Literary binges were a telltale sign of his benders, with Question Mark quoting whatever author currently inspired him.

And when he heard him yell, "Fucking Halpern!" he knew Mark was angry at a guy who'd tied up one of his screenplays in a legal battle. It was a dark story about an early pioneer family in Kansas that had killed and robbed travelers, and Mark was wanting to shop it to producers.

Louis grabbed Tavy's hand and crossed the street. He knocked on the door just as Mark yelled:

"*I am my own God!*"

They heard him make an enormous burp and Tavy giggled, completely unafraid. Mark was a big guy, fit, muscular, and he had a loud presence, but Tavy just loved him.

"You want to wait out here?" Louis asked quickly, but the young girl shook her head and looked up when the door slid back, revealing a dark room that appeared like a gloomy cave.

"Good morning, Question Mark," she said when he filled the doorway, leaning drunkenly. He stood there in a bathrobe, unshaved with messy hair. At 6'2" and two hundred and forty pounds he towered over the little girl.

He grinned. "Why Tavy-Two-Tone, how are you today?"

"I'm good, but you sound a little crazy."

Mark laughed uproariously and said, "*Some people never go crazy. What truly horrible lives they must live.*"

Tavy watched him, unsure, and Mark ruffed up her hair.

Still quoting Bukowski, Louis thought. When Mark was on a roll he could go on for hours quoting not just writers and poets, but politicians and other famous people, making their words apply to whatever subject he needed.

"*Never get out of bed before noon,*" he said and turned into his house, motioning for Louis and Tavy to follow. The floor of the kitchen was covered with pistachio shells, and Mark dismissively pointed at them and muttered, "Watch your steps."

Then he began to complain about Halpern.

"Did I tell you the latest?" he asked Louis.

Tavy interrupted him. "Question Mark, do you hate people?"

This pulled him out of his rant. He crouched down next to her and said softly, "*I don't hate them... I just feel better when they're not around.*"

Tavy looked at him with eyes that were filled with acceptance and his anger melted away. He pulled her into a hug.

"*I no doubt deserve my enemies,*" he said, "*but I don't believe I deserve my friends.*"

"So we're on to Whitman now?" asked Louis, thinking it might be a good turn in the conversation.

Mark smiled. "No need to start Tavy's day with my spectacle. So what can I do for you on this fine day?"

Louis took his turn to complain. He gave Mark the full story of how his landlord, in his eyes, had swindled them.

Mark swayed until the fridge stopped him.

He collected himself. When he spoke he sounded surprisingly sober.

"Listen," he said, "a lot of homeowners are underwater on their mortgages and they're desperate. I'm sure before this is all done she'll have convinced herself you guys were just negligent."

"So you're saying I should just walk away from it?"

Mark shrugged. "You like the new place you're moving into?"

Louis nodded. "Yeah, it's great."

"Then cut your losses and move on. Forget about this place. *You have to die a few times before you can live.* I'll miss having you as a neighbor, but I'm sure we'll still hang out."

"Well, I feel like I should fight for my money," said Louis.

"What matters most is how well you walk through the fire," he said.

"Aha. Bukowski again."

"Sure," grinned Mark. "One last one because it's relevant. All that's really important is how you act now — what your girls witness. Just roll with it and down the line it will fade away."

He smiled, and Tavy said, "I like you better when you're happy?"

Mark held up his arms like he was surrendering and said, *"Henceforth I ask not good fortune. I myself am good fortune."*

He led them to the door, winking at Louis, and said, "Had to end on Whitman."

He patted Tavy's head as she walked out and said, "When you get bigger, Tavy-Two-Tone, old Question Mark is gonna tell you all about Uncle Walt."

"Okay," she said and waved goodbye.

Suddenly, Mark grasped the doorframe for support; the evening's buzz, the morning hangover, and his fervent pontificating were catching up with him.

He looked pale as he slightly swayed in the door frame.

Tavy looked at him, then looked up at Louis. Her eyes held the same caution as when she'd stared at the bull moose emerging out of the fog by the hot spring boardwalk in the Yukon.

Louis heard an echo of that morning as she again whispered, "We should go."

When Dee returned they loaded the Vinniman with the yard toys and drove to their new house on Trails End Drive.

The DeMayo family – Trail's End - 2013

Epilogue

Trail's End, Sedona
(Feb. 2010)

On a beautiful spring morning, Louis stood in the backyard of their new rental on Trails End Drive, listening to the creek flow by a few hundred feet away.

The cape-style house would have looked more at home back east, with its gables and second story; and the four-foot wall that surrounded it added to that feeling, making it feel quaint and secluded. The wall was painted olive green, which helped it blend into the surrounding trees, most of which were towering sycamores.

There were two lawns, one in front the other in the back, and the back yard also had a small building that Louis claimed as an office. The office was raised on a platform, and when he was sitting at his desk he could look beyond the wall to a cluster of trees in an empty lot between their place and the creek, and if he watched long enough he'd often see movement in the shadows.

Three mule deer does hung out there most days, staying in the cool shade, not venturing forth until the sun was down and the humans had left the creek. Louis liked watching them, because they made him think of the Chase house on the lake which they'd left behind, now almost ten years ago. He could still remember clearly watching the doe nibbling on the blueberry bush from the canoe with Tavy.

The front yard had a large dead tree that leaned against the wall, and on their first day Tavy spotted an owl nesting in it. The bird watched silently from its nest, about ten feet off the ground, but stayed mostly hidden during the day.

This house by the creek was another place where time stood still. Tavy was ten, Scout eight, and the summers on Trails End seemed to last forever. There was a pristine swimming hole along a trail beside the creek, and almost every day of that summer they splashed around in it, filling their days with sparkling water and butterflies.

Along with the deer there were also raccoons, ringtail cats and about a million squirrels. Blue herons stood in the upper branches along the creek, and mourning doves cooed gently from the underbrush.

The girls had made new friends from Miss Danielle's dance class. Tavy now did everything with a young girl named Annie by her side. Scout had likewise met a girl her age named Savi—short for Savana—and together they explored the creek and the surrounding woods.

At night, Louis and Dee lay in bed with a view out their window of the owl's nest. When the sky darkened the little bird would shuffle to the edge of its hole in the tree and appear to watch them.

Mario, the Apache jeep driver, warned that owls were a symbol of death. "Even to hear one hooting is considered an unlucky omen."

But Dee loved the little bird and didn't think anything bad could come of it. I like to imagine when they did finally hear the owl, it was asking a question: its, "Who? Who?"

Because then I could say, "I'll tell you who—it was me!"

As it turned out, Dee became pregnant within a few weeks of sleeping under the little owl's gaze, and nine months later I was born.

The pregnancy inspired them to research owls more seriously, and they soon discovered the Native Americans had a rich mythology associated with the bird and not all associations were as negative as

Mario's. Some tribes believed owls were protective spirits, others considered them the souls of the recently departed.

But the day after Dee discovered she was pregnant, the owl left, never to be seen again. They continued to talk about it, half-convinced it had something to do with the pregnancy.

At a checkup they learned they were having another girl. This brought an Inuit legend about owls into their discussions.

According to the legend, a beautiful young girl was kidnapped and magically changed into a bird with a long beak. She became frightened and while attempting to escape flew into a wall, which flattened her face and beak into that of an owl.

Tavy and Scout were old enough now to excitedly followed the stages of the pregnancy, and every night they talked about what they might name their sister when she finally arrived. They never seemed to sit still when they were talking, and often fluttered about the kitchen like the owl-girl in the Inuit legend.

Names—like nicknames—had deep meaning in their family.

Their younger daughter Saydrin Scout was born on the same day as her maternal grandfather, but her first name came from her paternal grandfather, Pip.

Pip was of Italian descent, and Louis always joked that you could have taken him off the set of *The Sopranos*. He was the last person Louis figured would find any symbolism from a dream, but that's where they got her first name.

In Pip's dream, he was talking to a young girl. They talked a long time, about all sorts of things, and at the end of the dream the girl told Pip that she was his granddaughter, and that her name was Saydrin.

When he woke, he climbed out of bed and wrote the name down.

And the name of their oldest—Tavish—came out of what Louis always described as one of the fullest days of his life.

*

When they were camping on the Stampede Trail, just outside of Denali National Park, Louis and Dee had decided to make a baby. They set a date: one month after the Cantwell Music Festival, and during that time they smoked no weed, drank no alcohol, and ate healthy.

Dee made Louis use protection that month, too.

"I'm not getting pregnant until you get those mushrooms out of your system," she said shortly after the festival.

Louis often spoke of the day of Tavish´s conception, when it finally rolled around. "So I started the day getting laid," he said. "How could that not be a good day?"

Afterwards he met Ryan and Killer to play a round of golf on a small course in Healy. The course only had seven holes so you had to play two of them twice, but from a different direction.

Ryan and Killer were drinking from a six-pack of Alaskan amber and stood on one of the greens watching a large raven try to steel Ryan's golf ball. "Fuckin' bird. If he flies off with that I'm marking it down as a hole in one," said Ryan and swilled down the rest of his beer.

Louis decided to break his fast and have a beer. He was young and confident and assumed Dee would get pregnant right away — as it turns out she was.

This was one of Louis´ first days off in a while, and he'd arranged both a free rafting trip down the Denali River and a free flight around McKinley — or Denali as the locals called it. Most of the tour operators out here offered comps to front desk staff and bartenders in the hopes that they would advertise the tours to their patrons, and Louis finally found the chance to take them up on this.

The rafting trip down the canyon left him exhilarated and wet. Louis had optioned for a Paddle Raft, where each passenger had to paddle under the direction of a guide. There were five other people in his boat, all park service employees also taking advantage of comps.

The rapids were mostly Grade 3, with one Grade 4, and there were rocks and freezing water and those dangers kept him focused. It was a professional operation, and the ride was nothing like his canoe trip with Ryan — other than the freezing water."

"Yikes, that's cold," he said the first time a wave swamped him.

The guide nodded. "Yeah, don't fall in — you're not wearing a wet suite and you don't want to catch hypothermia."

It took two action-packed hours to get through the eleven miles of the canyon, crashing through rapids with names like Coffee Grinder, Ice Worm and Cable Car.

In the parking lot he changed his clothes, had a beer with the other paddlers, and then drove to the small airport for his flight. In mid-summer in Alaska there was close to twenty hours of sunlight, and the day seemed to go on forever.

The flight around Denali was haunting. On the approach, braided rivers fanned out across the land, flashing when the sun made a rare appearance. Dark gray clouds hoovered below them, and crept up the ridges of the mighty mountain when they got closer.

"On that crest," said the pilot while pointing, "a plane crashed a few years ago and you can still see one wing."

The pilot seemed competent and Louis never feared they would crash, but the sharp, snowy ridge intimidated him, bringing back scary moments from his climbs in Africa and South America. On every ridge they passed he stared hard, trying to decide what route he would take down if he somehow survived a crash and ended there.

"Did anyone survive?" asked Louis.

The pilot shook his head. "If they weren't killed on impact they would have died from the cold soon after."

After circling the mountain, they returned and landed in Healy. On shaky legs—wigged out by all the adrenaline—Louis drove to visit Dee, who was busy with a lunch shift at the Denali Smoke Shack.

Lorenzo, the French dishwasher, was sneaking back from the parking lot with a cloud of smoke trailing him when Louis drove up. He grinned at Louis and said, "America has no hash and fat women, but I love it here."

From inside they could hear one of the waitresses—Deb—angrily shouting at two customers who were walking out.

"Go on! Get out of here!" she yelled. "It only means I don't have to serve your miserable asses."

Lorenzo covered a giggle and ran into the kitchen after the disgruntled customers walked by.

Louis hopped out of the van and entered the restaurant. He saw Dee and flagged her over.

"How's your day going?" Louis asked her with a smirk.

She glanced at Deb. "Oh, just peachy. Ryan and Simone ran to Fairbanks for supplies and this place is falling apart."

Louis nodded at the deck. He was having a great day and didn't want to get caught up in work drama.

"I'm gonna read the paper on the deck. Got time to join me?"

Just then Deb threw her apron on the ground and stormed out the door. "Ya'll can kiss my ass!" she shouted.

"Not likely," said Dee and walked into the kitchen.

So Louis sat in the sun by himself and read the current issue of *USA Today* to catch up on what was happening around the world.

One article caught his eye: It was about three young boys, nicknamed Ace, Marky and Tavish, who had died by a fire bomb in Northern Ireland. He looked at the anguished expression on the father's face and felt all the air flow from his lungs. His exhilaration had vanished.

He set down the paper, feeling restless. Eventually Dee popped out to say hi and noticed his frown. "You okay?" she asked.

He scratched his stubbly chin. "How long before you get off?"

She glanced at the clock forlornly. "Not for another five hours."

He folded the newspaper in half.

"I'll see you then — I'm gonna do a hike."

With hours of sunlight still ahead of him, Louis decided to hike Bison Gorge. You could see the steep ravine from the Parks Highway, and from the parking lot it only took him about an hour and a half to hike through tall pines and sprawling alders to reach the top.

As he climbed out of the steep gorge and onto the summit he was greeted by a different world. Beyond the gorge the mountainside tilted down in a long, grassy slope. Islands of clouds floated by, a large cloud heading toward him. He sat down and let the fog envelop him. For minutes, he was sitting alone in a white mist that swirled around him.

When the cloud lifted at least twenty mountain goats were standing around him, silently grazing. He didn't move, and if they noticed him they didn't show it.

It was here that he remembered the article. When the next gust of wind blew the clouds back in, he again sat in the silent white vapor, and then he heard the name Tavish in the breeze.

This was the moment he decided he wanted to name his firstborn Tavish, whether it was a boy or a girl. Whenever I asked him to elaborate on his decision, he only said, "one candle goes out, another gets lit".

*

I was born on one — one one — one one. That's January eleventh, 2011. Pretty cool, huh? And yes, the girls eventually came up with a name for me, and like everyone else in this family, I got a nickname, too.

So for now you can call me Tikibear.

Unfortunately, I can't remember back that far so for a few more pages we're gonna have to stick with the stories I was raised with.

The first one is how Louis dealt with me when I cried.

When Louis was alone with me, and I became inconsolable, he would pick me up, walk into the back yard and stand in the cool night air with me.

Then he would hold me up to the moon so I could marvel at its pale wonder.

According to my sisters this always worked — just as it had for them.

In August of that year John Bradshaw sold A Day in the West and Louis was layed off. It shouldn't have been a surprise; the company had struggled through the recession, but it still threw Louis for a loop.

He sat in his little shed and pondered his future. The worry about how to pay the bills ate at him. Over the last ten years he always seemed to have struggled financially, never quite getting ahead. He was deeply frustrated.

Dee still had her little office on Jordan Road, but there were only so many massages she could do in a week. Her job had physical limitations.

Louis trudged out to his office and sat in his chair. He looked around at all the little knickknacks which he'd picked up during their many crossings of North America. On his desk sat a railroad spike from the *White Pass Railroad*, and by it was a tip of an elk antler he'd found in Colorado; and plenty of other trinkets cluttered his desk: shells from Baja, a pottery shard from Rimrock, a photo of him sitting astride Timber.

He reached out and fondled a few of them, tenderly, as if they might offer advice. The bookshelf behind his desk was stuffed with guidebooks from Alaska, the Southwest and Baja, with popular fiction about those places, and with a large collection of natural history.

He took down Krakauer's *Into the Wild* and flipped through it, pausing at the chapter about Everett Ruess, the young vagabond who'd disappeared in Utah in 1934.

He put it back, then grabbed a book by William Sewall about his time in the Maine woods with young Teddy Roosevelt. Louis glanced at a photo of him and Cleo Sewall sitting on the porch of the family cabin which was tacked on a corkboard by the desk

There were so many memories in his office, and he didn't quite know what to do with them. As he spun his chair slowly around his foot caught on a box of travel journals from before he'd met Dee, and he browsed them as well. Eventually he closed the box because they were making him restless.

He closed his eyes. His travels flashed before him, those from his younger days, the journeys with Dee, and the long road they'd taken the girls on from New Hampshire to Sedona. From when they first left the little house on the lake up until when they finally settled on Trail's End Drive, they must have driven twenty-five thousand miles.

So many memories, and thoughts, and ideas. Are they all supposed to just fade away now? Louis had written stories and poetry for years, and he'd had articles published since 1988 when he worked as a foreign correspondent for *The Telegraph*, but he realized now he'd never really written about the things that were important and close to him. He'd never in print expressed the things he felt were truly important.

Maybe, he thought with a growing sense of excitement, it was time.

He spent the next week in the office taking notes, and at the end of the week he sat with Dee and shared a glass of wine while they listened to two flickers squawking above them in the thick, pale branches of a sycamore tree.

"I've decided I'm gonna write about it," he said.

Dee gave him a strange look. "About what?" she asked.

"All of it. My early travels, our travels together, our journeys with the girls—I want to write about it. And there are other stories, too. I want to finally write something about Teddy Roosevelt and his time in northern Maine, and that young artist, Everett Ruess, who disappeared in Utah—I want to write it all."

Dee scratched her head. "That's going to be one big novel."

Louis set down his wine glass. "No, it'll be more than one. I'm thinking I have four—maybe five—novels in me."

"How long will that take?" said Dee, looking worried. "I've known guys who are on the same novel for ten years. How long will five novels take?"

Louis glanced at his shed. "Well, I've been thinking about these stories so long I bet they just flow out of me. But just to be safe, I'll set a deadline of five years."

Dee smiled at him. "You think you can write five novels in five years?"

For the first time in a long time, Louis smiled confidently and said, "I can do whatever I set my mind to."

Dee clinked glasses with him. "Good luck, honey."

But then she furrowed her brows. She was serious when she spoke next. "Yesterday I stopped by the office next door—it's for rent now. The space has four treatment rooms, a bathroom and an atrium with a fountain."

Louis felt his pulse quicken with anxiety.

"How much is the rent?"

Dee sighed. "It's three times our current office rent, but I can bring in other therapists for treatments."

Louis looked up at one of the flickers that had landed on a suet feeder. For a moment he collected his thoughts.

Dee didn't wait for him to speak. "I'm all for you writing novels, but you have to trust me on this. It'll be a much bigger machine, but I think I can make it work."

Louis took a deep breath, let all the air out of his lungs and said, "Let's do it."

Three months later, on Halloween Day, Tikibear crawled over the front lawn while Louis and Dee watched from a blanket. Saydrin and Savana played with her, trying to encourage the baby to stand, but each wobbly effort ended with her falling back on her diaper-padded bottom.

In one of the tall sycamores above them a flicker called out repeatedly, sounding more like a squeaky toy than a bird, and Tikibear seemed more concerned with the bird than walking on two legs.

"Come on, Tika," encouraged Saydrin. "You can do it."

Dee disappeared in the house for a moment, and then reemerged with a battery-powered CD player. Soon Lyle Lovett's scratchy voice filled the yard.

Through the gate in the yard Tavish and her friend, Annie, came into view, zipping down a hill on their bikes. "I got an A!" shouted Tavish and hopped off the bike, holding a paper in her hand. She ran over to Dee and showed it to her.

Saydrin and Savana had left Tika to the birdsong and were now doing cartwheels, spinning across the lawn until they were dizzy. They had a contest on who could do a hundred consecutive ones first, but every few minutes they had to pause until the world stopped swirling around.

Louis watched the scene, feeling content. The last few months he'd been working on a collection of stories about his early travel days, and a part of him had despaired that those days were over.

But now, watching his girls, a sense of domestic bliss overcame him, and at least for a few minutes he was satisfied.

Next to him, Dee nudged Tavish and said, "Tell your dad what your report is about."

Tavish cleared her throat, and then the eleven-year-old began in her most professional voice. "The monarch butterfly is the only known butterfly to make a two-way migration," she said. "Some of these butterflies fly as much as three thousand miles."

Louis ruffed up her hair and smiled at her, and encouraged, the girl continued. "It takes multiple generations to complete this migration. One generation is born in Mexico from butterflies that wintered over there, but it will take three or four generations of them to reach the northern United States and Canada—each one completes a segment of the journey."

Tavish kept reading, but Louis' mind was drifting off, suddenly overcome by what she was saying.

Multiple generations? he asked himself. His mind was spinning— just like the girls cartwheeling behind him—as he processed this. None of the butterflies were aware of the final destination, just their part in the journey.

He wondered if they saw a bigger picture, and suddenly realized he wasn't really thinking about the butterflies, but about his own family and their travels.

Maybe he was only completing his portion of the journey, and his girls were meant to complete the rest—or at least their segment of it.

Maybe he was never meant to do and see it all.

Maybe...

He was pulled away by a shout of "Heyyyy!!!" and he glanced sideways to see Tikibear in the process of standing straight up, unassisted.

Saydrin dropped out of a cartwheel and came running over. Tavish let go of her paper and clapped, and Dee squealed with delight.

Tikibear stood straight and her legs held. She swayed, grinning, but didn't fall.

That's right, I stood.

And from now on this is my story.

I'd love to tell you how things progressed from there. I could go on about Tavish and Annie's plans to share the position of captain on the cheerleading team, or Saydrin getting into aerial silks or playing the upright base in the school orchestra.

Or I could go on about Dee's successful business, Uptown Massage, or Louis' writing career, but I'm just gonna say that what you are reading is Louis' fifth novel. And just as he promised Dee, he completed it just shy of five years.

But like I said, it's my story now so you can just wait until I'm ready to tell it.

So for now just stay with me a moment longer, on the soft lawn in front of the little house at the end of Trail's End Drive, where the soft trickle of the creek floated in the air, interspersed with birdsong, and the sun never seemed as harsh.

And enjoy this timeless moment when the red rocks of Sedona converged with the cloudless blue sky to create what I call home. My home. Our home.

The DeMayo family 2013

Robert (Louis), Diana (Dee), Tavish (Pookey Bear),
Saydrin (Say Say) & Martika (Tikibear).

Tavish

Conceived on soft taiga,
the Alaskan winds call your name.
Up Bison Gorge I hike
with my mind on your future.

I've nothing to give you, my unborn daughter.
I own a motorcycle, a laptop, and a tent — that's it.
I've chased my dreams for years,
but I don't even know if I ever caught any.

Clouds enter the gorge far below
and ascend to white me out.
Sharp drop-offs to the left,
but the ridgeline continues.

There is no sound at the top.
I am alone, but I am with you.
Unstable screes and damp earth,
Loose rocks underfoot, slippery with moss.

All you need to learn is in the mountains.
They will treat you as friends
but friends aren't always kind.
Long slopes slow you down,
like the lies you'll believe.
Uphill stretches burn your muscles,
like the work that life requires.

Mountain goats graze soundlessly at the top,
I watch from within the clouds.
My descent is announced as rocks skip free.
I am exposed.
The dense brush repeatedly throws me to the ground
and I feel alive.
A cut hand leaves a trail of blood,
and I think of the bears it may attract.

But the rush of walking the ridgeline is my elixir.
It's like my hand on my pregnant wife's stomach.
And the creaking of the pines sounds like
the amused voices of spirits.
They also talk through the old and young.

In the wind up there you can hear secrets.
I've heard a few – I heard your name once.
Snow covered peaks and alpine beauty.
I stand in awe as I think of you, my Tavish.

(Bison Gorge, Alaska – September 98)

The author, on House Mountain, Sedona

Robert Louis DeMayo took up writing at the age of twenty when he left his job as a biomedical engineer to explore the world. Over the coming years he traveled to every corner of the globe, experiencing approximately one hundred countries. He is a member of The Explorers Club and The Archaeological Institute of America. During his travels he worked extensively for the travel section of *The Telegraph*, out of Hudson, NH.

For three years he worked as marketing director for Eos, a company that served as a travel office for six non-profit organizations, and offered dives to the *Titanic* and the *Bismarck*, Antarctic voyages, African safaris and archaeological tours throughout the world. Following this, Robert worked for three years as a tour guide in Alaska and the Yukon during the summers, and as a jeep guide in Sedona, Arizona, in winter.

He was general manager at A Day in the West, a Jeep tour company in Sedona before he decided to write full time. He is the author of four novels: *The Making of Theodore Roosevelt*, *The Light Behind Blue Circles*, *The Wayward Traveler*, and *Pledge to the Wind; the Legend of Everett Ruess*.

He has also published a novella that takes place in Sedona, AZ entitled, *The Cave Where the Water Always Drips*. This adventure tale is set in modern and colonial times and combines many of the local legends. Many of his experiences while traveling were captured in *Random Thoughts from the Road*, a collection of poetry and prose.

His novel, *The Wayward Traveler*, won a Pinnacle Book Achievement Award. This memoir-based story follows, Louis, a young adventurer, who runs out of money while abroad and creates a list of Rules for Survival to get by.

His most recent novel, *Pledge to the Wind, the Legend of Everett Ruess*, is a historical fiction account of the young man's exploration of the southwest between 1931 and 1935. This novel won a Silver medal in the eLit Awards, and another Historical Fiction Award by the Pinnacle Book Awards.

Currently he resides in Hollis, N.H. and Sedona, AZ, with his wife Diana and three daughters: Tavish Lee, Saydrin Scout, and Martika Louise.

Also by Robert Louis DeMayo

"Reading this exquisitely written work should inspire anyone to want to live a simpler life with an endearing respect for nature. It is almost unfathomable that someone as young as Everett Ruess could have such a profound look at society and the way it can strangle the purity and life out of so many. Robert Lois DeMayo captures both the beauty of the country and an individual's quest for beauty in its simplest form. This book makes one want to pack up and visit the glorious beauty of the southwest in a similar fashion, to try to even remotely see life through the unadulterated eyes of a young man who dared to live life on his own terms."

–Tim Glover

PLEDGE TO THE WIND, THE LEGEND OF EVERETT RUESS

Eighty years ago a young man disappeared in the Utah wilderness. A large manhunt followed, but all they turned up was his last camp and a couple burros. Numerous historical books have been published that attempt to prove what happened to Everett, but his fate remains one of the biggest mysteries of the southwest. *Pledge to the Wind, the Legend of Everett Ruess* follows the adventures of Everett Ruess from his appearance in the southwest in 1931 when he was barely seventeen, until his disappearance in 1934, shortly before he turned 21. This historical fiction novel focuses more on how he lived from day to day, the adventures he experienced, and the language he used to express them. Upon reading it, Brian Ruess wrote, "In this work of fiction ... I saw Everett for the first time, as he might actually have been."

Historical Fiction.
Wayward Publishing.
Available in print, eBook & audiobook.

Also by Robert Louis DeMayo

"This book explores an aspect of Theodore Roosevelt's life that is not usually addressed when it comes to information regarding this president. Although this is a fictionalized story, DeMayo perfectly presents the essence of a young Roosevelt. The story is based on local recollections of Roosevelt's visits to the wilds of Maine where he learned the ways of the woods. DeMayo seamlessly captures the local vernacular and paints an accurate picture of the time in which the story is set. The story is an enjoyable read that is appropriate for young adults as well as adults."

–Kathleen Kallfelz

THE MAKING OF THEODORE ROOSEVELT

This a fictionalized account of a true story – the tale of how two rough Maine woodsmen took a young Theodore Roosevelt under their wing in 1878 and introduced him to the beautiful but unforgiving woodlands of the Northeast. Under their guidance, the frail but strong-willed New Yorker becomes a worthy outdoorsman, an experience which significantly shaped the world view of the man poised to become the 26th President of the United States thirteen years later.

Historical Fiction.

Wayward Publishing.
Available in print, eBook
& audiobook.

Also by Robert Louis DeMayo

"I enjoyed this book immensely. It is a way to see the world from the safety of your home and yet feel like you are experiencing the thrills, adventures, fears and exhilaration along with the main character, Louis. This book is so well-written that I didn't want to put it down as I followed Louis's adventures around the world. He met every type of person...from the dangerous to the glorious and everything in between. His descriptions of animal encounters left me breathless and envious for the same experiences. If you have any interest in traveling and a general guideline for that and for life, you should read this book! I was so inspired, I applied for my passport...although I doubt I would ever be as willing to jump into adventure as Louis did."

–Heidi Benson

THE WAYWARD TRAVELER

This memoir-based novel follows the adventures of Louis, a young American who, in 1985, is determined to travel the world. The story takes place in forty countries and spans ten years: from the deck of a felucca on the Nile to the scorched dunes of India's Thar Desert to the powerful Beni River in the Amazon Basin. Louis feels disenchantment with his former life, and a yearning to understand the foreign lands he encounters on his travels. He's broke most of the time and spends considerable effort trying to get by. Along the way he develops a list of Rules to help him get by, and yet, there's a restlessness to his travels. He continues to wander into new countries, and through it all his Rules save him.

Fiction.
Wayward Publishing.
Available in print or eBook.

Made in the USA
Columbia, SC
01 February 2018